Child Labor in the Developing World

Alberto Posso
Editor

Child Labor in the Developing World

Theory, Practice and Policy

palgrave
macmillan

Editor
Alberto Posso
School of Economics, Finance & Marketing
RMIT University
Melbourne, VIC, Australia

ISBN 978-981-15-3105-7 ISBN 978-981-15-3106-4 (eBook)
https://doi.org/10.1007/978-981-15-3106-4

This Palgrave Macmillan imprint is published by the registered company Springer Nature Singapore Pte Ltd.
The registered company address is: 152 Beach Road, #21-01/04 Gateway East, Singapore 189721, Singapore

Acknowledgements

The studies in this volume were originally presented at the *Understanding Child Labour in Agriculture* Workshop held in RMIT University, Melbourne, Australia on 8th – 9th April 2019. The workshop was kindly hosted by The Australian APEC Study Centre at RMIT University. We are thankful to all Centre members for their input and are particularly grateful to Sally Parkes-Mcclay for her work, organizational skills and patience both before and after the workshop. We would also like to thank Simon Feeny, Nobu Yamashita, Aaron Soans and all workshop participants for their invaluable comments during the workshop as well as Palgrave Macmillan's anonymous reviewers for their insights. We remain grateful to Palgrave Macmillan professional staff for their support.

Contents

Notes on Contributors

Roselaine Bonfim de Almeida has a doctorate in applied economics from the University of São Paulo. She is Adjunct Professor of Economics at the Federal University of Grande Dourados in Brazil. In her research she uses econometric techniques to study the following topics: labour economics, education and child labour.

Lorena Vieira Costa was born in Minas Gerias, Brazil. At present, is Professor of Economics of the Department of Rural Economics at Federal University of Viçosa. The Professor Costa Vieira received her PhD in Economic from the Federal University of Viçosa in 2016. E-mail: lorenavclelis@gmail.com. More info: http://lattes.cnpq.br/4459571064066337.

Eva Rodríguez Cuevas was born in Santo Domingo, Dominican Republic. Master's degree in Applied Economics at the Federal University of Viçosa (2018). Graduation *Cum Laude* in Economic Sciences of the Autonomous University of Santo Domingo, Dominican Republic (2013). Currently work in the Ministry of Finance of the Dominican Republic. E-mail: evrodriguezc@gmail.com. More info: http://lattes.cnpq.br/0259829109244207.

Afreen Gani Faridi is a PhD candidate at the Centre for the Study of Law and Governance, Jawaharlal Nehru University. His research seeks to locate the interstices of constitutionalism and conflict for determining the impact on work practices in Kashmir. His writings include poetry on conflict, trauma and memory. Besides wielding a pen, he is busy whipping up food recipes to counter fascism.

Trinh Q. Long is a project consultant at the Asian Development Bank Institute (ADBI), Tokyo. He is also a researcher at the Faculty of Finance and Banking, Tôn Đức Thắng University, Vietnam. Before joining the ADBI, he had worked as an economist at the Central Institute for Economic Management, Vietnam, for more than 10 years. His research topics include implications of financial development and international trade on firm performance and household welfare.

Dakhina Mitra has been conducting research on child rights and child well-being for more than 15 years. She specialises in using participatory research approaches to highlight the voices of children, families and vulnerable communities. She has worked on several child-focussed projects for international agencies. She is the Knowledge Building (Research) Practice Lead at the Centre for Excellence in Child and Family Welfare which is a peak sector body for children and family services in Victoria, Australia. She is also a member of two child protection global alliances/ working groups which work on both development and humanitarian settings.

Peter J. Morgan is a senior consulting economist and vice-chair of Research at the Asian Development Bank Institute (ADBI). Previously, he had 23 years of experience in the financial sector in Asia, most recently serving as the Chief Asia Economist for HSBC. His research interests are macroeconomic policy and financial sector regulation, reform, financial development, financial inclusion, fintech, financial literacy and financial education.

Alberto Posso is Professor of Economics at the Centre for International Development and Principal Research Fellow at the Australian APEC Study Centre, RMIT University, Australia. Posso holds a PhD in Economics from the Australian National University with specialisations in economic development and applied econometrics. He has over 40 peer-reviewed publications, including papers in *World Development*, *The Journal of Development Studies* and *The Review of Development Economics*.

Posso has also authored reports for governments and international organisations, including Oxfam, Plan International, the United Nations and the Fred Hollows Foundation.

Joydeb Sasmal is Former Professor of Economics at Vidyasagar University in India. Presently, he is an honorary research scholar of the Centre for Training and Research in Public Finance and Policy (CTRPFP) at CSSSC, India. His teaching and search areas are natural resource and agriculture, economic growth, public economics, international trade and child labour. He has authored many articles in various topics of Economics and nearly 50 papers have appeared in reputed journals, and he has authored one book, published by Springer. He has presented his papers in international conferences in the country and abroad including the USA, the Netherlands, Spain, France, Italy, Australia, China, Turkey and Morocco.

Ritwik Sasmal is a researcher in business, marketing and sales promotion. He has obtained his MSc degree in Economics from the University of Calcutta, India, and just completed his master's programme in Politics and Public Administration at the University of Konstanz, Germany. His master's thesis in the University of Konstanz is 'Role of Information & Communication Technology on Dimensions of Governance-A Cross country Analysis'. His papers in the field of public expenditure, economic growth and poverty alleviation have appeared in many journals and books. He has expertise in computer programming and data analysis.

Fabien Sundjo is an economist and political scientist, lecturing at the Department of Economics of the Higher Teacher Training College, under the University of Bamenda. Dr. Sundjo is a visiting lecturer at the Universities of Buea and Yaounde II, Soa, and at the Rome Business School. Sundjo has occupied the post of Chair and Dean of studies at the School of Business and Public Policy of the St. Monica University.

Indrajit Thakurata is an assistant professor at the Indian Institute of Management, Indore, India. His research interests include life cycle optimization models, portfolio choice and DSGE models. He teaches Macroeconomics and Monetary Economics.

List of Figures

List of Tables

1

Introduction

Alberto Posso

1.1 Purpose and Scope

The aim of this volume is to present new information to complement existing work on child labour. There is a large literature on child labour, which has attracted thorough reviews, most comprehensive of which is Edmonds (2007).

Edmonds (2007) decomposes the child labour literature into two categories. The first focuses on defining child labour, which discusses issues related to legal definitions that help statistical agencies to account for child labour. This research also preoccupies itself with scoping different activities that should or not be included in the child labour definition.

The second major part of this literature focuses on understanding why children work. This strand of the literature focuses on both the theory and practice of child labour, usually from an economic perspective. This literature primarily defines child labour in terms of time allocations, which is usually preferred by academics for empirical work. It studies the determinants of child labour to inform policymakers as to how to

A. Posso (✉)
RMIT University, Melbourne, VIC, Australia
e-mail: alberto.posso@rmit.edu.au

A. Posso (ed.), *Child Labor in the Developing World*,
https://doi.org/10.1007/978-981-15-3106-4_1

eradicate the phenomenon. This literature focuses on how family characteristics affect child work as well as how exogenous shocks, such as income or price changes as well as policies, affect it. This literature often discusses the consequences of child labour, focusing on health and well-being outcomes, for example (Posso 2019).

This volume primarily fits into the second strand of this literature. While defining child labour is important, each chapter adopts its own definition often aiming to facilitate empirical analysis. The volume presents both theoretical and empirical approaches to understanding child labour, primarily from an economic perspective.

The volume is made up of three sections. The first section builds on the existing literature and provides new theoretical insights into child labour. Section 1.2 provides empirical evidence from both quantitative and qualitative case studies on child labour from across Asia, Africa and Latin America. This section provides information from studies conducted in Brazil, Cameroon, the Dominican Republic, India and Vietnam. Section 1.3 provides policy recommendations.

The remainder of this chapter sets the stage for the ensuing analysis by first discussing how governments usually define child labour. Then, the chapter discusses the most commonly known consequences of child labour to highlight why communities should care about it. Finally, the chapter discusses leading policies identified as negatively impacting child labour. Given that comprehensive reviews exist, the focus of this chapter is to discuss the latest thinking on the topic.

1.2 How Do Governments Usually Define Child Labour?

The United Nations Sustainable Development Goals (SDGs) include a commitment to eradicate child labour in all its forms by the year 2025 (Goal 8.7). However, child labour, according to UN guidelines, generally does not refer to all work activities that a child undertakes. In 2008 at the 18th International Conference of Labour Statisticians, convened by the ILO, the UN system agreed on a definition of child labour to allow for the collection and analysis of data. Accordingly, a child is considered a labourer when he or she lies within the following categories: (1) is between the ages of 5 and 11 and undertakes at least 1 hour of economic work or 21 hours of unpaid household services per week; (2) is aged 12 to 14 years and undertakes at least 14 hours of economic work or 21 hours of unpaid household services per week; and (3) is between the ages of 15 and 17 years and undertakes at least 43 hours of economic or unpaid household services per week (UNICEF 2017). A child is also identified as a labourer if she/he is engaged in the worst forms of child labour, which include slavery, forced labour, prostitution, trafficking or exposure to hazards.

It is using these definitions that we now know that despite declining in recent decades, the latest estimates suggest that approximately 168 million children aged between 5 and 17 are engaged in some type of child labour (UNICEF 2019). Figure 1.1 presents the percentage of children aged 5 to 17 years in child labour, by sex and region. The figure highlights that using this definition, approximately 30% of children in Southern

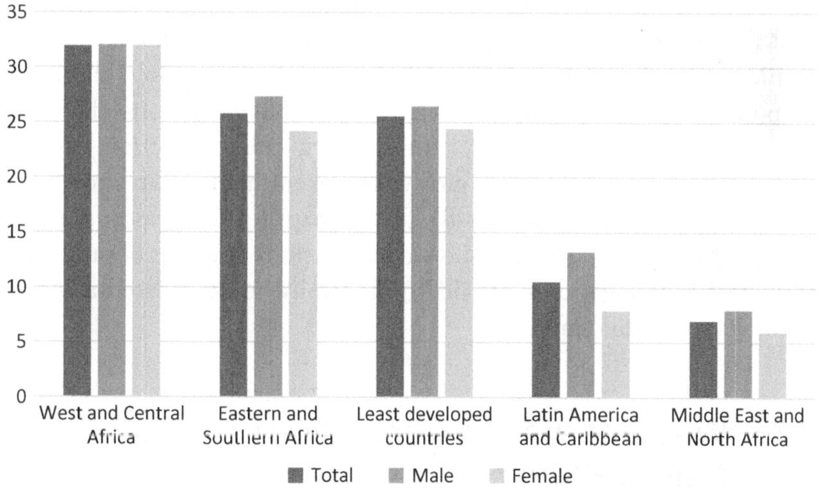

Fig. 1.1 Percentage of children aged 5 to 17 years in child labour, by sex and region. (Source: UNICEF (2017). Notes: Regional estimates represent data from countries covering at least 50% of the regional population of children aged 5 to 17. Data coverage was insufficient to calculate a global estimate and regional estimates for East Asia and the Pacific, Eastern Europe and Central Asia, North America, South Asia and Western Europe)

and Western Africa are engaged in child labour, compared to between 5% and 10% in the Latin America and the Caribbean and the Middle East and North Africa. On average, using this definition generates data that also suggests that boys are more likely to work than girls. This issue is dealt with below.

There are at least two important problems with this definition. The first problem is related to the stepwise definition of child labour. For example, if an 11-year-old child is working in a family farm for an hour a week, he or she is a worker. However, that same child ceases to be a worker on their 12th birthday. This ad hoc distinction assumes that child well-being, lifestyle and pressures can arbitrarily and drastically change from one day to the next. Perhaps adopting a more linear approach would be useful. Indeed, economic researchers aim not to classify child labour in a dichotomous fashion. Rather, many economists employ child work hours to test the relationship between child work and various outcomes (Posso 2019).

The second problem is related to the distinction between work activities and unpaid household services. The current definition structures treat unpaid household work as less problematic for children than economic work. The issue with this definition is that household chores can be potentially harmful by exposing children to dangerous chemicals, tools and abuse (Posso 2019). Importantly, this distinction can also underplay the extent to which girls work, given that they are more likely to work at home (Bhukuth 2008). It is perhaps for this reason that Save the Children (2019) defines child work to include all kinds of productive or domestic work, paid or unpaid, in the family home or externally, both in rural and urban contexts.

1.3 Why Should We Care About Child Labour?

Child labour is both a symptom and a cause of poverty. Low-income households use child labour to meet their basic needs, using child labour to boost income to help achieve a minimal subsistence standard (Basu and Van 1998). The problem is that child labour can also have important long-term consequences for adults once they grow up. Child labour is associated with adverse health consequences, which can last until adulthood, and lower levels of educational attainment and has been found to lead to lower earnings in adulthood (ILO 2015; Posso 2017, 2019).

As a result, child labour not only plagues the poor but can potentially condemn poor children into a life of poverty, generating a vicious poverty cycle. Basu (1999) conceptualises a model that explains how this works. Mainly, poor households that are unable to meet a minimal subsistence standard send their children to work. In turn, work deprives children of education and skill acquisition. Consequently, the generation of child workers become poor, unskilled adult labourers. This cycle of poverty fuels child labour in the next generation.

1.4 What Can We Do About Child Labour?

Policies that aim to ban child labour are likely to be ineffective for two reasons. First, it is difficult to ban child labour when it predominantly occurs in the informal economy (Bhukuth 2008). Family businesses, domestic work and artisan work mostly fall outside of the regulatory framework of governments, particularly in developing countries and in rural areas. This is particularly so for the rural sector, where most child labour exists (UNICEF 2019). As a result, children that work are not protected by existing legislation.

Second, child labour occurs in relatively poorer households, such that banning may propel households further into poverty. Many households survive thanks to the financial or in-kind contributions made by children's work; consequently, banning such support would risk pushing households below a minimum subsistence standard (Bhukuth 2008). Bharadwaj et al. (2013) examine the consequences of India's Child Labor (Prohibition and Regulation) Act of 1986, which banned child labour. Using survey data conducted before and after the ban, they show that the ban decreased child wages, which in turn resulted in an increase in child labour. Their results suggest that families use child labour to reach a minimum subsistence standard, so when child wages decrease, poor families utilise more child labour.

In the absence of effective government policies, many suggest that goods made by child workers should be banned or boycotted in other countries. However, this can backfire because boycotting goods can reduce wages, pushing households to increase child labour supply to meet their required subsistence standards (Basu and Zarghamee 2009).

Policies that aim to directly affect the root causes of child labour are going to be more effective than banning it or boycotting products. Eradicating child labour can be achieved only by eradicating poverty, so policies that tackle poverty, particularly child poverty, are more effective.

There is a large economic literature that shows that even small cash transfers, which increase household income, can lead to sharp falls in both paid and unpaid economic activity of children (Del Carpio et al. 2016). Conditional cash transfers, for example, provide the household with cash injections if children attend school and have regular health check-ups. The policies recognise that helping children accumulate human capital through schooling and health interventions can lift them out of poverty. The evidence suggests that cash transfers are indeed associated with declining incidences of child labour (Kabeer and Waddington 2015). Overall, the evidence suggests that policies that are associated with factors that can potentially help households increase their income, including better access to credit markets and loans, are associated with declines in child labour (Chakrabarty 2015). Conversely, economists have found that child labour increases during difficult economic times for families (Del Carpio et al. 2016). Overall, when budgetary and financial constraints of poor households are alleviated, households become less likely to rely on child labour.

Studies have also found that investing in quality education is associated with declining child labour, as households perceive a higher opportunity cost of working (Del Carpio et al. 2016). Consequently, policies that lower both direct (school fees) and indirect (travel time) costs of formal schooling as well as aim to improve its quality can decrease child labour (Edmonds and Shrestha 2014).

However, many studies continue to uncover heterogeneity on the impact of various policies, including absolute or conditional transfers on child labour. This literature points to the fact that context matters. Household characteristics and cultural factors can be particularly relevant, as child labour may be more acceptable in some societies over others (Bandara et al. 2015). Within households, children's age, gender and birth order also seem to make a difference (Kantarevic and Mechoulan 2006). Finally, factors like access to credit can potentially increase child labour when they create new employment opportunities, particularly when educational alternatives are poor (Bandara et al. 2015).

This level of heterogeneity calls for further research into child labour. It is important to understand the complex context in which it operates. This volume provides new evidence of the theoretical and empirical causes and consequences of child labour. In so doing, the chapters provide a unique set of policy prescriptions that are applicable to both the developing countries that make up the case studies of the volume and other countries more broadly. The volume is constructed to inform policy with rigorous analysis.

1.5 Volume Content

To present a revised theoretical framework, Section 1.1 of this volume discusses child labour from both a macroeconomic and microeconomic point of view. In Chap. 2, Joydeb Sasmal and Ritwik Sasmal discuss child labour from a macroeconomic perspective. The chapter begins with a review of the literature on child labour. Then, it theoretically presents the vicious poverty cycle in which child labour exists. Child labour is primarily caused by poverty. In turn, working children, deprived of education, grow up to become poor, which results in a child-labour-induced poverty trap. The chapter addresses potential pro-poor and pro-growth macroeconomic policies, which could potentially curtail the child labour problem. The authors present a classical argument in economics that sustains that shifting employment from the low-productivity agricultural sector to high-productivity manufacturing is likely to reduce child labour.

Chapter 3 builds on this framework with a microeconomic perspective of child labour. In this chapter, Indrajit Thakurata develops a life-cycle microeconomic model various financial and human-capital parameter playing a role in the incidence of child labour in developing countries. The chapter frames child labour as a coping strategy and explores three income categories, with different levels of financial access and human-capital investment options, and examines a two-generation, multi-period, finite lifetime problem of an altruistic parent valuing the human capital of their offspring. The problem is solved using dynamic programming where life-cycle profiles are generated using simulations. Simulations replicate child labour as an optimal strategy of very poor households, and income support remains the only policy initiative to bootstrap education. The study shows that for the highest income category, there exists space for resource transfer without compromising on net human-capital production.

Section 1.2 of the volume discusses new qualitative and quantitative empirical evidence. In Chap. 4, Dakhina Mitra focuses on cultural factors that may be propagating the child labour problem. The author asks if there is a culture of child labour and looks at the decision-making process of working, with special reference to the girl beedi rollers in Jhalda region of Purulia, West Bengal. This chapter utilises primary data collected from a traditional agro-forest industry, beedi making, in Jhalda, West Bengal, India. The chapter aims to inform about children's perceptions of work, their level of awareness of hazardous or exploitative working conditions, the amount of consultation that working children receive regarding the labour decision and broad cultural factors that can be used to justify work. The study uses an ethically approved methodology, which documents life stories of children. Given that children are socialised by families, peer groups and the society, their stories are deconstructed against the backdrop of the discourses of the family and larger society. The study argues that children socialised in a particular manner tend to accept their reality as fate. The study finds that child workers belong to sections of society, which are considered different at multiple levels from the others in that society. This distinction is observed in their physical spaces, living conditions, socio-economic status. Children are found to internalise the distinction and exhibit a sense of powerlessness and vulnerability. Their ability to exercise agency is inhibited by the societal discourses of caste hierarchies, cultural practices, traditional norms surrounding gender and structural neglect. This and much more contribute to the decision-making process of working among these children. The chapter concludes that unless there are external influences (e.g. practical educational initiatives, civil society and government partnerships, regulation of exploitative conditions, context-specific alternative approaches) that work to break these barriers, such cycles become intergenerational, and the culture of child labour develops.

In Chap. 5, Eva Rodriguez Cuevas and Lorena Vieira Costa expand the empirical microeconomic literature, by studying how income shocks affect child labour in the Dominican Republic. This chapter builds on a large literature in applied economics that investigates the relationship between negative income shocks, child labour and school attendance. It begins with a theoretical mode and then tests its propositions using survey data from the Dominican Republic, one of the most vulnerable economies in Latin America. The chapter applies rigorous econometric techniques to model households' decision to allocate children's time to work and/or study. The results suggest that economic assets at home improve the human capital formation of children and adolescents and concomitantly reduce their probability of work, regardless of gender and age. The authors suggest that policies to combat child labour and to develop human capital in rural areas should not be limited to fighting poverty. The chapter ends with policy recommendations.

In Chap. 6, Peter J. Morgan and Trinh Q. Long contribute to our understanding of child labour by investigating it vis-à-vis another common phenomenon in developing countries, migration. Building on a literature that investigates the child well-being impacts of migration, this chapter uses Vietnamese household survey data to examine the effect of migration on left-behind children's education and labour in Vietnam. Since decisions to attend school and to work are jointly determined, the authors use a simultaneous equation modelling approach to estimate the effect of migration on child education and labour. Since migration also affects household welfare, they integrate household welfare into a system of equations. They find that migration of other family members does not affect a child's decision to attend school directly but does so indirectly through an increase in time spent at work. However, migration might increase household income, and this may also have a positive effect on child education and reduce child labour.

As in Chaps. 5 and 6, Chap. 7 also studies the nexus between child labour and educational attainment. In this chapter, Roselaine Bonfim de

Almeida evaluates the effect of the child labour on educational attainment using data from Brazil. The study builds a pseudo-panel at the state level to understand how the proportion of child workers is associated with aggregated educational attainment of successive generations. The indicator of educational attainment is the probability of that a given generation in a given state finishes eighth grade of elementary school without any delay in a given year. The results show that child labour decreases the probability of attainment by approximately 70 percentage points. The chapter concludes with policy suggestions.

In Chap. 8, Fabien Sundjo explores the heterogeneity of child labour participation by focusing on parent's characteristics. The chapter uses individual records of the 2007 Cameroon household consumption survey. The chapter pays specific attention to subjective and objective poverty measures and how they affect child labour. The study uses several empirical methods to find that an increase in child wage increases the number of hours worked by a child and that child labour in Cameroon is poverty driven as indicated by both objective and subjective measures of poverty. Hence, placing a legal restriction on the employment of children as stated by the 1992 Labour Code of Cameroon in a context where poverty is pervasive may lead to a larger cost if not accompanied by other measures.

Section 1.3 of the study includes two chapters on policy recommendations. In Chap. 9, Afreen G. Faridi studies child labour in a pastoral tribe of Jammu and Kashmir. This chapter calls into question those recommendations using a case study from a unique group of individuals in a conflict-affected zone. It focuses on the distinct social and economic realities that enculture and shape work practices in isolated communities, while locating perspectives which shape child labour legislation. The chapter argues that most of the studies on child labour in India and other developing nations employ a legal-positivist approach while determining the incidence of child labour across social groups. Even as ethnographic studies on scheduled tribes highlight the distinct cultural nature of their work practices, most of the analysis of child labour amongst tribes continues to rely on the universal definition of child labour prescribed within child labour legislation to determine the success or failure during its implementation. Thus, there exists a need to 'embed' state institutions and policy frameworks within the cultural practices of a tribe to determine their efficacy in plugging child labour within a particular socio-economic reality. The chapter conceptualises the need to locate the social prejudice within the definition of child labour in legislative and the customary values that affect child work amongst tribes. It provides for the rationale that directed the researcher to embed and analyse child labour legislation within a tribe rather than any other social group in India. Using institutional analysis and development framework to analyse state policy in a zone of conflict, the study highlights the extent of work undertaken by tribal children in Jammu and Kashmir and the impact of such customary work practices on their lives. The study embeds child labour legislation and state policy against cultural notions of child work using a case study of a pastoral tribe in Jammu and Kashmir. It reviews the extant legislation and policies for a critical analysis of child labour laws and policies in India to analyse the implicit assumptions of 'child' and 'work' in the legal framework.

In the final chapter, Alberto Posso provides a summary of the overall policy findings from all the previous chapters. This chapter reviews the policy recommendations of the previous chapters, providing a generalised view of how to curb child labour in developing countries. It warns that over-generalisations can be counter-productive, while highlighting the need for comprehensive nation, regional and international policies that aim to wholeheartedly address this phenomenon.

References

Bandara, A., R. Dehejia, and S. Lavie-Rouse. 2015. The impact of income and non-income shocks on child labor: Evidence from a panel survey of Tanzania. *World Development* 67: 218–237.

Basu, K. 1999. Child labor: Cause, consequence, and cure, with remarks on international labor standards. *Journal of Economic literature* 37 (3): 1083–1119.

Basu, K., and P.H. Van. 1998. The economics of child labor. *American Economic Review* 88: 412–427.

Basu, K., and H. Zarghamee. 2009. Is product boycott a good idea for controlling child labor? A theoretical investigation. *Journal of Development Economics* 88 (2): 217–220.

Bharadwaj, P., L.K. Lakdawala, and N. Li. 2013. *Perverse consequences of well intentioned regulation: Evidence from India's child labor ban*. National Bureau of Economic Research Working Paper No. w19602. Cambridge, MA: National Bureau of Economic Research.

Bhukuth, A. 2008. Defining child labour: A controversial debate. *Development in Practice* 18 (3): 385–394.

Chakrabarty, S. 2015. A nexus between child labour and microfinance: An empirical investigation. *Economic Papers* 34 (1–2): 76–91.

Del Carpio, X.V., N.V. Loayza, and T. Wada. 2016. The impact of conditional cash transfers on the amount and type of child labor. *World Development* 80: 33–47.

Edmonds, E.V. 2007. Child labor. *Handbook of Development Economics* 4: 3607–3709.

Edmonds, E.V., and M. Shrestha. 2014. You get what you pay for: Schooling incentives and child labor. *Journal of Development Economics* 111: 196–211.

ILO. 2015. *Child labour and education: Progress, challenges and future directions*. Geneva: International Labour Organisation. http://www.ilo.org/ipec/Informationresources/WCMS_IPEC_PUB_26435/lang%2D%2Den/index.htm.

Kabeer, N., and H. Waddington. 2015. Economic impacts of conditional cash transfer programmes: A systematic review and meta-analysis. *Journal of Development Effectiveness* 7 (3): 290–303.

Kantarevic, J., and S. Mechoulan. 2006. Birth order, educational attainment, and earnings: An investigation using the PSID. *The Journal of Human Resources* 41 (4): 755–777.

Posso, A. 2017. Child labour's effect on long-run earnings: An analysis of cohorts. *Economic Modelling* 64: 465–472.

———. 2019. The health consequences of hazardous and nonhazardous child labor. *Review of Development Economics* 23 (2): 619–639.

Save the Children. 2019. *Child labour*. Toronto: Save the Children Canada. https://www.savethechildren.ca/what-we-do/global-programs/protection/child-labour/.

UNICEF. 2017. *Child labour*. New York: United Nations Children's Fund. https://data.unicef.org/topic/child-protection/child-labour/.
———. 2019. *Child protection from violence, exploitation and abuse: Child labour*. New York: United Nations Children's Fund. https://www.unicef.org/protection/57929_child_labour.html.

2

Economic Growth, Structural Change and Decline of Child Labour in Agriculture: A Theoretical Perspective

Joydeb Sasmal and Ritwik Sasmal

2.1 Introduction and Literature Review

Child labour is a serious socio-economic problem at the global level, especially in the developing world. International organizations like UN, UNICEF and ILO, the national governments, NGOs and various

The authors are indebted to Prof. Sugata Marjit for his help in writing this chapter. The valuable comments on the chapter received from the participants of the workshop on 'Understanding Child Labour in Agriculture' jointly organized by the Australian APEC Study Centre and RMIT University at RMIT University in Melbourne, Australia, on April 8–9, 2019, are gratefully acknowledged.

J. Sasmal (✉)
Department of Economics with Rural Development, Vidyasagar University, Midnapore, India

Centre for Training & Research in Public Finance and Policy at CSSSC, Kolkata, India

R. Sasmal
Department of Politics & Public Administration, University of Konstanz, Konstanz, Germany

A. Posso (ed.), *Child Labor in the Developing World*,
https://doi.org/10.1007/978-981-15-3106-4_2

voluntary organizations are very much concerned with this problem, and all are searching for effective policy measures to solve this problem. Legal ban, direct intervention of the government and incentive-based schemes have been suggested by scholars, researchers and policy makers as effective measures to combat this problem. Among the factors responsible for child labour, poverty is considered to be the most important one. Basu (1999), in seminal work, demonstrates that if the wage of the poor parents is less than a critical minimum level, they will send their children to work for family earning instead of sending them to school for education. As the children of the poor parents are deprived of education and acquiring skill, they grow up to become unskilled adult workers. That means the families will remain poor in the next generation also, and they will send their children to work again. Thus a child labour trap is formed due to persistence of poverty in a dynamic perspective (Basu 1999). Basu and Van (1998) assume that parents are altruistic and they want children's education. Two axioms have been considered in their analysis here—luxury and substitution. The luxury axiom asserts that if the parents are poor, they will send their children to work. Under this axiom, leisure is a luxury for the family, whereas under substitution axiom, adult and child labour are substitutes. In this theoretical model, there are two equilibria, one is with child labour where adult wage rate is low and the other is without child labour where adult wage rate is high.

The ILO states that child labour deprives children of their childhood, and it hampers their access to education and skill formation (Basu 1999; Burra 2005; Venkatanarayana 2004). Educational failure is an important cause of poverty and child labour (Sasmal and Guillen 2015). However, not all educational failures can be attributed to the incidence of child labour. Burra (2005) shows that nearly 100 million children in India in the age group 5–14 years are out of school, but all of them cannot be termed as child workers even though schooling and formation of human skill can play an important role in solving the problem of child labour. Another important measure towards this problem is complete ban on child labour. But success of this measure depends on proper enforcement and effectiveness of the prohibition laws. It is generally difficult to implement such prohibitive laws in poor countries. For example, the Child Labour (Prohibition and Regulation) Act was passed in India in 1986 along with many supplementary measures. But this Act did not have much success, especially in the informal sector of the economy. Another route to curb child labour is direct intervention of the government in the labour market. The government may pass laws to raise the wage rate of the poor adult workers. The argument is that if Minimum Wage Act is enforced properly, poverty will decline, and with decline of poverty, the parents will be in a situation to send their children to school. But there are different views on the issue of enactment of minimum wage law. It is apprehended that minimum wage legislation may make the situation worse. As a result of enforcement of the Minimum Wage Act, employment of adult workers may decline leading to greater employment of child labour (Basu 2000). Chaudhuri and Mukhopadhyay (2010) show in a theoretical model that adult labour and child labour are perfect substitutes. If wage rate increases, supply of child labour will increase because leisure will be costly and substitution effect will outweigh the income effect. Besides, sanction on the export of child labour-tainted goods in the international market is suggested as a policy instrument to curb child labour. Baland and Duprez (2009) and Basu and Zarghamee (2009), however, have expressed doubt in the effectiveness of this policy. Basu and Zarghamee are of the opinion that boycott of child labour-tainted goods may have adverse impact on child labour as it reduces the wage of child workers. Baland and Duprez, on the other hand, show that the policy of label may divert the children to the works of the domestic sector as a result of displacement effect. Thus the condition of the poor children may even worsen as their working opportunities are reduced by this policy. Another policy instrument to curb child labour suggested in this context is to provide benefits like mid-day meal at school and provision for free books and study materials for greater schooling and education of the poor children. But, these measures are not found to create sufficient incentives for the poor parents to send their children to school. In that case, Conditional Cash Transfer (CCT) benefit scheme is suggested to be a more effective measure for the schooling of the poor children (Ravallion and Wodon 2000; Sasmal 2013; De Hoop and Rosati 2013). Under the CCT scheme, the family of the poor child will be provided a direct cash benefit on the condition that the child is sent to school. The minimum years of schooling necessary for imparting skill in the child may be ensured by increasing the amount of direct cash payment, and such scheme has been found to be fruitful in some countries of the developing world (Ravallion and Wodon 2000; De Hoop and Rosati 2013).

The child workers are not only deprived of education and human skill, they are very often subject to exploitation and inhuman behaviour. In a model of exploitative child labour, Rogers and Swinnerton (2008) show that the child workers are paid wage less than the value of marginal product. So, there is scope for policy intervention to protect the children from exploitation. They have suggested a system of inspection and fines to stop such practice.

Schooling, education and human capital formation are important aspects of the literature of child labour. So long as poverty persists, children are deprived of acquiring human skill, and the poor children grow as unskilled adult workers who earn low wage in future life. Thus child labour trap continues in a dynamic perspective. Apart from schooling and education, sufficient financial investment on education is also necessary to impart skill in the child which the poor households cannot afford. Galor and Zeira (1993) and Basu (2002) demonstrate using overlapping generations models that expenditure on education has to cross a minimum threshold level in order to impart skill in labour and making the investment meaningful. These models show that such investment will take place for human capital formation if inheritance or bequest exceeds some critical value. But in poor households, bequest or inheritance is almost nil. Naturally, poverty and child labour continue over generations. Glomm (1997) makes an important comment in this context. According to him, an individual when young can make decisions about investment on his/her education. But at the school level, it is the parent who decides whether the child will go to school and for how many years. The child has no say in this matter. In this context, Ermisch and Francesconi (2001) find that parents' education and income are important determinants of child's education.

Most of the existing theoretical literature on child labour has emphasized children's study time as the only input in their human capital accumulation. So, it implies that child labour necessarily reduces children's human capital. The paper by Fan (2004) extends the literature by considering that a child's human capital is determined by the financial resources spent on his/her education in addition to study time. With reference to financial resources, the author shows that if the children's labour market participation increases in response to changes of the relative wage/productivity between child labour and adult labour, it may raise the financial resources spent on education, and thereby it can enhance children's human capital. In the literature of financial problem in human capital formation of the poor children, the credit market has a role. Baland and Robinson (2000) show that resource constraint of the household and credit market imperfection may be a cause of child labour. Using a two-period model, they demonstrate theoretically that child labour may arise in equilibrium even though it is socially inefficient, and parents are altruistic if capital markets are imperfect and family bequests are zero. With reference to the role of credit market in human capital formation, the theoretical model of Ranjan (1999) shows that in education-child labour trade-off in the developing countries, the child is most likely to be out of school. However, if the credit market is informal, the problem of child labour will arise because informal credit market mainly provides short-term credit, whereas the poor households need long-term credit to overcome financial constraints for children's education (ILO/IPEC—SIMPOC 2007).

2.2 Child Labour in Agriculture

We have so far discussed different aspects of child labour in general. Now, our focus will be on the problem of child labour in agriculture, in particular. According to ILO estimates, there are 152 million child labourers at the global level, 60% of which are employed in agriculture (ILO 2016). That means 60% of the child workers are engaged in farming, fishing, forestry and livestock management in global perspective. The types of work they generally do in agriculture are plantation, irrigation works, pest control, harvesting and procurement of crops, processing of products, cattle grazing, fuel collection, collection of forest products, fishing, sales of agro-products in the market and so on. These works are mostly hazardous and they put huge stress on the child's health and mind. Agricultural child workers are not only deprived of education and acquiring human skill, but also they become demoralized for their future life. In the non-agricultural sector, on the other hand, the child labourers work as table boys in hotels and restaurants; remain engaged as workers in brickfields, garage and repairing shops, manufacturing of fire crackers and works of artisans; and also work as domestic help (servant) and labourers in small industries using harmful chemicals. Using children in such activities are not only inhuman, it bears huge socio-economic costs in the form of loss of dignity, skill, health, productivity and future income. According to the ILO report 2012–2016, out of 152 million child labourers, 73 million are employed in hazardous works. Edmonds (2003) finds that majority of child workers are involved in agriculture although much of the research has been focused on the employment of child labour in the industrial sector.

With reference to child labour in agriculture, we need to differentiate between two categories of child workers in agriculture. In the first category, there are child workers who work in their family farms on part-time basis, generally, without having any adverse impact on their schooling and education. On the contrary, they may gather experience, self-esteem, confidence and intergenerational professional skill for their family business or occupation. The other category of child workers employed in agriculture are those who work at the cost of acquiring education and skills for future life. These child workers belong to poor families, and their parents send them to work for wage earning instead of sending them to school. This second category of child workers remain engaged in different activities of agriculture mostly on full-time basis due to poverty, and this put huge cost on the society in the form of loss of skill, productivity, income and growth. Moreover, they lose confidence and self-esteem and get demoralized forever.

The objective of this chapter is to address the problems of the second category in agriculture in the developing countries. This study will concentrate on the problems of child labour in agriculture where the root cause of child labour is poverty. Poverty is generally higher in the rural sector of less developed countries. The reasons behind higher poverty in rural areas are small size of land holding, excessive dependence on agriculture, low productivity in agriculture, lack of alternative employment opportunities and lack of education and human skill. Even large numbers of rural people do not have any land of their own. They are just agricultural labourers and their livelihood depends only on their wage earning. Since productivity is low, wage of the workers is also low. In such a situation, the poor parents are rather forced to send their children to work for family earning.

This chapter intends to address the problem of child labour from macro perspective. It attempts to show that if growth takes place in the country, there will be structural change in the economy with declining importance of agriculture in respect of employment and income generation. In its place, the non-agricultural sector (manufacturing and services) will expand with higher productivity and higher wage rate. In effect, the adult workers will be gradually shifted from agriculture to the non-agricultural sector where they will get higher wages. As the workers will get higher wage in the non-agricultural sector, poverty will decline, and this will lead to decline of child labour as a whole and also in agriculture. Thus decline of child labour in agriculture will be the natural outcome of economic growth and structural change in the economy. This is reflected in ILO report also. According to the ILO report (2018) on global estimates of child labour 2012–2016, low-income countries (per capita income US $ 1045 or less) account for 19.4% of total child workers in the world, whereas only 1.2% of the total child labour in the world are employed in high-income countries (per capita income US $ 12,736 or more). The report also notes that there has been sharp decline of child labour in the world from 245 million in 2000 to 152 million in 2016. The greater opportunities for schooling of poor children and various welfare measures have been helpful in reducing child labour. At the same time, rise in income and resultant decline in poverty have been effective in solving the problem at the global level. Since poverty is known to be the major cause of child labour, Grootaert and Kanbur (1995) show that economic growth and equitable distribution of income can be the most sustainable way of reducing child labour.

In this chapter, a theoretical model has been constructed to demonstrate that economic growth and structural change help reduce child labour in the economy. Since education and schooling of the children enhance skill and wage earning of the children in adulthood, an analytical framework has also been provided in Sect. 2.2 to show how schooling and skill formation can break the child labour trap in a dynamic perspective. In Sect. 2.3, a three-sector trade theoretic general equilibrium model has been developed to show that as formal sector expands, the less productive agricultural sector shrinks leading to decline of child labour in agriculture. It has been demonstrated that as workers are being transferred from agriculture to the formal non-agricultural sector with higher wage rate, child labour declines in the economy as a whole. As the agricultural sector shrinks, child labour in agriculture also declines. The summary results and policy implications have been provided in Sect. 2.4.

2.3 Theoretical Exposition: On Elimination of Child Labour Through Education and Human Skill Formation

2.3.1 The Model

In this chapter we are basically considering child labour caused by low income and poverty. Basu (1999) shows that if the wage of the parent falls below certain critical minimum level (say, subsistence level), parent will send children to work to earn income for the family. As the child goes to work, she/he is deprived of education and acquiring human skill. The child then grows to become an unskilled adult worker, and his/her wages remain low in the next generation. Thus, a vicious circle of poverty, child labour, lack of education and low income is created in the system. This circle can be broken if the child can acquire necessary skill to earn high wage in his adulthood through education and adequate schooling. It is assumed that the parent wants child's education, and in the utility function of the parent, child's education has positive contribution. Here, utility function of the parent can be expressed as:

$$U = U\left(C, E_1\right) \tag{2.1}$$

where C is consumption of the family and E_1 is years of education of the child in period 1. Each individual lives for two periods—in period 1, the individual is child, and in period 2, he is adult. Total years in childhood (5–14 years) is T which may be used in work for earning of the family or in education for acquiring human skill. It is like an overlapping generations model where at each period there are two generations—parent and child—and the parent takes the decision whether the child will go to school and for how many years.

Here,

$$T \geq E_1 \geq 0$$

If $E_1 = T$, the child does not go for work at all, and he goes to school for education for the whole period of childhood. If $E_1 = 0$, the schooling of the child is zero. For simplicity, child's education has been taken in years. It may be taken in hours per day also.

The parent takes decision regarding child's education and his budget constraint is

$$C = W_1 + W_C\left(T - E_1\right) \tag{2.2}$$

where W_1 is wage earning of the parent in period 1 and W_C is wage rate of the child worker per unit of time (year). $(T - E_1)$ is the amount of child labour. The family has no other source of income and the whole income is spent on consumption.

The wage rate of the adult worker depends on his human skill (H), and it depends on his education in childhood. So, the wage rate in the next period when the child is adult is W_2, and it depends on the education in childhood (i.e. E_1). Therefore, we can write

$$W_2 = W_2\left(E_1\right) \tag{2.3}$$

where

$$W_2'\left(E_1\right) \rangle\, 0, W_2''\left(E_1\right) \langle\, 0,$$

That is, W_2 is an increasing function of E_1 with concavity.

The objective of the parent in period 1 is

$$\begin{aligned}&Maximize\ V = W_1 + W_C\left(T - E_1\right) + W_2\left(E_1\right)\\&E_1\quad \text{S.t. } E_1 \le T\end{aligned} \tag{2.4}$$

The parent wants maximum family income in period 1, and he also wants that his child gets higher income as adult worker in the next period.

First order conditions for maximization of V are

$$\frac{\partial V}{\partial E_1} = -W_C + W_2'\left(E_1\right) = 0 \tag{2.5}$$

The sufficiency condition of maximizing V is

$$\frac{\partial^2 V}{\partial E_1^2} = W_2''\left(E_1\right) \langle\, 0 \tag{2.6}$$

The sufficiency condition is satisfied by the concavity of the function in (2.3). The conditions (2.5) and (2.6) determine the optimal level of education of the child $\left(E_1^*\right)$ in period 1. In equilibrium, the wage rate of child labour will be equal to the increase of adult wage in period 2 due to higher skill from education in childhood, that is, $W_C = W_2'\left(E_1\right)$.

Suppose the critical minimum level of education necessary to impart skill in the child is $\overline{E}_1$. The child will be a skilled worker in his adult age if $E_1^* \rangle\, \overline{E}_1$. But there is no guarantee that this condition will be fulfilled. In order to break the child labour trap in a dynamic perspective, E_1^* has to cross $\overline{E}_1$. Following Basu (1999), we may express E_2 (child's education in the next period) as a function of the education of the adult worker in his childhood, E_1, that is,

$$E_2 = E_2\left(E_1\right) \tag{2.7}$$

It is assumed that E_2 function takes a logistic shape as in Fig. 2.1, implying that it is convex in the first part and concave in the second part and then converges to a maximum value.

There are two equilibria in the dynamic perspective—e_1 and e_2. e_1 is unstable and e_2 is stable. If child's education in period 1 (i.e. E_1) falls

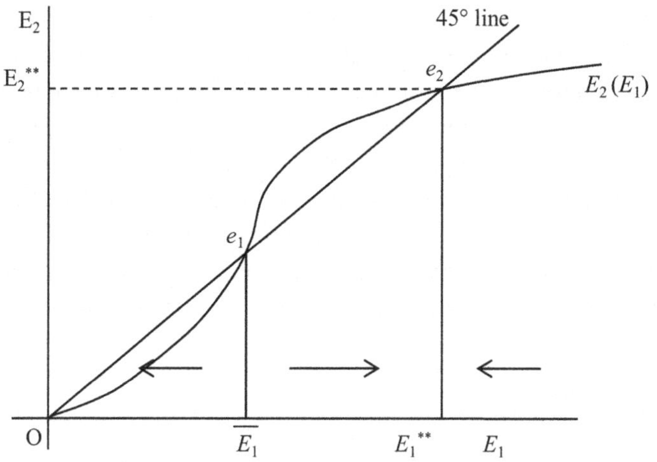

Fig. 2.1 Breaking the child labour trap through education

below $\overline{E_1}$, no skill will be formed in child. The wage rate will be low again and the family will remain poor for generations, and E_1 will decline to zero for all periods. But if E_1 can cross $\overline{E_1}$, it will stabilize at E_1^{**} where the child will not go to work and he or she will continue in school for education for the whole period of childhood, that is, $T = E_1$, and this will continue for all periods. If this equilibrium can be achieved, child labour will be eliminated, and it will break the child labour trap. If E_1^{*} cannot cross $\overline{E_1}$ in an automatic process of decision-making of the parent, policy manipulation may be helpful here. Anyway, it demonstrates that schooling and skill formation of the child can break the child labour trap.

2.4 Economic Growth, Structural Change and Decline of Child Labour in Agriculture: A Theoretical Explanation

This chapter is considering the problem of child labour caused by poverty and the household is poor due to low wage income of the adult worker (parent). Here, it is proposed that if economic growth takes place in the economy, non-agricultural sector (both formal and informal) will expand, and relative importance of agriculture will decline. In the formal non-agricultural sector (both manufacturing and services), wage rate is higher. Therefore if more and more labour can be transferred from agriculture to the non-agricultural sector through economic growth and structural change, poverty will decline, and this will lead to decline of child labour in the economy as a whole and also in agriculture. A theoretical explanation can be provided on this proposition by using a three-sector general equilibrium model of international trade in the line of Jones (1965).

2.4.1 The Model

We are considering an economy with three sectors—(1) informal agricultural sector, (2) formal manufacturing and services sector and (3) informal manufacturing and services sector. There are three factors of production—adult labour, child labour and capital. For simplicity, land has not been included in the model, and also land is not our focus of analysis in the present context. However, land can be incorporated in the model especially with respect to the agricultural sector. X, M and Z are the respective products of the above three sectors. L, L_C and K are adult labour, child labour and capital, respectively. L and K are used in all three sectors and L_C is used in X and Z only. There is perfect competition in the markets and production functions are characterized by CRS. a_{ij} is the requirement of ith factor in per unit production of jth product. X, M and Z—all are traded goods and their prices are P_X, P_M and P_Z, respectively. So, under small country assumption, prices of X, M and Z are given. Z is used in the production of M as intermediate input. The domestic demand for Z is $a_{ZM} \cdot M$. If production of Z is greater than its domestic demand, that is, $Z > a_{ZM} \cdot M$, there will be export of Z, and in the reverse situation, there will be import of Z. The supply of capital is K, and K is equal to $K_d + K_f$ where K_d is domestic capital and K_f is inflow of foreign capital. W is wage rate of adult labour in informal sector, r is rate of interest and W_C is wage rate of child labour. $\overline{W}$ is wage rate in the formal sector, and it is fixed due to trade union or any other economic reason. $\overline{W}$ is always higher than W. That means, if an adult worker gets employment in the formal sector, he always gets higher wage, $\overline{W}$. Total supply of adult labour is $\bar{L}$. The number of adult labour employed in M is $a_{LM} \cdot M = L_M$, and $(\bar{L} - L_M)$ is employed in informal sectors X and Z. Since W is less than $\bar{W}$, a section of the workers employed in the informal sectors will send their children to work due to poverty. Let us write $\alpha\left(\bar{L} - L_m\right) = l$ and $L_C = \phi(l)$ where α is the fraction of the number of the adult workers not employed in the formal sector and $\phi'(l) > 0$. So, $\alpha < 1$ and $\varphi'(l) > 0$ implies that if L_m increases, it means that a greater number of labourers are transferred to high income brackets. In effect, the number of poor workers, l, will decline with the result that L_C will also decline.

The full-employment conditions are

$$a_{LCX} \cdot X + a_{LCZ} \cdot Z = L_C \tag{2.8}$$

$$a_{LX} \cdot X + a_{LM} \cdot M + a_{LZ} \cdot Z = \bar{L} \tag{2.9}$$

$$a_{KX} \cdot X + a_{KM} \cdot M + a_{KZ} \cdot Z = K \tag{2.10}$$

The price equations are

$$a_{LCX} \cdot W_C + a_{LX} \cdot W + a_{KX} \cdot r = P_X \tag{2.11}$$

$$a_{LM} \cdot \bar{W} + a_{KM} \cdot r + a_{ZM} \cdot P_Z = P_M \tag{2.12}$$

$$a_{LCX} \cdot W_C + a_{LZ} \cdot W + a_{KZ} \cdot r = P_Z \tag{2.13}$$

P_X, P_M and P_Z are given in (2.11), (2.12) and (2.13). Given P_Z, Eq. (2.12) determines r. After r is determined, W and W_C are determined from (2.11) and (2.13). Here, product prices determine factor prices. Once factor prices are determined, the factor coefficients (a_{ijs}) are also determined. Now, output in three sectors X, M and Z are determined from (2.8), (2.9) and (2.10). So, the whole system is determined.

It is assumed that M is more capital-intensive than Z and Z is more capital-intensive than X compared to labour, that is,

$$\left(\frac{a_{KM}}{a_{LM}}\right) > \left(\frac{a_{KZ}}{a_{LZ}}\right) > \left(\frac{a_{KX}}{a_{LX}}\right)$$

Let us now consider the effect of economic growth on the three sectors and child labour in agriculture. $\hat{X}$, $\hat{M}$ and $\hat{Z}$ are relative changes in the production of *X*, *M* and *Z*, respectively, as described in Jones (1965). Suppose, supply of capital (*K*) increases due to inflow of foreign capital or increase of domestic savings. Now, given the product prices unchanged, capital-intensive sector (*M*) will expand, and labour-intensive sector (*X*) will shrink due to Rybczynski effect.

As product prices are unchanged, factor prices will also remain unchanged. But reallocation of factors will take place between the sectors. That means adult labour will be transferred from agriculture to the expanding non-agricultural sectors *M* and *Z*. Similarly, child labour will be transferred to *Z* sector from agriculture as *Z* sector expands. Thus child labour in agriculture will decline as a result of economic growth and structural change.

Let us now derive the effect of economic growth on the three sectors of the economy.

Total differentiation of Eqs. (2.8), (2.9) and (2.10) gives

$$da_{LCX} \cdot X + a_{LCX} \cdot dX + da_{LCZ} \cdot Z + a_{LCZ} \cdot dZ = dL_C \quad (2.14)$$

$$\begin{aligned} & da_{LX} \cdot X + a_{LX} \cdot dX + da_{LM} \cdot M + a_{LM} \cdot dM + \\ & da_{LZ} \cdot Z + a_{LZ} \cdot dZ = dL \end{aligned} \quad (2.15)$$

$$\begin{aligned} & da_{KX} \cdot X + a_{KX} \cdot dX + da_{KM} \cdot M + a_{KM} \cdot dM + \\ & da_{KZ} \cdot Z + a_{KZ} \cdot dZ = dK \end{aligned} \quad (2.16)$$

Equation (2.14) can be rearranged as

$$\begin{aligned} & \frac{da_{LCX}}{a_{LCX}} \cdot a_{LCX} \cdot X + a_{LCX} \cdot X \cdot \frac{dX}{X} + \frac{da_{LCZ}}{a_{LCZ}} \cdot a_{LCZ} \cdot Z + \\ & a_{LCZ} \cdot Z \cdot \frac{dZ}{Z} = dL_C \end{aligned} \quad (2.17)$$

or

$$\hat{a}_{LCX} \cdot \lambda_{LCX} + \lambda_{LCX} \cdot \hat{X} + \hat{a}_{LCZ} \cdot \lambda_{LCZ} + \lambda_{LCZ} \cdot \hat{Z} = 0 \quad (2.18)$$

Here, '∧' indicates relative change, and

λ_{ij} indicates factor share of *i*th factor in *j*th product (see Jones (1965)). Here, the factor is L_C and products are X and Z. Since L_C is given, $dL_C = 0$. Following the same procedure, (2.15) and (2.16) can be written as

$$\hat{a}_{LX} \cdot \lambda_{LX} + \lambda_{LX} \cdot \hat{X} + \hat{a}_{LM} \cdot \lambda_{LM} + \lambda_{LM} \cdot \hat{M} + \hat{a}_{LZ} \cdot \lambda_{LZ} + \lambda_{LZ} \cdot \hat{Z} = 0 \quad (2.19)$$

$$\hat{a}_{KX} \cdot \lambda_{KX} + \lambda_{KX} \cdot \hat{X} + \hat{a}_{KM} \cdot \lambda_{KM} + \lambda_{KM} \cdot \hat{M} + \hat{a}_{KZ} \cdot \lambda_{KZ} + \lambda_{KZ} \cdot \hat{Z} = dK \quad (2.20)$$

Equations (2.18), (2.19) and (2.20) can be expressed in matrix form as

$$\begin{bmatrix} \lambda_{LCX} & 0 & \lambda_{LCZ} \\ \lambda_{LX} & \lambda_{LM} & \lambda_{LZ} \\ \lambda_{KX} & \lambda_{KM} & \lambda_{KZ} \end{bmatrix} \begin{bmatrix} \hat{X} \\ \hat{M} \\ \hat{Z} \end{bmatrix} = \begin{bmatrix} A \\ B \\ C \end{bmatrix} \quad (2.21)$$

where

$$A = -\{ \hat{a}_{LCX} \cdot \lambda_{LCX} + \hat{a}_{LCZ} \cdot \lambda_{LCZ} \}$$
$$B = -\{ \hat{a}_{LX} \cdot \lambda_{LX} + \hat{a}_{LM} \cdot \lambda_{LM} + \hat{a}_{LZ} \cdot \lambda_{LZ} \}$$
$$C = dK - \{ \hat{a}_{KX} \cdot \lambda_{KX} + \hat{a}_{KM} \cdot \lambda_{KM} + \hat{a}_{KZ} \cdot \lambda_{KZ} \}$$

As factor prices are constant, there will be no change in factor coefficients. So, all $\hat{a}_{ijs} = 0$. Therefore, $A = 0$, $B = 0$, $C = dK$. The determinant of the coefficient matrix in (2.21) is

$$|\Delta| = \lambda_{LCX}\begin{bmatrix} \lambda_{LM} & \lambda_{LZ} \\ \lambda_{KM} & \lambda_{KZ} \end{bmatrix} + \lambda_{LCZ}\begin{bmatrix} \lambda_{LX} & \lambda_{LM} \\ \lambda_{KX} & \lambda_{KM} \end{bmatrix}$$

or

$$|\Delta| = \lambda_{LCX}\{\lambda_{LM}\cdot\lambda_{KZ} - \lambda_{LZ}\cdot\lambda_{KM}\} + \lambda_{LCZ}\{\lambda_{LX}\cdot\lambda_{KM} - \lambda_{LM}\cdot\lambda_{KX}\} \quad (2.22)$$

$|\Delta| \langle 0$ in (2.22) on the condition that M is highly capital-intensive and the greater share of child labour is employed in agriculture. That means the value of λ_{KM} is very high and $\lambda_{LCX} > \lambda_{LCZ}$. These are plausible assumptions.

Now, using Cramer's Rule, we solve the relative change in X, M and Z as

$$\hat{X} = \frac{|\Delta_X|}{|\Delta|} = \frac{-dK\{-\lambda_{LM}\cdot\lambda_{LCZ}\}}{|\Delta|} \langle 0 \quad (2.23)$$

because $|\Delta_X| \rangle 0$

$$\hat{M} = \frac{|\Delta_M|}{|\Delta|} = \frac{dK\{\lambda_{LCX}\cdot\lambda_{LZ} - \lambda_{LX}\cdot\lambda_{LCZ}\}}{|\Delta|} \rangle 0 \quad (2.24)$$

Here, $|\Delta_M| \langle 0$ on the condition that X is highly labour-intensive and the value of λ_{LX} is very high. Here, $(\lambda_{LX}\cdot\lambda_{LCZ})$ outweighs the value of $(\lambda_{LCX}\cdot\lambda_{LZ})$.

Finally, we get

$$\hat{Z} = \frac{|\Delta_Z|}{|\Delta|} = \frac{-dK\cdot\lambda_{LCX}\cdot\lambda_{LM}}{|\Delta|} \rangle 0 \quad (2.25)$$

From comparative static results, we get $\hat{X} < 0$, $\hat{M} > 0$ and $\hat{Z} > 0$. To support the expansion of capital-intensive M sector, labour is released from agriculture indicating that more labourers are now employed in M sector and they are getting higher wage $\bar{W}$. As $a_{LM} \cdot M = L_M$ increases, l declines. Since L_C is an increasing function of l, total child labour in the economy (L_C) declines with decline of l. Another implication of the result is that since Z sector supplies intermediate inputs to M sector, Z sector also expands with M sector. To allow the expansion of Z sector, child labour will be transferred from agriculture to the Z sector. Moreover, as X falls, $a_{LCX} \cdot X$ will decline. That means not only child labour declines in the economy but also it declines in agriculture. This follows from economic growth and structural change in the country.

2.5 Summary and Policy Implications

Child labour is a serious socio-economic problem, particularly in the developing countries. Many factors are responsible for this problem, but poverty and low income of the parent is considered to be the main cause of child labour in most cases. This chapter analyses the problems of child labour in general and also in agriculture, in particular, using theoretical models. We assume that parents want child's education and skill formation. Basu (1999) shows that if the parent's income (wage) is less than certain critical minimum level, she/he is forced to send the child to work. In that case the child is deprived of schooling and education and grows to become an unskilled adult worker. Naturally, she/he earns low wage in the next generation also and the family remains poor again. Thus, a vicious circle of poverty and child labour is formed in a dynamic perspective. For skill formation of the child, a threshold level of education is necessary, and if the child can complete this minimum years of schooling to acquire skill, he becomes able to earn higher wage as skilled worker in his adult age. Then it will no longer be necessary to send the child to work for earning of the family, and thus the child labour trap breaks down.

Different measures for child's education, legal ban on child labour and legal provision for minimum wage of the adult worker, trade sanction and boycott of child labour-tainted goods in the export market, provision of Conditional Cash Transfer to the poor family and various other measures have been suggested to solve the problem. Schooling and skill formation of the child has been prescribed as a very effective measure to combat this problem. But poverty of the household and credit market imperfection are found to be big hurdles to that goal. The employment of child labour in agriculture is very high in low-income countries. It is also found from theoretical and empirical literature that the incidence of child labour declines as income increases in the country. This chapter proposes that if economic growth and structural change takes place in the country, the share of agriculture in GDP will decline and the non-agricultural sector including manufacturing and services will expand and as a result adult workers will be transferred from agriculture to the non-agricultural sector where the wage rate is higher. This will lead to decline of poverty, and as poverty declines, child labour will also decline in the country. This chapter has developed a theoretical framework using a three-sector general equilibrium model of international trade to demonstrate that as non-agricultural sector including manufacturing and services expands due to inflow of foreign capital or accumulation of domestic savings, the agricultural sector shrinks. As a result, child labour declines in the country as a whole and also in agriculture. Thus it theoretically shows that child labour in agriculture declines as a result of economic growth and structural change. The implication is that economic growth can be a sustainable way of reducing child labour. This chapter also develops a model to show that sufficient schooling and skill formation of the child can break the child labour trap indicating the importance of schooling and education of the child to combat the problem of child labour.

References

Baland, J.M., and C. Duprez. 2009. Are labels effective against child labour? *Journal of Public Economics* 93: 1125–1130.

Baland, J.M., and J.A. Robinson. 2000. Is child labour inefficient? *Journal of Political Economy* 108 (4): 663–679.

Basu, K. 1999. Child labour: Cause, consequences and cure with remarks on international labour standards. *Journal of Economic Literature* 37 (3): 1083–1119.

———. 2000. The intriguing relation between adult minimum wage and child labour. *The Economic Journal* 110 (462): 50–61.

———. 2002. A Note on multiple general equilibria with child labour. *Economics Letters* 74 (3): 301–308.

Basu, K., and P.H. Van. 1998. The economics of child labour. *American Economic Review* 88 (3): 412–427.

Basu, K., and H. Zarghamee. 2009. Is product boycott a good idea for controlling child labour? A theoretical investigation. *Journal of Development Economics* 88: 217–220.

Burra, N. 2005. Crusading for children in India's informal economy. *Economic and Political Weekly* XXXVIII (46): 5199–5208.

Chaudhuri, S., and U. Mukhopadhyay. 2010. *Revisiting the informal sector – A general equilibrium approach*. New York, Heidelberg, London: Springer.

De Hoop, J., and F.C. Rosati. 2013. *Cash Transfers and child labour*. Discussion paper No. 7496, Institute for the study of labour (IZA), Bonn, Germany.

Edmonds, E.V. 2003. *Child labour in South Asia, OECD social, employment and migration*. Working Paper No. 5, May, (OECD), Paris.

Ermisch, J., and M. Francesconi. 2001. Family matters: Impacts of family background on educational attainments. *Economica* 68 (270): 137–156.

Fan, C.S. 2004. Relative wage, child labour and human capital. *Oxford Economic Papers* 56 (4): 687–770.

Galor, O., and J. Zeira. 1993. Income distribution and macroeconomics. *Review of Economic Studies* 60 (1): 35–52.

Glomm, G. 1997. Parental choice of human capital investment. *Journal of Development Economics* 53 (1): 99–114.

Grootaert, C., and R. Kanbur. 1995. Child labour: An economic perspective. *International Labour Review* 2 (134): 187–203.

ILO. 2016. World Employment Social Outlook –Trends 2016. International Labour Office, Geneva.

———. 2018. *Global estimates of child labour: Results and trends 2012–2016*.

ILO/IPEC—SIMPOC. 2007. Explaining the demand supply of child labour: A review of the theories, Geneva, January 18.

Jones, R.W. 1965. The structure of general equilibrium models. *Journal of Political Economy* 73 (6): 557–572.

Ranjan, P. 1999. An economic analysis of child labour. *Economics Letters* 64 (1): 99–105.

Ravallion, M., and Q.T. Wodon. 2000. Does child labour displace schooling? Evidence on behavioural responses to an enrollment subsidy. *The Economic Journal* 110 (462): C158–C175.

Rogers, C.A., and K.A. Swinnerton. 2008. A theory of exploitative child labour. *Oxford Economic Papers* 60 (1): 2–41.
Sasmal, J. 2013. Breaking the child labour trap through conditional cash transfer – A theoretical note. *Artha Beekshan* 22 (2): 20–28.
Sasmal, J., and J. Guillen. 2015. Poverty, Educational Failure and Child Labour Trap: The Indian Experience. *Global Business Review* 16 (2): 270–280.
Venkatanarayana, M. 2004. Out of school children – Child labourers or educationally deprived? *Economic and Political Weekly* XXXIX (38): 4219–4221.

3

Child Labour and Human Capital in Developing Countries: A Multi-Period Stochastic Model

Indrajit Thakurata

3.1 Introduction

Why are some countries poorer than others? This question has been at the centre of a fecund research agenda in the field of economic growth and development. Whilst recognizing the role played by culture, geography, natural resources, government, openness and institutions, the differences in growth across nations are factored into differences arising from the accumulation of physical capital, technology and human capital. With regard to human capital, it has been documented that countries with higher per

This chapter is a reprinted version of the original article "Child Labour and Human Capital in Developing Countries: A Multi-Period Stochastic Model" published in *Economic Modelling*, 2018 (with Prof. Errol D'Souza as co-author). Please refer to the original paper for details. The author thanks the Editor Prof. Sushanta K. Mallick and Elsevier for the permission to reprint the journal article. Link to the original paper: https://www.sciencedirect.com/science/article/pii/S026499931730353X.

I. Thakurata (✉)
Indian Institute of Management Indore, Indore, India
e-mail: indrajitt@iimidr.ac.in

A. Posso (ed.), *Child Labor in the Developing World*,
https://doi.org/10.1007/978-981-15-3106-4_3

capita output have a more educated population (Mankiw et al. 1992). However, this does not translate into a straightforward policy guideline that countries should focus their energies on better educational systems as that is associated with larger output per capita. This is because it disregards the point that it is individuals that make choices with regard to investments in human capital under the influence of different forces and constraints.

Human capital investments are usually made in the early stages of the life cycle when children are not free agents and their parents decide for them. Regions of the world with low levels of income also have a high incidence of child labour, and this impedes the ability of children to receive an education and accumulate human capital (Strulik 2004; Basu and Tzannatos 2003). Posso (2017) shows that children engaged in child labour earn significantly lower than their peers as adults. It is therefore important to study household decision making with respect to human capital investment and child labour in a unifying framework in order to understand an important part of the dynamics of economic development.

In the literature, some of the early models on family influence and human capital acquisition[1] were developed by Becker and Tomes (1979), Becker and Tomes (1986) and Loury (1981). These studies incorporated altruism and credit market imperfections and contributed towards understanding the role of initial conditions in determination of income mobility across generations. Galor and Zeira (1993) showed the existence of multiple steady states in the presence of credit market imperfections and non-convexities in human capital investments. Among the multi-period quantitative models which this study focusses on, Aiyagari et al. (2002) developed a framework incorporating altruism and incomplete credit markets to show that credit constraints and lack of insurance do not necessarily lead to underinvestment in human capital. Cunha and Heckman (2007) have looked at the technology of capability development while studies like Keane and Wolpin (2001) and Lochner and Monge-Naranjo (2012) have investigated the presence of borrowing constraints in influencing college education.[2] Other models (Caucutt and Kumar 2003)

[1] Related literature but not the focus of this study explores fertility decisions along with human capital (Becker et al. 1990; Hazan and Berdugo 2002; Doepke and Zilibotti 2005; Galor and Moav 2002; Moav 2005).

[2] See also Todd and Wolpin (2003), Cunha and Heckman (2008), Lee and Seshadri (2014) and Carneiro and Heckman (2002).

have introduced uncertain pay-offs in human capital acquisition and the role of early investment period in children in determining later period's college decisions (Restuccia and Urrutia 2004).

While the multi-period quantitative studies with a focus on developed countries do not find a strong impact of market imperfections on human capital outcomes, the same may not be true for developing countries where banking access is limited to only 30% of the households and due to extreme poverty: instead of investing in the human capital of children, households are forced to rely on their labour to augment the low family income.

This study's innovation is the provision of a framework to enable us to consider how income, child labour and investment in human capital are co-determined in the backdrop of poverty, uncertainty, parental altruism, differential access to financial markets and human capital investment constraints. Through a novel seventy period discrete time[3] life cycle model, the study attempts to track household decisions on present/future consumption and child labour versus various types of human capital acquisition from time and non-time educational inputs. This study's extension of the literature is in the joint consideration of risky income and returns to financial savings, as well as differential access to finance and human capital investment options. This study's framework enables an understanding of the importance of income deficiency as separate from financial exclusion or high cost of education as a determinant of child labour and participation in an educational institution.

To account for differences in education of the head of the household, the study works with three types of households: those where the head is either uneducated or has completed a secondary school education or an undergraduate degree. In line with studies that link financial access with levels of education, this study associates an uneducated head of household with financial exclusion, the secondary school educated head of household with access to a bond market and the college educated head of household with access to both bond and stock markets. Sensitivity analysis with respect to education and income provides confidence to the discrete choice of levels of education and financial access.

[3] The choice of the span of the time period is to mimic the life expectancy associated with a typical household in the developing world.

The study also examines the consequences of various policy interventions which aim to limit if not eliminate child labour. Lack of financial inclusion has been advanced as a reason for child labour being inefficiently high (Baland and Robinson 2000) as parents can neither borrow nor have sufficient assets to sell. Child labour has also been reported to increase with the cost of access to education. The study examines the impacts of various types of policies such as income support, higher returns on savings, discounts and subsidies on the costs of educational inputs such as books, improvements in access to education and self-financed loans to households, on the supply of child labour and participation in an educational institution.

In the literature on human capital and child labour, the impact of wage income on parental investments in childrens' human capital and child labour is considered in a deterministic scenario. For example, Basu and Van (1998) look at the effect of a reduction in the adult wage and predict that this results in sending children to work. The study extends the analysis to a dynamic setting where wage income is assumed to be stochastic. The study finds that an increase in the risk to income has no impact on the schooling of children from families where the head of the household has no education. Such a family responds by increasing precautionary savings and reducing pre-school consumption that affects the early stage development of children. Households where the head has a secondary school or college education respond with more financial savings as well as an increase in human capital investments.

The study extends the literature by inquiring into how financial access affects the acquisition of human capital of the young. Earlier studies have shown how financial widening positively affects education (Dehejia and Gatti 2005). This study shows that this result does not hold for those families where the head of household is uneducated. This study argues that it is low income and not financial access that influences the decision of this type of family. Financial access to bond markets affects the uneducated household asset holding and increases later period's consumption. For other households who already had financial access, the increase in the portfolio of assets they can save in results in an increase in human capital investment as well as consumption.

Subsidies on the cost of education such as cheaper books are seen to induce middle-income households with prior financial access to invest more in human capital. The study shows that these subsidies can be financed by transfers from high-income households without affecting their decisions regarding investments in human capital. However, the study finds that even completely financed educational resources are not strong enough to induce the uneducated household category to send its offspring to school.

Our results support some of the empirical findings in the literature whilst providing some new insights. For instance, the income effect of human capital investment is brought out in Edmonds and Schady (2012) who show that the extent of child labour falls with cash transfers. Transitory negative income shocks have been reported to reduce schooling and induce child labour in the studies of Edmonds (2005), Edmonds and Turk (2002), Kazianga (2005), Beegle et al. (2006) and Bandara et al. (2015). In addition, studies such as Baland and Robinson (2000), Ranjan (2001) and Alvi and Dendir (2011) document that when external credit is unavailable and households are financially excluded, they make children work rather than invest in human capital. The role of education subsidies in the form of free uniforms, textbooks, scholarships and fee exemptions in promoting school enrolment is a feature of studies such as Kremer et al. (2002), Kremer et al. (2009) and Grogan (2009). Other studies have explored the impacts of trade liberalization (Jafarey and Lahiri 2002), labour market reform and inflow of foreign capital (Chaudhuri 2011; Dwibedi and Chaudhuri 2010), migrants' remittances (Bouoiyour et al. 2016) and child wage subsidies (Estevez 2011) on child labour.

Results of this study present important policy implications for stimulating the human capital investments of different household categories. The financially excluded uneducated households are seen to prefer financial assets with negative real returns over human capital investments in their offspring and consequently fall into an intergenerational poverty trap. While policies like financial inclusion and free educational inputs are ineffective, only income support which pushes the household beyond a minimum income threshold is effective in starting educational investments of this household category. Such income doles may be funded through direct transfers or withdrawal of educational subsidies from college educated households, in which case one college educated household can start educational investments of 10.9 and 2.4 uneducated households through these policies, respectively. Simulations indicate that households with a secondary level of education of the household head and access to basic financial services display higher preference for human capital investments over financial savings. For these households, targeted policies like subsidized education and access to more educational resources are much more efficient in raising human capital than income support. While stock market participation increases human capital acquisition by 5.8% and life cycle loans impact it positively with elasticity of 2.23, subsidised higher returns on savings are not that effective as it is seen to promote child labour.

This study's work indicates the importance of extending the framework in the future towards understanding decision making that includes the household making fertility choices as well as choices with regard to the quality and quantity of human capital. The structure of the paper is as follows: Sects. 3.2 and 3.3 outline the model. Section 3.4 presents results for the three benchmark education categories of households. Section 3.5 discusses the marginal impacts of various financial and human capital parameters on education and consumption. The mathematical solution and solution algorithm are included in the supplementary material.

3.2 The Environment

This study builds a seventy time periods, two generation, non-dynastic life cycle model with per-period financial and human capital investment constraints. Downward altruism and explicit valuing of human capital are the drivers of parental investment in the offspring. Wages and stock returns are stochastic, and human capital is assumed to be a two-input production function of education time and books.

The list of symbols in Table 3.1 will be used in the description of the model:

The model assumes a single parent (dad/father) with a single offspring (son) both of whom would be jointly referred to as the household. Time is discrete and the life cycle model starts from time, $t = 1$, when the son is just an infant (age = 1) and the dad has started working (age = 21). There are seventy time periods in the model (Fig. 3.1).

Table 3.1 List of variables with their benchmark values

Variable	Description	Variable	Description
t	Time period in years, $t \in [1, 70]$	*age*	Age of the person in focus
ξ	Coefficient of risk aversion, $\xi=5$	β	Time-discounting parameter, $\beta=0.98$
ρ	Downward altruism parameter, $\rho=0.7$	*pen*	Father's affinity for human capital parameter, *pen*=2.55
θ	Son's innate ability parameter, $\theta=0.16$	*aa, bb, cc*	Human capital production function parameters, values 0.75, 0.75, 0.2
δ	Depreciation rate of human capital, $\delta=1.8\%$	$\bar{H}$	Base level of human capital, set at 1.0
$H_{s,t}$	Human capital level of the son at time t	H_{relv}	The relevant, age dependent, child labour wage rate
H_{matric}	Human capital level at matriculation, equal to 2.0	H_{dad}	The human capital level of the father
λ_t	Fraction of time the son spends studying at time t, $0 \leq \lambda_t \leq 1$	λ_{max}	Maximum possible per-period time investment in education
b_{max}	Maximum possible books' investment at any time t	b_t	Books invested at time t, $0 \leq b_t \leq b_{max}$
s	Fraction of the books' investment that the household has to bear, $0 \leq s \leq 1$	$\bar{G}$	Exogenous per year growth rate of real income, equal to 1%
e_t	Wage shock at time t	γ_t	Shock to stock return at time t
Ω_t	Joint state of wage shock, e_t, and stock return shock γ_t at time t	$\pi(\Omega_t)$	Probability of joint state Ω_t at time t
corr	Correlation between wage and stock shocks	τ	Contributed-pension-fund deduction rate, $\tau \in [0, 25\%]$
R_0	Gross real bond return, equal to 1.04	R_{γ_t}	Gross real stock return at t for shock γ_t
α_t	Fraction of stock in the portfolio savings at time t, $0 \leq \alpha_t \leq 1$	$R_{p,t}$	Gross real portfolio return at t
μ	Excess return on stocks, equal to 5%	$f()$	Human capital production function
$X_{f,t}, X_{s,t}$	Resources-in-hand with father/son at time t: includes returns from previous period's assets and current period's earnings	$C_{f,t}, C_{s,t}$	Father/son's consumption at time period t
$pension_{f,t}$	Pension earning of the retired father at time t	$pension_{s,t}$	Pension earning of the retired son at time t
$PF_{f,t}$, $PF_{s,t}$	Contributed-pension-fund level of father/son at time t	a'_t, a'_{st}	Father/son's savings at the end of time period t
$V^{(t)}()$	Value function of joint household at time t	$V_j^{(t)}()$	Partial derivative of value function with respect to the jth argument

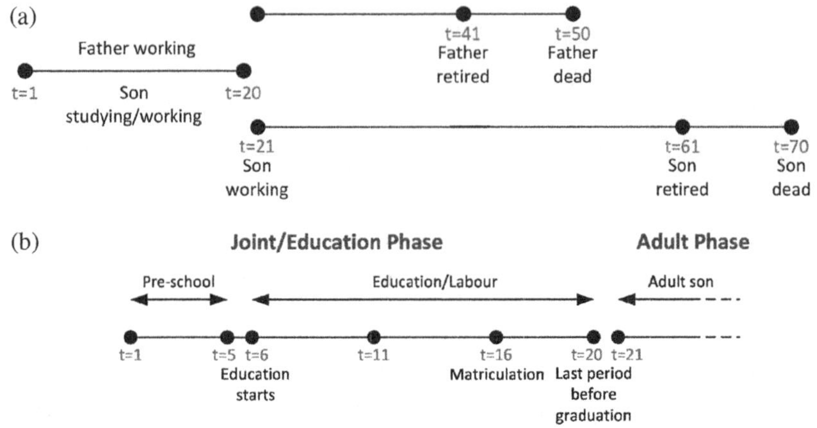

Fig. 3.1 Time-line (from Thakurata and D'Souza 2018). **(a)** Two-generation, seventy time periods' life cycle. **(b)** Important points in son's education phase

A phase is defined as the son's phase in life: education phase and adult phase. The first twenty time periods ($1 \leq t \leq 20$) have been defined as the education phase when the father and son live jointly. The terms "education phase" and "joint phase" are used interchangeably. Adult phase starts from $t=21$ onwards. In the first 5 years (pre-school stage), there are neither education nor labour options available to the son. Simulations assume equal dad-son consumption expenditures as health expenses of the child are not explicitly modelled. From $6 \leq age \leq 20$ the son can go to school or work in the informal child labour market to augment the family income. At $t=21$ the independent, grown-up son enters the formal labour market and separates from the dad. From $t=21$ the dad and son have no economic interaction except a last-period bequest. At time $t=41$ the dad starts retired life at age 61 and dies at $t=50$ (age 70). He leaves a predetermined constant fraction of his last period's wealth as bequest to his son. The son starts his adult life with zero financial assets and begins retired life at $t=61$ and dies at $t=70$ which is also the last period of the model. The model stays away from a dynastic set-up by not including further generations.

Human Capital

From $6 \leq t \leq 20$, the dad can either educate the son or send him for child labour or pick a combination of both. The son is endowed with a unit amount of time in each period. The fraction of time devoted to education in time period t is denoted as λ_t. The dad also decides the amount of books b_t to be invested in each time period. The son's future income as an adult depends on the level of human capital accumulated in the education phase.

It is assumed that the dad cannot borrow against his son's future labour income due to moral hazard problems and can't borrow against his own future labour income due to labour income risk.

The father's human capital, $H_{f,t} = H_{dad}$, is assumed constant over time. Human capital of the son is represented by a standard (Ben-Porath 1967) production function where the child's human capital at period $t+1$ depends on previous period's human capital $H_{s,t}$, innate ability level θ, time fraction spent studying λ_t, books invested b_t and the rate of depreciation δ:

$$H_{s,t+1} = f(\theta, \lambda_t, H_{s,t}, b_t) = H_{s,t}(1-\delta) + \theta(\lambda_t)^{aa}(H_{s,t})^{bb}(b_t)^{cc} \tag{3.1}$$

Since the nutritional effect on human capital is not modelled in the pre-school stage, human capital is assumed to remain at the base level $\overline{H}$ up to age 6 after which human capital acquisition can start. Also, since the dad is solving the life cycle model at $t=1$ and assumes the son will be a separate household from age 21, he ignores human capital acquisition through on-the-job training and only takes into account formal education up to graduation.[4]

At any time period t, the maximum human capital the child can enter the next time period corresponds to $\lambda_t = \lambda_{max}$ and $b_t = b_{max}$ where $\lambda_{max} = 0$ at pre-school stage and equal to 1 thereafter till $t=20$.

$$\begin{aligned} H_{s,t+1}(\lambda_{max}, b_{max}) &= f(\theta, \lambda_{max}, H_{s,t}, b_{max}) \\ &= H_{s,t}(1-\delta) + \theta(\lambda_{max})^{aa}(H_{s,t})^{bb}(b_{max})^{cc} \end{aligned} \tag{3.2}$$

b_{max} is the maximum investment possible in books at any time t. b_{max} is zero at pre-school and then constant for a given income category. It varies for different income categories to reflect the inaccessibility of good schools/educational inputs for the poor households. The presence of b_{max} makes lost

[4] Refers to 15 years of education in developing countries like India: 12 years in school and 3 years in college, which is similar to undergraduate in the US.

human capital investment options in the earlier time periods irreversible and precludes possibilities of infinite investment in books just before the son enters the labour market.

Similar to Jafarey and Lahiri (2002), the dad has an explicit per-period utility from the educational inputs (education time and books) that he invests in his child's human capital production. The utility is assumed to have the following functional form:

$$u(\lambda_t, b_t) = pen.(H_{s,t+1}(\lambda_t, b_t) - H_{s,t+1}(\lambda_{max}, b_{max})) \quad (3.3)$$

where *pen* is a constant number signifying the amount of utility gain per-unit of additional human capital produced. Studies like Behrman et al. (2001) and Azam and Bhatt (2015) based on Latin American and Indian data report a 75% probability of the son of a person with a secondary level of education to attain a secondary level or higher. In the model *pen* was accordingly calibrated such that a dad with a matriculation[5] level of education, on average (10,000 simulations), teaches his son up to matriculation or higher in 75% of the trials.

Thus $u(0, 0) = -pen.H_{s,t+1}(\lambda_{max}, b_{max})$ and $u(\lambda_{max}, b_{max}) = 0$, and u is an increasing function of the inputs with an upper bound of zero.

The formulation of the model assumes six important life cycle events in the father/son set-up from a developing country perspective: pre-school, pre-matriculation, post-matriculation, adult son and working father, adult son and retired father and finally retired son. Hence, the minimum number of time periods the study could have assumed was six as life cycle consumption patterns, savings and human capital investments would be dictated by these unique life cycle events. In that event, twenty to thirty time periods would have been condensed into a single time period with no consideration for less than perfectly substitutable human capital and physical investments between time periods. Solving even a six-period model with financial and human capital constraints in the presence of risk would have precluded any possibility of analytically tractable solution. Therefore, the study assumes a more representative seventy periods' life cycle model for accurate results. The study consciously errs on the side of accuracy at the expense of making the model complex. The results of the study are more representative of the developing world where informal child labour markets exist as also do various financial and human capital restrictions on different education/income strata.

[5] Matriculation refers to the secondary level of education in developing countries.

Dad's Wage

Wages are subjected to a per-period wage shock e_t which can take two discrete values, $e_t=\{e_{low}, e_{high}\}$, such that $\mathbf{E}[e_t]=1$. The actual wage of an adult with human capital H_{dad} at time t, for a given wage shock realization e_t and exogenous growth in expected wage rate $\overline{G}$, is represented by the following:

$$WAGE(H_{dad},t,e_t)=\overline{G}^{t-1}H_{dad}e_t \tag{3.4}$$

The minimum expected adult wage corresponds to that of an adult with the base level of human capital ($\overline{H}$) and is equal to 1[6] at $t=1$ and grows exogenously at $\overline{G}$. In monetary terms 1 would be equivalent to \$2/day.

Child Labour Wages

ILO (2007) documents the wage differentials between adult wages and children's wages based on surveys in Ghana, India, Philippines and Uganda. According to the study, the fishing industry in Uganda pays children one-third less than adults while auto repair industries in Delhi and Patna pay 60–66% less than an adult. Similarly, the Indian Zardosi industry pays children up to 80% less than adults.

This study assumes a 66% lower wage rate for children between 6 and 10 years and 50% lower wage rate for children between 11 and 15 years as compared to the minimum adult wage. From $16 \leq age \leq 20$, the minimum adult wage rate applies if human capital of the son is less than the matriculation/secondary level, else the matriculation wage rate is applicable (200% of the minimum adult wage rate).

At any given time t, for human capital of son $H_{s,t}$ and time fraction spent in school λ_t, the child labour wage earning (CLWAGE) is equal to:

$$CLWAGE(H_{s,t},t,\lambda_t)=\overline{G}^{t-1}H_{relv}(1-\lambda_t) \tag{3.5}$$

where H_{relv} is the relevant, age dependent, child labour wage rate defined in Table 3.2. H_{matric} is the matriculation level of human capital and $\overline{H}$ is the base level of human capital.

To reduce one state variable, child labour wages are assumed as not subject to wage shocks. Since child labour wages are anyway a fraction of the

[6] $\overline{H}$ is normalized to be equal to 1.0.

Table 3.2 Child labour wage rates

	$0 \le age \le 5$	$6 \le age \le 10$	$11 \le age \le 15$	$16 \le age \le 20$	
H_{relv}	0	$0.33\bar{H}$	$0.5\bar{H}$	$H_{relv}=H_{matric}$ if $H_{s,t}>H_{matric}$	else $H_{relv}=\bar{H}=1$

minimum adult wage, the assumption wouldn't result in major discrepancies in net household income.

Financial Assets

Financial assets consist of a riskless one-period bond of gross real return R_0 and a risky one-period stock with gross real return R_{γ_t} which is subject to a per-period stock market shock:

$$R_{\gamma_t} = R_0 + \mu + \gamma_t \tag{3.6}$$

γ_t is the time *t* shock to the stock return which can take two discrete values $\gamma_t=\{\gamma_{low}, \gamma_{high}\}$ such that $\mathbf{E}[\gamma_t]=0$. μ is the excess return of stock over bond. Shocks to labour wage e_t and stock returns γ_t can be correlated.

Based on the dad's level of human capital, he is assumed to have no financial access, only bond market access or full financial access. A dad with no financial access would have negative real returns on savings, whereas a dad with only bond access doesn't participate in the stock market. Only a dad with full financial access would have a savings portfolio consisting of a bond and a stock. Section 3.3 includes literature support for the financial access assumptions which are quite common in the developing world.

Expected Utility Maximization

Let $\Omega_t = (\gamma_t, e_t)$ denote the vector of the wage shock e_t and stock market shock γ_t at any time *t*. Both e_t and γ_t are individually uncorrelated over time. However, they can be cross-sectionally correlated. Let $\Omega^{(t)} = \Omega_1, \Omega_2, \Omega_3 \ldots \Omega_t$ denote the history of joint shocks[7] up to time *t*.

At time $t=1$ and aggregate state Ω_1, for resources-in-hand $X_{f,1}$, human capital of son $H_{s,1}$ and contributed-pension-fund deposit $PF_{f,1}$, the dad seeks to maximize the expected utility from his and his son's lifetime consumption accounting for per-period utility from educational inputs in the education phase. Hence, the dad's optimization problem (subject to constraints) is:

$$\max_{C_{f,t}, C_{s,t}, \lambda_t, \alpha_t, b_t} ((u(C_{f,1}) + \rho u(C_{s,1}) + u(\lambda_1, b_1)) + \mathbf{E}[\sum_{t=2}^{20} \beta^{t-1} u(\lambda_t(\Omega^{(t)}), b_t(\Omega^{(t)}))] + \mathbf{E}[\sum_{t=2}^{50} \beta^{t-1} u(C_{f,t}(\Omega^{(t)})) + \rho(\sum_{t=2}^{70} \beta^{t-1} u(C_{s,t}(\Omega^{(t)})))])$$

The dad's decision problem is to determine the optimal amounts of his fifty time periods' consumption streams ($C_{f,t}$), his son's seventy time periods' consumptions ($C_{s,t}$) and, for each of the twenty joint periods, the fraction of time λ_t the son spends studying and the amount of books b_t (in terms of foregone consumption) to be invested in son's education. The dad also has to determine the optimal amount of fraction of savings, α_t, to be invested in stock for each of his fifty time periods if he has stock market access.

Utility from consumption has been modelled as a standard CRRA utility, $u(C)=C^{1-\xi}/(1-\xi)$, and the father's explicit utility from educational inputs at time t for education time λ_t and books b_t is modelled as $u(\lambda_t, b_t) = pen.(H_{s,t+1}(\lambda_t, b_t) - H_{s,t+1}(\lambda_{max}, b_{max}))$. Downward altruism parameter is represented by ρ and β is the time-discounting parameter.

[7] It must be noted that $\Omega^{(t)}$ is different from Ω_t (which denotes the realization of the joint shock at time t). An example of $\Omega^{(t)}$ for t=2 would be $\Omega^{(2)} = ((\gamma_{low}, e_{high}), (\gamma_{high}, e_{high}))$.

The dad faces several per-period constraints. The constraints are briefly discussed below:

Father's Current Period's Resources-in-Hand Balance

$$X_{f,t} + \overline{G}^{t-1} H_{relv}(1-\lambda_t) - s.b_t = C_{f,t} + C_{s,t} + a_t' \quad \text{for } 1 \le t \le 20$$
$$X_{f,t} = C_{f,t} + a_t' \text{ for independent-father for } t: 21 \le t \le 50$$

The LHS of the constraint is the net resources-in-hand post-child labour earnings ($\overline{G}^{t-1} H_{relv}(1-\lambda_t)$) and books' expenses ($s.b_t$), while the RHS is the expenditures on consumptions and savings. $(1-s)$ is the discount fraction on books. $X_{f,t}$ is resources-in-hand with father at time t, which includes returns from previous period's assets and his current period's (post-pension-fund deduction) wage earning. It does not include child labour earnings. The definitions of other variables are summarized in Table 3.1.

Father's Next Period's State-Contingent Resources-in-Hand

$$X_{f,t+1}(\Omega_{t+1}) = a_t' R_{p,t+1} + \overline{G}^{t} e_{t+1} H_{dad}(1-\tau) \quad \text{for } 1 \le t \le 39$$
$$\textit{where} \quad (R_{p,t+1} = R_0 + \alpha_t(R_{\gamma_{t+1}} - R_0))$$
$$X_{f,t+1}(\Omega_{t+1}) = a_t' R_{p,t+1} + pension_{f,t+1} \quad \text{for } t \ge 40$$

The RHS of the constraint is the $t+1$ time period portfolio returns ($R_{p,t+1}$) from previous period's savings (a_t') added to pension-deducted dad's earnings or pension annuity at time $t+1$. LHS is equal to $t+1$ period state-contingent resources-in-hand. $X_{f,t+1}(\Omega_{t+1})$ is state-contingent resources-in-hand with father at time $t+1$ for joint state Ω_{t+1}.

Son's Next Period's Human Capital

$$H_{s,t+1} = f(\theta, \lambda_t, H_{s,t}, b_t) = H_{s,t}(1-\delta) + \theta(\lambda_t)^{aa}(H_{s,t})^{bb}(b_t)^{cc}$$

The constraint is the next period's human capital of the son as a function of education time, books and current human capital.

Father's Next Period's State-Contingent Contributed-Pension-Fund Level

$$PF_{f,t+1}(\Omega_{t+1}) = PF_{f,t}R_0 + \bar{G}^t H_{dad} e_{t+1}\tau \text{ for } 1 \le t \le 39$$
$$PF_{f,t+1}(\Omega_{t+1}) = PF_{f,t}R_0 \text{ for } t = 40 \text{ or}$$
$$PF_{f,t+1}(\Omega_{t+1}) = PF_{f,t} \text{ for } t > 40$$

The dad's next period's state-contingent pension-fund level ($PF_{f,t+1}$ (Ω_{t+1})) is the sum of the next period's pension-fund deduction ($\bar{G}^t H_{dad}\, e_{t+1}\tau$) and the gross returns (at bond rate) on current period's accumulated pension fund. Next period's pension-fund deduction depends on the wage shock realization e_{t+1} but can still be written as a function of aggregate state Ω_{t+1}.[8] The pension funds accumulated at retirement (t=41) are used to fund pension annuities of the father till death ($pension_{f,t}$).

Adult Son's Current Period's Resources-in-Hand Balance

$X_{s,t} = C_{s,t} + a'_{st}$ for adult-son for t: $21 \le t \le 70$

Adult Son's Next Period's State-Contingent Resources-in-Hand

$$X_{s,t+1}(\Omega_{t+1}) = a'_{st} R_{p,t+1} + \bar{G}^t e_{t+1} H_{s,t}(1-\tau) \quad \text{for } 21 \le t \le 59$$
$$X_{s,t+1}(\Omega_{t+1}) = a'_{st} R_{p,t+1} + pension_{s,t+1} \quad \text{for } t \ge 60$$

Adult Son's Next Period's State-Contingent Contributed-Pension-Fund Level

$$PF_{s,t+1}(\Omega_{t+1}) = PF_{s,t}R_0 + \bar{G}^t H_{s,t} e_{t+1}\tau \text{ for } 21 \le t \le 59$$
$$PF_{s,t+1}(\Omega_{t+1}) = PF_{s,t}R_0 \text{ for } t = 60 \text{ or}$$
$$PF_{s,t+1}(\Omega_{t+1}) = PF_{s,t} \text{ for } t > 60$$

Borrowing Constraint

$a'_t \ge 0$ for all dad's time periods and $a'_{st} \ge 0$ for all adult son's time periods
The savings of dad/adult-son can't be negative.

[8] It will not vary with γ_{t+1}.

Non-Negativity Constraints: Stock Fraction and Time Fraction in Education

$0 \leq \alpha_t \leq 1$ applies for all dad's time periods

$0 \leq \lambda_t \leq 1$ for $1 \leq t \leq 20$

The stock fraction in savings (if there is stock market access), α_t, and fraction of the unit time the son spends in education, λ_t, have to lie between 0 and 1 (both values included).

Upper Limit on Books

$$b_t \text{ " } b_{max} \qquad \text{for } 1\text{" } t \text{ " } 20$$

There is an upper limit on the per-period amount of investment in books, b_{max}.

The son's future consumption and utility from consumption depend on his accumulated human capital level in the first twenty periods, and the dad cares about it through the downward altruism parameter ρ. Beyond the utility from consumption that human capital affords, the dad explicitly values the acquisition of human capital which the model captures through the utility from educational inputs term $u(\lambda_t, b_t)$. The dad solves the problem at $t=1$ assuming that the income from endogenous human capital he leaves the son with will be used to meet the consumption requirements of the adult son. The model stays away from a dynastic set-up by excluding future generations.

Solution Methodology and First-Order Conditions

This study employs dynamic programming (Bellman equations) to solve the problem where the value associated with each period would be recursively written as a function of that period optimum variable and the value in the subsequent period. The way to solve is using backward induction where the value at the last period is computed first and then iteratively the value at intermediate periods are computed.

At any time[9] $1 \leq t \leq 19$ (detailed proof in supplementary material), let $V^{(t)}(X_{f,t}, H_{s,t}, PF_{f,t})$ be the value, after the realization of the vector of joint shock $\Omega_t = (e_t, \gamma_t)$, of having resources-in-hand $X_{f,t}$, human capital level of the son $H_{s,t}$ and contributed-pension-fund deposit $PF_{f,t}$. The t superscript of $V^{(t)}$ is not power but just a notation for value at time t. Then, the optimization problem for any t such that $1 \leq t \leq 19$ can be recursively written as:

$$\begin{aligned} V^{(t)}(X_{f,t}, H_{s,t}, PF_{f,t}) = \max_{C_{f,t}, C_{s,t}, \lambda_t, \alpha_t, b_t} & u(C_{f,t}) + \rho u(C_{s,t}) + u(\lambda_t, b_t) \\ & + \beta \sum_{\Omega_{t+1}} \pi(\Omega_{t+1}) V^{(t+1)}(X_{f,t+1}(\Omega_{t+1}), H_{s,t+1}(\Omega_{t+1}), PF_{f,t+1}(\Omega_{t+1})) \end{aligned} \tag{3.7}$$

subject to the applicable time period t constraints previously discussed.

[9] Other time periods can be similarly solved.

3.2.1 First-Order Conditions for $1 \leq t \leq 19$

For any time period t in the joint phase, the primary trade-off is between five baskets: utility from current consumption of dad or son, increased next period's value due to higher cash in hand earned through asset returns or, alternatively, increased future value through higher human capital of the son because of investment in books or investment in education time by foregoing child labour earnings. The per-period optimum is the trade-off of all these incentives when constraints are non-binding. For binding constraints, the situation needs to be handled on a case-by-case basis.

Equation 3.8 represents the utility trade-off between the father's and son's current consumptions where ρ is the downward altruism parameter:

$$u_c(C_{f,t}) = \rho u_c(C_{s,t}) \tag{3.8}$$

The LHS of Eq. 3.9 is the loss of utility from a unit amount of foregone consumption of the dad. One unit of foregone present consumption leads to expected $R_{p,t+1}$ (portfolio returns) amount of additional resources-in-hand, and $V_1^{t+1}(.)R_{p,t+1}$ expected gain in future value.[10] At the optimum the loss in present utility should be equal to the gain in future value if borrowing constraint ($\mu_{borr,t}$) is not binding. When the household is borrowing constrained, these marginals won't equalize, and the household would consume all the current resources leaving zero savings:

$$u_c(C_{f,t}) = \sum_{\Omega_{t+1}} (\beta \pi(\Omega_{t+1}) V_1^{(t+1)}(.) R_{p,t+1}) + \mu_{bor,t} \tag{3.9}$$

Equation 3.10 presents that a unit increase in investment in books leads to s units lower consumption of father, leading to $s.u_c(C_{f,t})$ loss of utility. The extra unit of books would increase the son's next period's human capital by $f_4(.)$ (where $f()$ is the production function of human capital and

[10] $V_1^{t+1}(.)$ is the partial derivative of $V^{t+1}()$ with respect to the first argument.

$f_4()$ refers to the partial derivative with respect to books) and increase in next period's expected value by $f_4(.)V_2^{t+1}(.)$. Also, due to $f_4(.)$ units of extra human capital produced, the dad gets $pen.f_4(.)$ amount of additional utility due to his explicit valuing of the human capital production of his son through the $u(\lambda_t, b_t)$ term.[11] *pen* which is a constant equal to 2.55 denotes the gain in dad's utility for a unit amount of additional human capital of the son. At the optimum the loss in utility ($s.u_c(C_{f,t})$) should be equal to the expected gain ($f_4(.)V_2^{t+1}(.) + pen.f_4(.)$) if the upper limit on books' constraint ($\mu_{b,t}$) is non-binding. Otherwise the books' investment would be at the upper limit:

$$s.u_c(C_{f,t}) = f_4(.)\sum_{\Omega_{t+1}}(\beta\pi(\Omega_{t+1})V_2^{(t+1)}(.)) + pen.f_4(.) - \mu_{b,t} \qquad (3.10)$$

Similar to books, a unit increase in education time λ_t leads to $\bar{G}^{t-1}H_{relv}$ units of loss of child labour income, leading to $\bar{G}^{t-1}H_{relv}u_c(C_{f,t})$ loss of present utility of dad. However, the extra unit of λ_t increases the son's next period's human capital by $f_2(.)$ and next period's value due to human capital by $f_2(.)V_2^{t+1}(.)$ units. Also, due to $f_2(.)$ units of extra human capital, the dad gets additional $pen.f_2(.)$ amount of utility due to his explicit valuing of human capital. At the optimum, the loss in utility should be equal to the gain if the upper/lower limits of education time constraints are non-binding. In case of binding constraints, corner solutions would be utility maximizing:

$$\bar{G}^{t-1}H_{relv}u_c(C_{f,t}) = f_2(.)\sum_{\Omega_{t+1}}(\beta\pi(\Omega_{t+1})V_2^{(t+1)}(.)) + pen.f_2(.) + \mu_{\lambda_m,t} - \mu_{\lambda_x,t} \qquad (3.11)$$

Equation 3.12 can be interpreted as follows: the optimum portfolio choice is such that a unit change in fraction of savings in stock (α_t) leading to ($R_{\gamma_{t+1}} - R_0$) change in expected gross returns does not lead to any change in future expected value. Had there been any such possibility α_t wouldn't be the optimum:

[11] $u(\lambda_t, b_t) = pen.(H_{s,t+1}(\lambda_t, b_t) - H_{s,t+1}(\lambda_{max}, b_{max}))$ where $H_{s,t+1}(\lambda_t, b_t) = f(\theta, \lambda_t, H_{s,t}, b_t)$; $\frac{\partial u(\lambda_t, b_t)}{\partial b_t} = pen.f_4(.)$.

$$\sum_{\Omega_{t+1}}(\beta\pi(\Omega_{t+1})V_1^{(t+1)}(.)a_t^{'}(R_{\gamma_{t+1}}-R_0))+\mu_{\alpha_m,t}-\mu_{\alpha_x,t}=0 \quad (3.12)$$

The other time periods ($t \geq 20$) can similarly be solved.

3.3 Benchmark Parameters

3.3.1 The Three Benchmark Education/Income Levels

The primary aim of this study is to quantify the marginal impacts of various policy parameters like income support, financial inclusion, higher return on savings, educational subsidies and others on human capital investments, consumption and savings of households. Since the impact on life cycle variables will be different for different household brackets, this study takes three benchmark education levels of the parent for analysis:

1. The uneducated dad ($H_{dad} = 1.0$)
2. The matriculate/secondary dad ($H_{dad} = 2.0$)
3. The graduate[12] dad ($H_{dad} = 5.0$)

The summary of the three benchmark households is presented in Table 3.3. This study assumes a linear relationship between the expected income and human capital level. Therefore, the empirically reported ratios of incomes for different education levels have been used to set human capital levels. Studies on developing countries, like Agrawal (2012),[13] report that the average income level of an individual with matriculation (or secondary) level of education is roughly twice that of an illiterate person (zero schooling years) while a person with graduation level of education has roughly 4.5 times the income of an illiterate person. Hence, this study assumes the

[12] Refers to 15 years of education in developing countries like India: 12 years in school and 3 years in college, which is similar to undergraduate in the US.

[13] This study reports private returns to education for primary, middle, secondary, higher secondary and graduates as 5.47%, 6.15%, 11.38%, 12.21% and 15.87%, respectively. This translates to roughly 1.93 and 4.39 times wages of matriculation and graduate workers relative to illiterate workers.

Table 3.3 The three benchmark scenarios

	H_{dad}	Fin access	Discount on books	Max books	Pension deduction
Uneducated dad	1.0	None	50%	0.25	NA
Matriculate dad	2.0	Bond	50%	0.5	0
Graduate dad	5.0	Stock and bond	50%	1.0	0

human capital level of the matriculate dad as twice that of an uneducated dad and sets the human capital of graduate dad as five times that of an uneducated dad. To make the results generalizable, the study performs sensitivity analysis with respect to income and reports it in Sect. 3.5.

Apart from income disparity, access to banks is also not universal in developing countries. Claessens (2006) observes that while access to basic financial services in OECD countries is over 90%, the usage figure for developing countries is only 26% with the maximum at 30%. Other than income and wealth, several studies link education as a key variable in explaining lack of bank access (Pal and Pal 2012; Rhine and Greene 2013; Djankov et al. 2008). In line with literature, this study assumes a financially excluded uneducated dad while the matriculate dad has only bond market access. Even though stock market participation in developing countries is very limited even for households with graduation level of education, this study assumes that the graduate dad has both bond and stock market access.

Often low-education/low-income households have limited access to high-quality schools/hospitals due to distance, discrimination or other supply issues, and hence are constrained by the amount of investments they can make on their offspring. Shukla (2010) pegs private educational and health-related expenses of Indian households at 7.4 and 4.7%, respectively. Since this study doesn't model the health-related expenses which have an indirect impact on human capital through early period mental and physical development of the child, an upper cap on per-period private books' investment of 12.5%[14] of income for the

[14] Approximately equal to 7.4 + 4.7%.

uneducated and matriculate dad households is assumed. Upper cap on books is a proxy for the limited educational and health investment options that poor households in developing countries face. In other words, total books' investment (b_{max}) is capped at 25% of income (12.5% private expense due to 50% subsidy) for the uneducated and matriculate dads. For graduated dad, $b_{max} = 1$. Section 3.5 includes the sensitivity analysis of the financial and educational access assumptions for the three households.

This study keeps the set-up simple by including only transitory shocks. Including permanent shocks would slightly improve the quality of results by capturing the additional impact of shock persistence over time but would also add another state variable. Contributed-pension-fund savings are ignored in the benchmark scenarios but get considered in the parametric analysis. In all the three scenarios, the son's value function is computed with the assumption of bond market access to the son so as to keep it uniform so that differences in son's life cycle values arise out of differences in human capital levels of the son only.

3.3.2 Consumption and Human Capital Parameters from Literature

Tables 3.4 and 3.5 present the human capital and financial parameter values used in the study. All the financial and human capital parameter values, except parameter *pen* which the study calibrates, have been used from literature. Section 3.5 presents the sensitivity analysis of the results for changes in the values of parameters.

The study assumes a moderately risk-averse individual with $\xi = 5$. Ability, θ, and the other human capital production coefficients, *aa*, *bb*, *cc*, were used from Manuelli and Seshadri (2014) with minor modifications to give an average return of 11% when the child studies full-time with the maximum available books, $b_{max} = 1$. Due to non-inclusion of health expenses of the son, the dad's downward altruism coefficient ρ is assumed to be 1 in the joint phase ($1 \leq t \leq 20$) and 0.7 for the rest of the independent son's life cycle.

Table 3.4 Benchmark values of consumption and human capital parameters

ξ	θ	aa(=bb)	cc	δ	ρ	Discount	*pen*	$\bar{H}$	H_{matric}
5	0.16	0.75	0.2	1.8%	1/0.7	50%	2.55	1	2

Table 3.5 Benchmark values of financial parameters

r_0	Er_s	r_{nofin}	var(γ_t)	var($\log(e_t)$)	corr	β	τ	Bequest	$\bar{G}$
4%	9%	−5%	0.0246	0.085	0	0.98	0%	15%	1%

Calibration of Parameter *pen* Several studies in literature have reported high correlations between the parent and the child's educational attainment (Black et al. 2005). Studies like Behrman et al. (2001) and Azam and Bhatt (2015), for Latin American and Indian data, respectively, report around 75% probability of a son attaining matriculation/secondary level (or higher) of education for a father with matriculation level of education. The parameter *pen*, which is a constant number capturing the per-period dad's utility from unit gain in son's human capital, was calibrated to ensure that on average over 10,000 simulations a dad with secondary (matriculation) level of human capital ($H_{dad}=2$) would teach his son up to matriculation level or higher for 75% of the trials. After calibration it was set to $pen=2.55$. Section 3.5 presents the sensitivity of results for different values of *pen*.

3.3.3 Financial Parameters from Literature

The financial parameter values are close to that assumed in Cocco et al. (2005). A bond rate of $r_0=4\%$[15] and expected stock return of $\mathbf{E}[r_s]=9\%$[16] are assumed. $r_{nofin}=-5\%$ is the return on savings of the financially excluded uneducated dad. $var(\gamma_t)$ and $var(\log(e_t))$[17] are the variances of

[15] $R_0=1.04$.

[16] $\mathbf{E}[R_s]=1.09$.

[17] Where $E[\log(e_t)]=0$.

stock return shocks and logarithm of wage shocks. The correlation between income shocks and stock returns (*corr*) is set to zero. Time-discounting rate is set as $\beta = 0.98$. The dad leaves 15% of his last period's wealth as planned bequest to his son. The exogenous growth rate of income is assumed at $\bar{G} = 1\%$. Pension-fund deduction rate (τ) is zero in the benchmark, but gets considered in the parametric analysis.

3.4 Simulation Results: Three Benchmark Scenarios

The primary motivation of this study is to bring out the contrasting responses of different households to various policy initiatives like income support, educational subsidies, financial access, higher asset returns and others. Before analysing the effect of policy parameters on life cycle variables, the study first establishes the benchmark profiles of life cycle consumption, savings and human capital investments of the three representative households with different incomes and financial as well as human capital access levels. This section presents the simulation results for the three benchmark scenarios. Average consumption and human capital investment profiles were generated by drawing numerous (10,000) realizations of the income and stock return shocks.

The per-capita consumption levels in the joint periods ($C_{jnt(1-5)}$,[18] $C_{jnt(6-10)}$, $C_{jnt(11-15)}$ and $C_{jnt(16-20)}$[19]) and independent dad's working and retired period consumptions ($C_{dad(21-40)}$ and $C_{dad(41-50)}$) as well as educational investments of the three households are presented in Table 3.6. The twenty joint periods have been divided into four subperiods based on applicable child labour wage rates. The consumption, assets and human capital investment profiles of the three benchmark households are described in Table 3.6.

[18] Refers to mean per-capita consumption for the pre-school time interval $1 \leq t \leq 5$ in the joint phase.

[19] Refers to mean per-capita consumption in the post-matriculation time interval $16 \leq t \leq 20$ in the joint phase.

Table 3.6 Benchmark values of bequest, net education time, net books, human capital of son and per-capita consumptions

	Beq	*Edu (years)*	*Books (Tot)*	H_{son}	$C_{jnt(1-5,6-10,11-15,16-20)}$	$C_{dad(21-40,41-50)}$
Uneducated dad	0.11	0	0	1.00	0.49, 0.7, 0.84, 0.92	0.78, 0.64
Matriculate dad	0.40	8.74	4.18	2.41	0.96, 1.14, 1.21, 1.34	2.05, 2.24
Graduate dad	1.40	15	15	5.00	2.22, 2.52, 2.82, 3.38	5.69, 7.35

1.0 consumption unit is equivalent to \$2/day. Edu(years) and Books(Tot) refers to the total investment in education time and books for 15 years ($6 \leq t \leq 20$) in the education phase

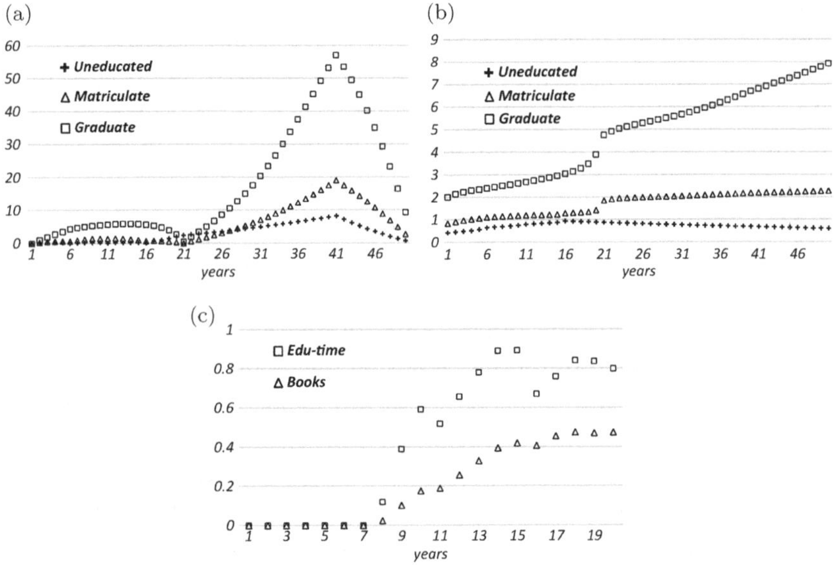

Fig. 3.2 Comparison of assets and per-capita consumptions of the three dads and human capital investments of the matriculate dad (from Thakurata and D'Souza 2018). **(a)** Assets. **(b)** Consumption. **(c)** Books and education time (matriculate)

Uneducated Dad ($H_{dad} = 1$) Figure 3.2 presents the per-capita consumptions and the starting assets' profiles for the fifty time periods of the three dads' lives. The first twenty time periods are the joint periods and the next thirty time periods are the independent dad's periods. The results presented in Table 3.6 show that the uneducated dad's son gets no schooling. Due to financial exclusion and binding borrowing constraints, the life cycle consumption trend is hump-shaped with assets in the joint periods close to zero, thus revealing that net income is entirely spent on consumption. After $t = 20$, assets follow the usual humped shape peaking the year before the dad's retirement. Without external intervention, this would be a self-perpetuating intergenerational poverty trap where the son, like dad, starts his adulthood with no education.

Matriculate Dad ($H_{dad} = 2$) This household category's son gets partial education during all time periods (Fig. 3.2c) and attains a human capital level of 2.41 (20% more than dad). The fraction of time devoted to education is low initially but increases gradually. As opportunity cost of education increases with age, a reconfiguration of investment in time and books is witnessed. The matriculate dad starts his independent phase with zero assets. The independent dad would have ideally borrowed resources from his independent and retired phases to fund his higher consumption and human capital expenses in the joint phase. However, due to strict borrowing constraints, the dad virtually runs two separate optimizations for the joint and independent phases as is reflected by the double-humped asset profile of the matriculate dad. A similar asset profile is also witnessed for the graduate dad.

Graduate Dad ($H_{dad} = 5$) The son of a graduate dad gets full education in all time periods with maximum permissible books' investment ($b_{max} = 1$) and attains a human capital of 5.0 (Table 3.6). Only higher ability or higher b_{max} can increase human capital further. For this income category, financial savings and portfolio choice are the more critical variables. Like the matriculate dad, the graduate dad also starts his independent phase with zero assets.

3.5 Parametric Analysis and Policy Discussion

This section explores the marginal impact of various intergenerational, financial and human capital parameters on the life cycle profiles of the three household categories. The first subsection explores the effect of intergenerational parameters while the second and third subsections explore the effect of financial and human capital parameters. The policy-maker's costs of raising human capital through different policies like income support, higher return on savings, discounted books, improvements in educational access and pension deductions have also been estimated. Unless mentioned, most of the parameters have been varied up to 25% in either direction from the benchmark values. Figures 3.3 and 3.5 present the consumption and books' investment profiles[20] for deviations in parameters from their benchmark values while Fig. 3.7 presents the elasticities of life cycle variables of the three households.

3.5.1 Intergenerational Parameters ρ and *pen*

3.5.1.1 Downward Altruism

In this study the downward altruism coefficient ρ, made famous by Becker (1974) and Cox (1987) and tested by Altonji et al. (1997), is the weight given by the dad to the independent son's rest of lifetime utility from consumption. This subsection tests the impact of ρ on life cycle variables from a multi-period optimization perspective with active financial and human capital constraints as often witnessed in developing countries. The simulation results find downward altruism as well as explicit valuing of human capital (*pen*) to be joint influencers of human capital investments. The moderate elasticity values of books' investment, education time and human capital (0.12, 0.15 and 0.1) of the matriculate dad household indicate that downward altruism alone doesn't have a very powerful impact on human capital outcomes of the offspring (Fig. 3.7a, b). For the uneducated dad household, there is no change in schooling or consumption for even a 100% increase in ρ. Its income levels are too low and the son gets no schooling as in the benchmark case. In contrast, the

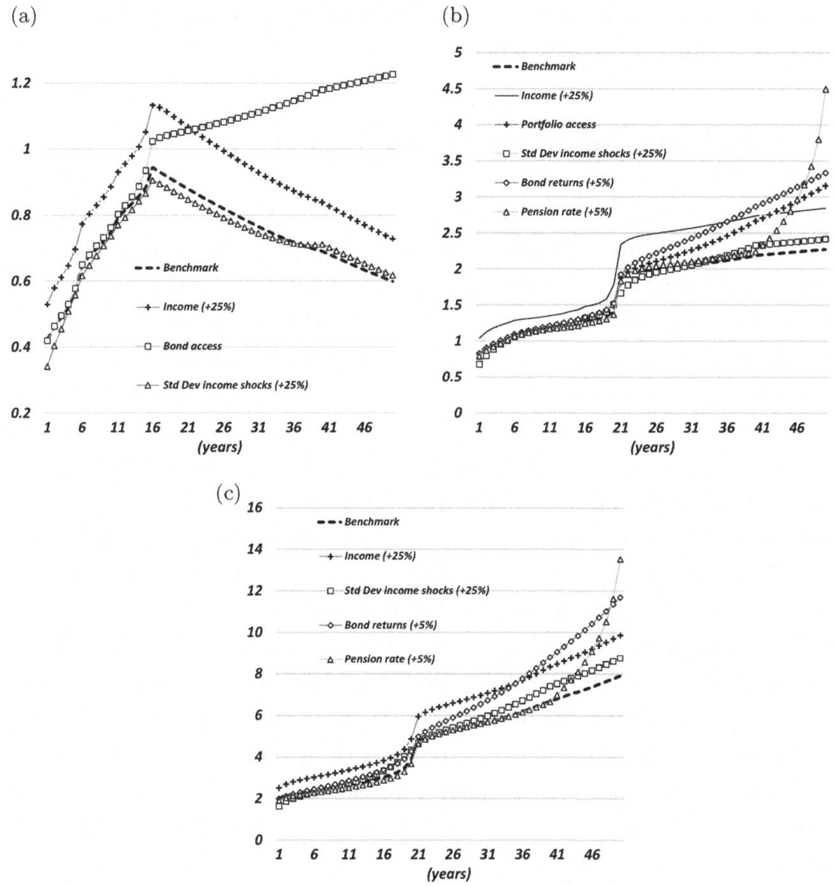

Fig. 3.3 Comparison plots of per-capita consumption profiles of the three dads for changes in parameters from benchmark values. Numbers in brackets are % deviations of parameters from benchmark values (from Thakurata and D'Souza 2018). **(a)** Uneducated dad. **(b)** Matriculate dad. **(c)** Graduate dad

graduate dad's human capital investments remain completely inelastic to fall in ρ in the given range. Higher values of altruism coefficient won't have any impact as its investments are already at the upper limit. The next subsection looks at the impact of *pen* on life cycle profiles. Figure 3.5c, d

[20] Education time profile will be very similar to books' investment.

presents the life cycle profiles of the matriculate dad household for a 25% increase in altruism coefficient.

3.5.1.2 Dad's Utility from Human Capital

A survey in Indian villages found that beyond economic motives, parents receive utility from seeing their children educated (De et al. 1999). The parameter "*pen*" captures the dad's affinity for human capital as separate from the consumption it affords. In the benchmark model *pen* was calibrated to 2.55 such that over 10,000 trials, a matriculate dad teaches his son up to matriculation or higher for 75% of the trials. The results show that the uneducated dad's income levels are too low and hence there is no impact of *pen* on schooling or consumption even when it is 100% higher. In contrast, the graduate dad's income levels are sufficiently high for human capital investments to remain completely inelastic to fall in pen in the considered range (25% around the benchmark value). The elasticities of education time, books and human capital of around 0.6, 0.49 and 0.46, respectively (Fig. 3.7c, d), for the matriculate dad household are about four times the corresponding elasticities for downward altruism coefficient ρ. Affinity for human capital, *pen*, clearly is a stronger driver of human capital investments than altruism. A discussion on the relative influence of *pen* and ρ is presented below. Figure 3.5c, d presents the consumption and books' investment profiles of the matriculate dad for a 25% increase in *pen*.

Table 3.7 summarizes the human capital and consumption outcomes when parameters ρ and *pen* are switched off. While the uneducated dad's life cycle outcomes remain unchanged, $pen = 0$ reduces the human capital outcomes of the graduate and matriculate dads significantly from benchmark values of 5 and 2.41 to 3.39 and 1.48, respectively (32.2% and 38.5% reduction). The reduction in human capital due to downward altruism not operating is relatively lower (0% and 9.5%) revealing that *pen* remains a stronger driver of human capital investments than ρ. The parameter *pen* was included in the baseline model as downward altruism doesn't completely predict the human capital outcomes as observed in data (Behrman et al. 2001; Azam and Bhatt 2015).

Table 3.7 Summary of consumption and human capital investments for cases when $\rho=0$ and *pen*=0 and when both are zero

	Joint-period per-capita consumption			Human capital of son			Books (total)			Education time (total years)		
Household	$\rho=0$	*pen*=0	Both zero	$\rho=0$	*pen*=0	Both zero	$\rho=0$	*pen*=0	Both zero	$\rho=0$	*pen*=0	Both zero
Uneducated	0.73	0.73	0.73	1.0	1.0	1.0	0	0	0	0	0	0
Matriculate	1.18	1.26	1.35	2.18	1.48	1.0	3.65	1.95	0	7.55	3.91	0
Graduate	2.73	2.87	3.10	5	3.39	1.0	15	8.08	0	15	12.33	0

The benchmark values of ρ and *pen* are 0.7 and 2.55, respectively

3.5.2 Financial Parameters

3.5.2.1 Dad's Income

A number of studies like Basu and Van (1998), Swinnerton and Rogers (1999) and Edmonds and Schady (2012) find significant effects of family income/wealth on children's education. The simulation results, while confirming that the matriculate dad's human capital investments are more sensitive to income change than consumption, also find the reverse to be true for the other income categories. Figure 3.4a reveals that the uneducated dad's extra income gets completely consumed and only after a threshold level of income which is 30% higher do the first human capital investments begin. Till then income significantly increases consumption with all elasticities higher than 0.66 (Fig. 3.7e, f). Initiatives like

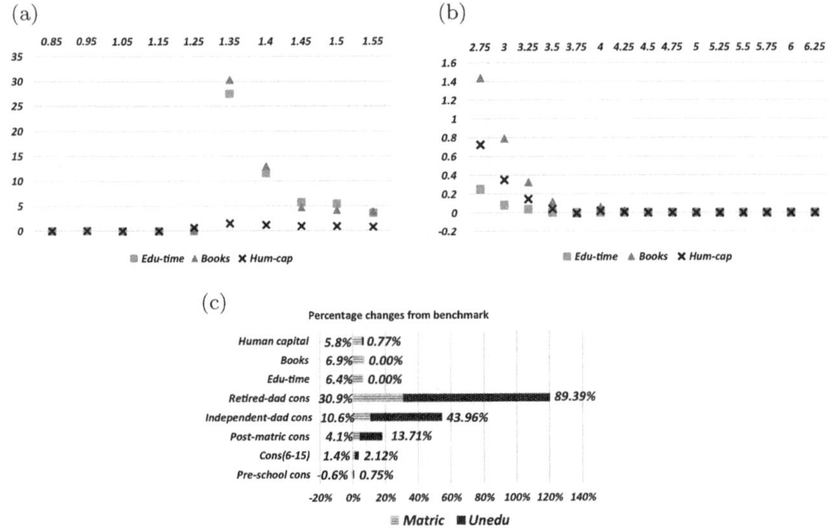

Fig. 3.4 Human capital elasticities of uneducated and graduate dads for different values of dads' incomes and % changes in uneducated and matriculate dads' variables from benchmark values due to bond market and portfolio access, respectively (from Thakurata and D'Souza 2018). **(a)** Uneducated dad: human capital elasticities. **(b)** Graduate dad: human capital elasticities. **(c)** Financial widening: % changes (uneducated and matriculate)

subsidized education, financial access, better schools and others will work only after crossing this minimum income threshold and hence income support remains the main parameter to begin human capital investments for this category. In contrast, the graduate dad's human capital investments remain completely inelastic up to 35% fall in income with books' investment more sensitive than education time (Fig. 3.4b). Till then, consumption gets sacrificed with elasticities around 1.0 (Fig. 3.7j, k). From a policy perspective, there exists space for transferring resources from the graduate dad to the uneducated dad without compromising on the net production of human capital of the graduate dad household. As opposed to the other income categories, the matriculate dad household's investments in human capital rises sharply with the first drop of extra income with elasticity of human capital around 2.83 (Fig. 3.7i). At lower income values, consumption elasticities are much lower than 1.0 as the extra income is getting funnelled into human capital investments (Fig. 3.7g). The consumption elasticities increase only after educational investments have picked up. Pre-school and independent dad's consumption elasticities remain close to 1.0 because of binding borrowing constraints and the non-existence of son's expenses, respectively. Figures 3.3 and 3.5a, b and e present the consumption and books' investment profiles for 25% increase in dads' incomes while Fig. 3.7e–k presents the elasticities of variables for a range of incomes of the three dads.

Policy Analysis At risk-free discounting rate, the present value of the matriculate dad's fifty periods' income amounts to 47.79 units and the present value of twenty joint periods' income is 30.7 units (Table 3.8, row 3). Since the dad doesn't carry forward assets from the joint phase into the independent phase, the independent periods' incomes are delinked from human capital investments and consumption in the joint phase. With elasticity of human capital with income at around 2.83, one consumption unit in present value terms raises human capital of the son by 9.2%.[21] Extra income funded by the policy-maker, though effective, turns out to be a costly way of raising human capital for this income cat-

[21] =2.83/0.307.

Table 3.8 Life cycle data of the three dads

	Pension rate	NI	PV(NI)	PV(NIjnt)	NS	PV(NS)	PV(NSjnt)	TB	PV(TB)
Uneducated dad	0%	48.85	23.90	15.35	143.27	42.19	5.95	0	0
Graduate dad	0%	244.39	119.55	76.78	855.61	244.01	57.68	15	9.5
Matriculate dad	0%	97.68	47.79	30.7	269.6	73.7	12.21	4.18	2.37
Matriculate dad	5%	–	47.79	29.17	–	–	–	–	–
Matriculate dad	10%	–	47.79	27.64	–	–	–	–	–

Pension rate: pension-fund deduction rate; NI (net income): sum of 50 periods' income; NIjnt: sum of twenty joint periods' income; NS (net savings): sum (for all 50 periods) of each period's bond market savings; NSjnt: total savings in twenty joint periods; TB (total books): sum of total books invested; '–': data not relevant. PV refers to the present value discounted at bond rate

egory as opposed to other policies like subsidized books or improvements in access to education.

The uneducated dad's investments in human capital start only after his income goes up by 25% which, in present value terms, amounts to 3.83 units (=15.35 × 0.25, Table 3.8, row 1) of additional resources in the twenty joint periods. On the other hand, the graduate dad's investments remain resilient to a 35% fall in income which in present value terms amounts to 41.84 units (=119.55 × 0.35, Table 3.8, row 2). Hence theoretically there exists space for transfer of resources from one graduate dad to 10.9 uneducated dads so that they can be pushed beyond the minimum income threshold after which human capital investments can start. Alternatively, the same resources can raise 91.6 matriculate dad households' human capital by 10% each,[22] if used as subsidies on books which is more efficient than income support in raising human capital for the matriculate dad category.

3.5.2.2 Financial Widening

Studies like Claessens (2006), Beck et al. (2008) and Pal and Pal (2012) have documented the lack of financial access of low-income, low-education households in the developing world. This subsection explores the impact of giving bond access to the unbanked uneducated dad and portfolio access to the non-stock-market-participant matriculate dad. Since the graduate dad already has both bond and stock market access in the benchmark scenario, financial widening for this category is not considered.

In the results, financial inclusion is seen to have no impact on the human capital of the uneducated dad's child as income levels are just too low. This confirms that no schooling in the benchmark case was due to low income and not financial exclusion. As a consequence of financial inclusion, later period's consumptions when asset levels are higher increase significantly while early periods' consumptions remain mostly unaffected due to binding borrowing constraints (Figs. 3.3a and 3.4c). The primary beneficiary is the independent dad with higher assets. Like

[22] 1 unit used on books' subsidy raises human capital by 21.9% (discussed in Sect. 3.5.3.1).

Dehejia and Gatti (2005) and Beegle et al. (2006), simulation results for the matriculate dad identify financial widening as one of the key variables for enhancing education. Extra returns earned through portfolio access are ploughed back into human capital leading to investments rising by around 6%. Most of the joint periods' consumption increases are insignificant while there is a significant rise in independent dad's consumptions due to his higher assets. Figures 3.3a, b, 3.4c and 3.5a and b present the relevant life cycle profiles and % changes in variables due to financial widening for the two households.

Policy Analysis Stock market participation of the matriculate dad raises his offspring's human capital by 5.77% which can otherwise be achieved with a 2.03% permanent income increase[23] of the dad.

3.5.2.3 Bond Returns

While there exists literature linking income/wealth to human capital, very few studies have linked human capital outcomes to return on safe assets. A possible reason may be the lack of variability in data on safe assets. This subsection explores the impact of bond returns on human capital and consumption for two income categories. The uneducated dad household doesn't get considered as this income group is assumed to be financially excluded.[24] For the matriculate dad, the study finds an interesting counterfactual where at low bond return levels, human capital elasticities are around −0.07 (Fig. 3.7u) as the parent is incentivised to increase child labour earnings to enhance savings to take advantage of rising returns. After a threshold, human capital elasticities turn positive (around 0.4) and are higher than consumption elasticities indicating that extra earnings through higher return on savings get primarily ploughed back into education. As indicated by the elasticity magnitudes, higher return on bond has a limited impact on this household. The results for the graduate dad household with portfolio access indicate a clear,

[23] = 5.77/2.83 where 2.83 is the income elasticity of human capital.

[24] The subsection on financial access considers a similar case where bond market access raises returns from −5% to +4%.

monotonic trend that the later period's consumption elasticities are higher than earlier period's consumption elasticities due to higher asset holdings in the later years (Fig. 3.7v and w). The primary beneficiary is again the independent and retired dad. For this income category, human capital remains completely inelastic to fall in returns including 0% returns. Figures 3.3b and c and 3.5a, b and e present the life cycle profiles for a 5% (500 bps) increase in bond return while Fig. 3.7s–w presents the elasticities of variables of the two households.

Policy Analysis The matriculate dad's investments in the bond market in all fifty time periods amount to 270 units which in present value terms amounts to 73 units (Table 3.8). The present value of his savings in the twenty joint periods amounts to 12.21 units. With elasticity of human capital with bond returns at around 0.4, a unit of present consumption leads to 3.2%[25] rise in human capital. Assuming the extra return on bonds are completely funded by the policy-maker, income support additional bond returns are only 34% as effective in raising human capital with the same cost in present value terms.

3.5.2.4 Standard Deviation of Income Shocks

There is a wealth of empirical literature linking negative income shocks to rise in child labour and fall in school enrolment (Kazianga 2005; Dehejia and Gatti 2005; Beegle et al. 2006). This subsection explores the impact of income shocks (negative and positive) on life cycle variables of the three households with different levels of income and financial access. For the uneducated dad household, there is no impact of wage shocks on the schooling of the son. With increasing standard deviation of wage shocks, due to higher precautionary savings, joint-period consumptions fall (assets increase) with pre-school consumption most affected (elasticity −0.44) which has implications on the child's early stage development (Figs. 3.3a and 3.7l and m). In contrast, the graduate dad household's human capital investments are able to withstand the impact of negative income shocks.

[25] 0.4/0.1221.

Expectedly, higher wage risk leads to higher precautionary savings in the two separate optimization zones for the father (joint and independent phases). Pre-school consumption falls while all other consumptions rise (Figs. 3.3c, 3.5e and 3.7q and r). For the matriculate dad household, increase in wage risk leads to higher precautionary savings in both the assets and financial and human capital. Precautionary financial savings' rise leads to fall in pre-school consumption and rise of post-matriculate consumption (Figs. 3.3b and 3.5b). Table 3.9 summarizes the fall in schooling variables when negative income shocks of different standard deviations hit the matriculate household. Consistent with literature, child labour increases as a response to negative shock in dad's wage. Education time and books are revealed to be more sensitive to negative shocks than consumption (initial elasticities 0.58 and 0.43). However, due to greater increase in educational investments for positive wage shocks, human capital investments overall rise with increasing standard deviation of income shocks, with elasticities touching 1.8 and 1.5 for education time and books (Figs. 3.5a and 3.7p). Figures 3.3 and 3.5a, b and e present the profiles of consumptions and books' investments for a 25% increase in standard deviation of income shocks. Figure 3.7l–r presents the elasticities of the three households' variables for a range of standard deviations of income shocks.

3.5.3 Human Capital Parameters

3.5.3.1 Discount on Books

Kremer et al. (2002), Kremer et al. (2009), Grogan (2009) and other studies have looked at the positive effects of free uniforms/textbooks/scholarships and fee exemptions on schooling. This subsection explores the role of discounted books on human capital and consumption. Discount (%) is defined as the percentage of books invested that is not borne by the household. If the household pays 100%, then discount percentage is 0%. For the uneducated dad household, there is no effect on schooling even for 100% discount on books, thus revealing that low income remains the reason for non-schooling and not explicit cost of education. Similarly, the graduate dad's human capital investments remain completely inelastic up to 0% discount revealing that these

Table 3.9 Matriculate dad: % fall in human capital investments and consumption when hit by negative income shocks of different standard deviations

% fall from mean	9%	19%	29%	39%	49%
Education time	10.12	15.89	20.97	22.39	23.51
Books	8.13	12.44	16.15	17.7	19.06
Joint consumption	0.67	2.13	3.46	4.76	5.66

The values are % fall from mean values of all shocks for the twenty joint periods, that is, (mean(all shocks) – mean (negative shocks))/mean (all shocks)

income categories' educational investments don't get altered by the cost of books (Fig. 3.7z). The matriculate dad's human capital elasticity of 0.65 and negative elasticity of C_{joint}(6–15) (around −0.04) indicate that beyond lower expenses on books, consumption is additionally cut by this household to further increase books' investment when price of education falls (Fig. 3.7x and y). Education time elasticity is low (0.66) due to substitution from time to books as a result of higher discount on books (elasticity 1.27). Figure 3.5c, d and f presents the profiles of variables for an additional 25% discount on books from the benchmark value of 50%.

Policy Analysis The total investment in books for the matriculate dad household is 4.18 units with present value of 2.37 units (Table 3.8). With elasticity of human capital for additional discount percentage at around 0.52, one unit of consumption in present value terms increases human capital by 21.9%.[26] Books' subsidy therefore is 2.3 times more effective in raising human capital than income support. On the other hand, complete withdrawal of discounts from the graduate dad household would release 9.5 units of resources in present value terms without compromising the human capital outcome of this category. Since it takes 3.83 units (discussed in Sect. 3.5.2.1) of additional resources to push the uneducated dad household beyond the minimum income threshold after which human capital investments can begin, the resources released by complete withdrawal of subsidies on books for the graduate dad household would be able to help unlock human capital investments of 2.4 uneducated dad households. Alternatively the same resources can raise the human capital of 20.8 matriculate dad households by 10% each.[27]

3.5.3.2 Upper Cap on Books

In developing countries, different income and education categories have different levels of access to educational inputs due to lack of good schools in neighbourhood, discrimination, entry barriers and others. As a result, they

[26] 0.52/0.0237.

[27] 1 consumption unit raises education by 21.9% so 9.5 units would raise human capital by 208.05% or of 20.8 households by 10% each.

are constrained by the maximum amount of inputs (school resources, quality teachers) they can invest. This study uses a two-input production function where the non-time input (books) is also a proxy for school resources and teacher quality which are not explicitly modelled. This subsection explores the impact of improvement in access to education (by raising b_{max}) on human capital outcomes. Simulations indicate that the uneducated dad remains unresponsive with no impact on schooling for up to 100% increase in b_{max}. In contrast, negative consumption elasticities (around −0.03) and positive human capital elasticities (around 0.16) of the matriculate dad indicate higher human capital investment appetite (Figs. 3.5c and d and 3.7aa and ab). Due to substitution effect, education time elasticity (0.11) is one-sixth of books' investment elasticity (0.64). The graduate dad also exhibits strong appetite for human capital where an extra unit of higher access is completely lapped up as indicated by the unit elasticity of books. Education time remains completely inelastic as it is at the upper limit and consumption elasticities are negative (Fig. 3.7ac and ad). The consumption and books' investment profiles for a 25% increase in b_{max} are presented in Fig. 3.5c, d and f and the elasticities for a range of b_{max} are represented in Fig. 3.7aa–ad.

Policy Analysis The total investment in books for the matriculate dad household is 4.18 units with present value of 2.37 units (Table 3.8). One per cent higher access to books costs $(0.0237/2) \times 0.6$ units of consumption in present value terms to the policy-maker (in simulations, in 60% of trials, the constraint is hit with 50% discount borne by the policy-maker). With elasticity of human capital for additional books' access at around 0.15, one unit of consumption in present value terms increases human capital by 21.18%.[28] Higher upper cap on books therefore is 2.3 times more effective in raising human capital than income support.

3.5.4 Contributed-Pension-Fund Savings

This subsection examines the effect of mandatory contributed-pension-fund deductions on life cycle profiles. The pension-fund savings are assumed to earn bond returns and, post retirement, the individual gets annuity payments

---

[28] 0.15/0.00711.

on the accumulated pension funds. Child labour wages are excluded. The independent son's value function is similarly computed in a regime with pension deductions. The very low-income, financially excluded uneducated dad household would normally not have access to such schemes and hence does not get considered. Results for the matriculate dad household show that pension deduction has a deleterious effect on education with elasticity of human capital touching −2.3. The distortion leads to independent dad's post-retirement consumption being very high while pre-school consumption gets severely hit (elasticity around −0.94). Other joint periods' consumptions are not hugely affected as the knock is taken primarily by educational investments in these periods (Fig. 3.7ae–ag). Due to liquidity distortions as a result of pension deductions, the asset profile of the dad undergoes interesting change (Fig. 3.6b) where at lower deduction rates it is a normal hump-shaped but gradually turns flat as the dad reduces his disposable assets owing to higher pension deposits. Unlike the matriculate dad, the graduate dad is able to absorb the knock of pension deductions on human capital. The elasticity of education time remains zero while at higher deduction rates, books' elasticity turns negative (−0.14) with marginal fall in human capital (Fig. 3.7ah–aj). The asset and consumption profiles are very similar to that of matriculate dad. Overall, not a big impact on this income category. Figures 3.3b and c and 3.5a, b and e present the consumption and books' investment profiles for a 5% higher pension deduction rate while Fig. 3.7ae–aj presents the elasticities of variables for a range of pension deduction rates.

Policy Analysis A relaxation of 5% in deduction rate for matriculate dad increases present value of joint periods' income by 1.53 units while keeping the present value of total income unchanged (Table 3.8, rows 4 and 5). The relaxation in deduction rate may be viewed as a self-financed loan. With elasticity of human capital with deduction rates at −2.23, a unit of self-financed loan by the policy-maker to the matriculate dad leads to 7.2%[29] rise in human capital which is 78% as effective as income support. In strict terms, they are not comparable as the loan is repaid in full with interest by the matriculate dad in the independent/retired phase. The loan by the policy-maker enables the dad to tide over the liquidity constraint in the joint phase, hence enabling higher educational investments.

[29] 2.23/(1.53/5).

3.6 Conclusion

This study focusses on the household decision problem to understand the co-determination of consumption, child labour and human capital investments in the backdrop of poverty, uncertainty, financial exclusion and parental altruism. Results of the study reveal that financially excluded households where the head of the household is also uneducated prefer financial assets with negative real returns over human capital investments in their offspring. These households consequently fall into an intergenerational poverty trap, and policies like financial inclusion and free education are not strong enough to induce human capital investments of this household category. Only income support which pushes the household income beyond a minimum threshold is effective in starting human capital investments. The study computes that full withdrawal of subsidies on educational inputs and direct transfer of income away from one single household with college educated head of the household can release resources which can launch human capital investments of 2.4 and 10.9 uneducated households, respectively, without lowering the former's human capital investments. Simulations indicate that households with secondary-level education of the household head and access to basic financial services display higher preference for human capital investments over financial savings. Targeted policies like subsidised education and higher access to educational resources are much more effective in raising human capital than income support. This study contributes to policy-making by computing the relative costs and human capital outcomes of policies like income support, subsidised educational inputs, higher access to educational inputs, life cycle loans and subsidised higher return on savings for different household categories. As a scope of future work, it will be useful to extend the framework towards understanding decision making that includes the household making fertility choices as well as choices with regard to the quality and quantity of human capital.

AcknowledgementsThe authors would like to thank the editor and anonymous reviewers for their constructive and elaborate comments.

Appendix: Figures and Graphs

See Figs. 3.5, 3.6 and 3.7.

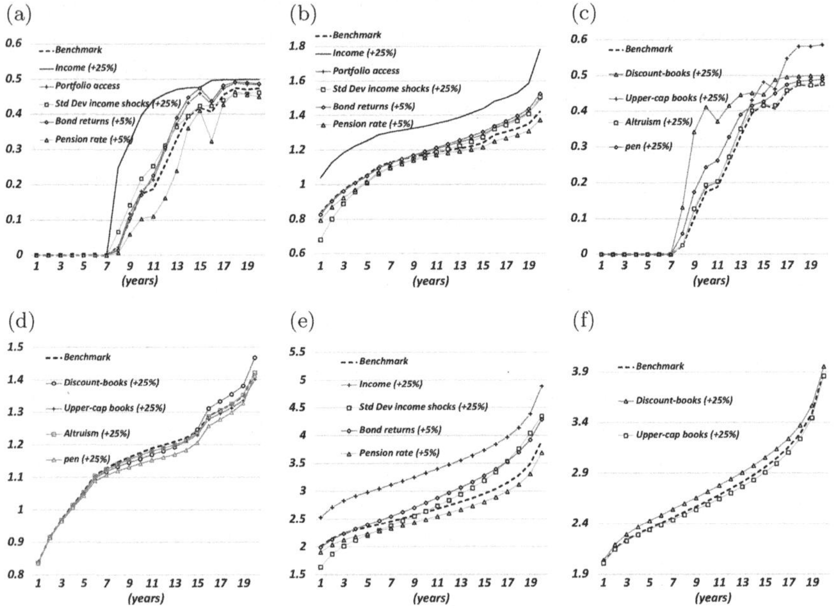

Fig. 3.5 Life cycle profiles of matriculate and graduate dads' households for different parameters. Numbers in brackets are % deviations of parameters from benchmark values. (**a**) Books' profile (Matriculate). (**b**) Joint-periods' consumption (Matriculate). (**c**) Books' profile (Matriculate). (**d**) Joint-periods' consumption (Matriculate). (**e**) Joint-periods' consumption (Graduate). (**f**) Joint-periods' consumption (Graduate)

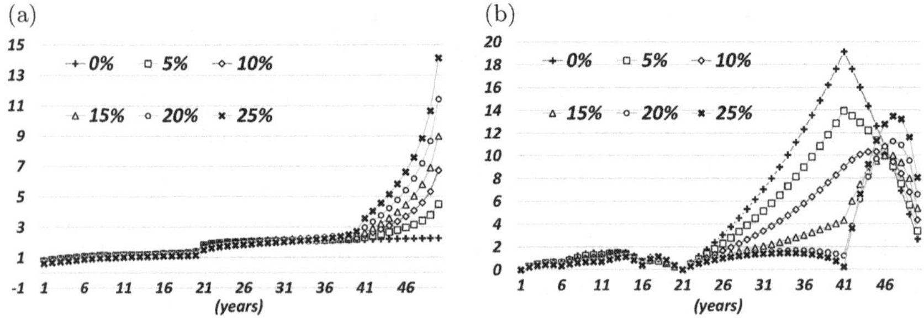

Fig. 3.6 Pension deduction rates: consumption and asset plots of matriculate dad for pension rates ∈[0%, 25%]. (**a**) Matriculate dad: per-capita consumption. (**b**) Matriculate dad: assets

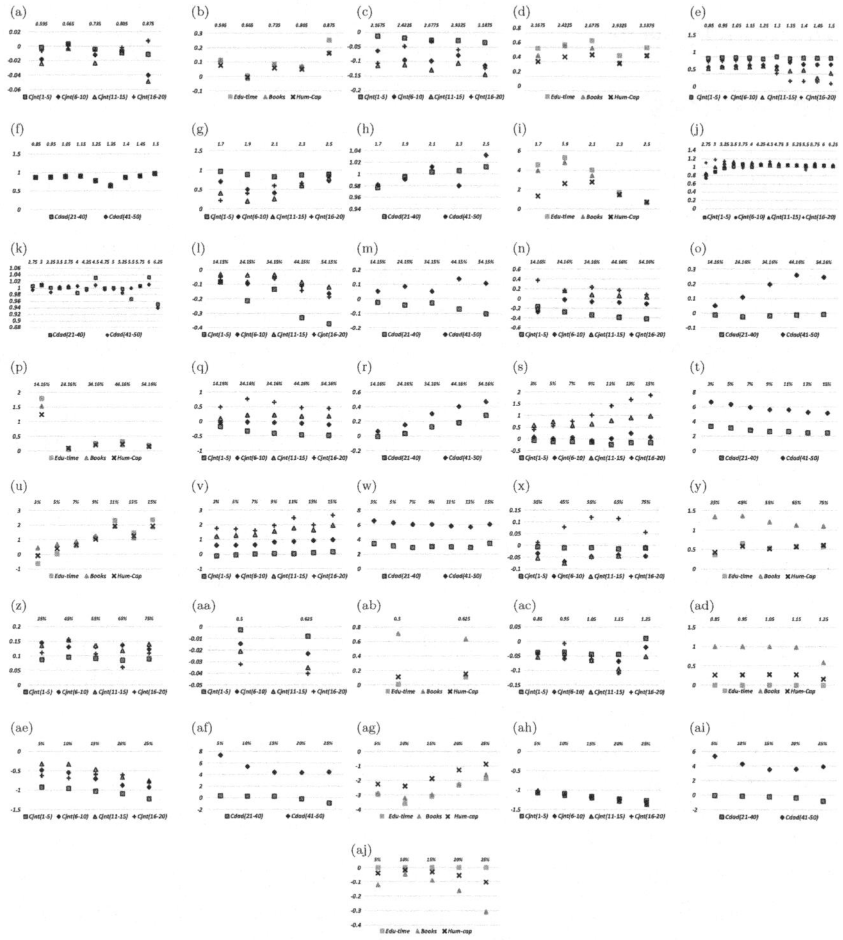

Fig. 3.7 Elasticities of joint-periods' consumptions (jce), independent dad's consumptions (idce), investments in education-time, books and human capital elasticities (hce) for different parameters. **(a)** Altruism: jce (matriculate). **(b)** Altruism: hce (matriculate). **(c)** pen: jce (matriculate). **(d)** pen: hce (matriculate). **(e)** Dad's income: jce (uneducated). **(f)** Dad's income: idce (uneducated). **(g)** Dad's income: jce (matriculate). **(h)** Dad's income: idce (matriculate). **(i)** Dad's income: hce (matriculate). **(j)** Dad's income: jce (graduate). **(k)** Dad's income: idce (graduate). **(l)** Income risk: jce (uneducated). **(m)** Income risk: idce (uneducated). **(n)** Income risk: jce (matriculate). **(o)** Income risk: idce (matriculate). **(p)** Income risk: hce (matriculate). **(q)** Income risk: jce (graduate). **(r)** Income risk: idce (graduate). **(s)** Bond returns: jce (matriculate). **(t)** Bond returns: idce (matriculate). **(u)** Bond returns: hce (matriculate). **(v)** Bond returns: jce (graduate). **(w)** Bond returns: idce (graduate). **(x)** Discount (books): jce (matriculate). **(y)** Discount (books): hce (matriculate). **(z)** Discount (books): jce (graduate). **(aa)** Upper-cap books: jce (matriculate). **(ab)** Upper-cap books: hce (matriculate). **(ac)** Upper-cap books: jce (graduate). **(ad)** Upper-cap books: hce (graduate). **(ae)** Pension rates: jce (matriculate). **(af)** Pension rates: idce (matriculate). **(ag)** Pension rates: hce (matriculate). **(ah)** Pension rates: jce (graduate). **(ai)** Pension rates: idce (graduate). **(aj)** Pension rates: hce (graduate)

References

Agrawal, T. 2012. Returns to education in India: Some recent evidence. *Journal of Quantitative Economics* 10: 131–151.

Aiyagari, S.R., J. Greenwood, and A. Seshadri. 2002. Efficient investment in children. *Journal of Economic Theory* 102: 290–321.

Altonji, J.G., F. Hayashi, and L.J. Kotlikoff. 1997. Parental altruism and inter vivos transfers: Theory and evidence. *Journal of Political Economy* 105: 1121–1166.

Alvi, E., and S. Dendir. 2011. Weathering the storms: Credit receipt and child labor in the aftermath of the great floods (1998) in Bangladesh. *World Development* 39: 1398–1409.

Azam, M., and V. Bhatt. 2015. Like father, like son? Intergenerational educational mobility in India. *Demography* 52: 1929–1959.

Baland, J.M., and J.A. Robinson. 2000. Is child labor inefficient? *Journal of Political Economy* 108: 663–679.

Bandara, A., R. Dehejia, and S. Lavie-Rouse. 2015. The impact of income and non-income shocks on child labor: Evidence from a panel survey of Tanzania. *World Development* 67: 218–237.

Basu, K., and Z. Tzannatos. 2003. The global child labor problem: What do we know and what can we do? *The World Bank Economic Review* 17: 147–173.

Basu, K., and P.H. Van. 1998. The economics of child labor. *American Economic Review* 88: 412–427.

Beck, T., A. Demirgüç-Kunt, and M.S.M. Peria. 2008. Banking services for everyone? Barriers to bank access and use around the world. *The World Bank Economic Review* 22: 397–430.

Becker, G., and N. Tomes. 1979. An equilibrium theory of the distribution of income and intergenerational mobility. *The Journal of Political Economy* 87: 1153–1189.

Becker, G.S. 1974. A theory of social interactions. *Journal of Political Economy* 82: 1063–1093.

Becker, G.S., K.M. Murphy, and R. Tamura. 1990. Human capital, fertility, and economic growth. *Journal of Political Economy* 98: S12–S37.

Becker, G.S., and N.Tomes. 1986. Human capital and the rise and fall of families. *Journal of Labor Economics* 4: S1–S39.

Beegle, K., R.H. Dehejia, and R. Gatti. 2006. Child labor and agricultural shocks. *Journal of Development Economics* 81: 80–96.

Behrman, J.R., A. Gaviria, M. Székely, N. Birdsall, and S. Galiani. 2001. Intergenerational mobility in Latin America. *Economica* 2: 1–44.
Ben-Porath, Y. 1967. The production of human capital and the life cycle of earnings. *The Journal of Political Economy* 75: 352–365.
Black, S.E., P.J. Devereux, and K.G. Salvanes. 2005. Why the apple doesn't fall far: Understanding intergenerational transmission of human capital. *The American Economic Review* 95: 437–449.
Bouoiyour, J., A. Miftah, and E.M. Mouhoud. 2016. Education, male gender preference and migrants' remittances: Interactions in rural Morocco. Economic Modelling 57: 324–331. https://doi.org/10.1016/j.econmod.2015.10.026. http://www.sciencedirect.com/science/article/pii/S0264999315003223.
Carneiro, P., and J. Heckman. 2002. The evidence on credit constraints in post-secondary schooling. *The Economic Journal* 112: 705–734.
Caucutt, E.M., and K.B. Kumar. 2003. Higher education subsidies and heterogeneity: A dynamic analysis. *Journal of Economic Dynamics and Control* 27: 1459–1502.
Chaudhuri, S. 2011. Labor market reform and incidence of child labor in a developing economy. *Economic Modelling* 28: 1923–1930.
Claessens, S. 2006. Access to financial services: A review of the issues and public policy objectives. *The World Bank Research Observer* 21: 207–240.
Cocco, J., F. Gomes, and P. Maenhout. 2005. Consumption and portfolio choice over the life cycle. *Review of Financial Studies* 18: 491–533.
Cox, D. 1987. Motives for private income transfers. *The Journal of Political Economy* 95: 508–546.
Cunha, F., and J. Heckman. 2007. The technology of skill formation. *American Economic Review* 97: 31–47. https://doi.org/10.1257/aer.97.2.31. http://www.aeaweb.org/articles?id=10.1257/aer.97.2.31.
Cunha, F., and J. Heckman. 2008. Formulating, identifying and estimating the technology of cognitive and noncognitive skill formation. *Journal of Human Resources* 43: 738–782.
De, A., J. Dréze, and A.S. Kumar. 1999. Public report on basic education in India. Oxford University Press, New Delhi.
Dehejia, R.H., and R. Gatti. 2005. Child labor: The role of financial development and income variability across countries. *Economic Development and Cultural Change* 53: 913–932.
Djankov, S., S. Sharma, E. Seira, and P. Miranda. 2008. Who are the unbanked? World Bank Policy Research Working Paper No. 4647. Available at http://papers.ssrn.com/sol3/papers.cfm?abstract_id=1149580.

Doepke, M., and F. Zilibotti. 2005. The macroeconomics of child labor regulation. *The American Economic Review* 95: 1492–1524.

Dwibedi, J.K., and S. Chaudhuri. 2010. Foreign capital, return to education and child labour. *International Review of Economics & Finance* 19: 278–286.

Edmonds, E., and C. Turk. 2002. Child labor in transition in Vietnam. Policy Research Paper 2774. World Bank, Macroeconomics and Growth, Development Research Group, Washington, D.C.

Edmonds, E.V. 2005. Does child labor decline with improving economic status? *Journal of Human Resources* 40: 77–99.

Edmonds, E.V., and N. Schady. 2012. Poverty alleviation and child labor. *American Economic Journal: Economic Policy* 4: 100–124.

Estevez, K. 2011. Nutritional efficiency wages and child labor. *Economic Modelling* 28: 1793–1801.

Galor, O., and O. Moav. 2002. Natural selection and the origin of economic growth. *The Quarterly Journal of Economics* 117: 1133–1191.

Galor, O., and J. Zeira. 1993. Income distribution and macroeconomics. *The Review of Economic Studies* 60: 35–52.

Grogan, L. 2009. Universal primary education and school entry in Uganda. *Journal of African Economies* 18: 183–211.

Hazan, M., and B. Berdugo. 2002. Child labour, fertility, and economic growth. *The Economic Journal* 112: 810–828.

ILO. 2007. Child labour wages and productivity: Results from demand-side surveys. International Labour Office. https://books.google.co.in/books?id=IZfJlgEACAAJ.

Jafarey, S., and S. Lahiri. 2002. Will trade sanctions reduce child labour?: The role of credit markets. *Journal of Development Economics* 68: 137–156.

Kazianga, H. 2005. Income risk and schooling decisions in Burkina Faso. Mimeo, Earth Institute, Columbia University, New York.

Keane, M., and K. Wolpin. 2001. The effect of parental transfers and borrowing constraints on educational attainment. *International Economic Review* 42: 1051–1103.

Kremer, M., E. Miguel, and R. Thornton. 2009. Incentives to learn. *The Review of Economics and Statistics* 91: 437–456.

Kremer, M., S. Moulin, and R. Namunyu. 2002. Unbalanced decentralization. Mimeo, Harvard University. Cambridge, MA. Available online at http://econ.bu.edu/dilipm/40-kremounam.pdf.

Lee, S.Y., and A. Seshadri. 2014. Nature and nurture in the transmission of economics status. University of Wisconsin Working Paper.

Lochner, L., and A. Monge-Naranjo. 2012. Credit constraints in education. *Annual Review of Economics* 4: 225–256.
Loury, G.C. 1981. Intergenerational transfers and the distribution of earnings. *Econometrica* 49: 843–867.
Mankiw, N.G., D. Romer, and D.N. Weil. 1992. A contribution to the empirics of economic growth. *The Quarterly Journal of Economics* 107: 407–437.
Manuelli, R.E., and A. Seshadri. 2014. Human capital and the wealth of nations. *The American Economic Review* 104: 2736–2762.
Moav, O. 2005. Cheap children and the persistence of poverty. *The Economic Journal* 115: 88–110.
Pal, R., and R. Pal. 2012. Income related inequality in financial inclusion and role of banks: Evidence on financial exclusion in India. Technical Report. Indira Gandhi Institute of Development Research, Mumbai, India.
Posso, A. 2017. Child labour's effect on long-run earnings: An analysis of cohorts. *Economic Modelling* 64: 465 – 472. http://www.sciencedirect.com/science/article/pii/S026499931630390X. https://doi.org/10.1016/j.econmod.2017.02.027.
Ranjan, P. 2001. Credit constraints and the phenomenon of child labor. *Journal of Development Economics* 64: 81–102.
Restuccia, D., and C. Urrutia. 2004. Intergenerational persistence of earnings: The role of early and college education. *The American Economic Review* 94: 1354–1378.
Rhine, S.L., and W.H. Greene. 2013. Factors that contribute to becoming unbanked. *Journal of Consumer Affairs* 47: 27–45.
Shukla, R. 2010. How India earns, spends and saves: Unmasking the real India. SAGE Publications India, New Delhi.
Strulik, H. 2004. Child mortality, child labour and economic development. *The Economic Journal* 114: 547–568.
Swinnerton, K.A., and C.A. Rogers. 1999. The economics of child labor: Comment. *The American Economic Review* 89: 1382–1385.
Thakurata, I., and E. D'Souza. 2018. Child labour and human capital in developing countries-a multi-period stochastic model. *Economic Modelling* 69: 67–81.
Todd, P., and K. Wolpin. 2003. On the specification and estimation of the production function for cognitive achievement. *The Economic Journal* 113: F3–F33.

4

Is There a Culture of Child Labour? The Decision-Making Process of Working Among Girl Beedi Rollers in Jhalda Region of Purulia, West Bengal

Dakhina Mitra

4.1 Introduction

Abedun, a 14-year-old girl from Jhalda city of Purulia District, West Bengal, told me that beedi rolling was a way of life for her (Fig. 4.1). She cannot remember clearly when she started, but now she can roll up to 800 beedis a day. From morning to late evening, she sits in one position, in the courtyard of her house to roll beedis, and thinks that her labour is indispensable for her family's survival. Abedun and the other children I met during my fieldwork accepted this reality of working from a young age and consider it natural to economically add value to the family income. But why do children accept these hazardous and exploitative working conditions? Are they consulted in making the decision of working? Is there a culture of child labour which rationalises and justifies their work?

D. Mitra (✉)
Social Researcher, Melbourne, VIC, Australia

A. Posso (ed.), *Child Labor in the Developing World*,
https://doi.org/10.1007/978-981-15-3106-4_4

Fig. 4.1 Abedun rolling beedis, Jhalda. ©Dakhinamitra

The child participants in my fieldwork were not born as labourers, but they were born into families where multidimensional poverty dictated life. These families belonged to the lowest caste and class hierarchies of the Indian society. Their socio-economic conditions and socialisation encouraged them to accept that they had to work as a paid/unpaid labourer to support their family income. Pierre Bourdieu (Mitra 2014) calls such an acceptance of one's conditions as the habitus which is a cognitive set of principles guiding action in a way that it appears to be instinctive and natural. Bourdieu argues that a habitus is not just there; it is produced by discourses, societal structures and the material as well as immaterial possessions that an actor owns in the world (p. 15). These children therefore have a habitus that encourages their naturalisation into the role of a child labourer (Mitra 2014).

This chapter utilises data collected from participant observation and conversations with children working on the streets of Kolkata, domestic and daily-wage earners in Purulia and an agroforest industry, beedi[1]-making, in Jhalda—all located in the state of West Bengal, India. It aims to shed a light on their perspectives of life and work which are embedded in their family discourses and surrounding social structures. In the next section, I will discuss the background for the chapter and research methodology. This will be followed by a description of the beedi industry and

[1] Beedi or Bidi/Biri is a thin, South Asian cigarette filled with tobacco flakes and wrapped in a 'tendu' leaf tied with a string.

the stories of child labourers in their own words. I will analyse and deconstruct these stories using the narratives that surround them. This includes documenting the structural barriers in their physical environment, perceptions of their parents and the community as well as sociocultural norms of the Indian society. Finally, I will conclude with a short discussion on potential solutions and recommendations.

4.2 Child Labour: Background

Child labour is a global phenomenon. A 2017 ILO report reveals that there are about 152 million child labourers around the world. Of these 73 million are engaged in hazardous work. About 58% of the 152 million are boys and 42% are girls. Forty-eight per cent of the children fall in the age group of 5–11 years old, while 70.9% are engaged in agriculture or agro-based industries (ILO 2017). The report further states that even though there has been a decline in the global numbers of child labour since 2000, the progress has been slow, and the rate of decline in the recent years has decreased.

Child labour is a complex issue caused by the interplay of socio-economic factors such as poverty, inequality, illiteracy, political instability and natural disasters which make families vulnerable. In the absence of social security nets or savings, global challenges such as climate change, thriving informal economies, migration, rapid urbanisation and digitalisation further contribute to the vulnerability of families, and children get pushed into the labour market. Child labour predominantly occurs in the unorganised and unregulated sectors such as agriculture, fishing, weaving, construction work, sweatshops, mines and other labour-intensive industries. The implications of child labour from long hours of work and mild to extreme hazardous conditions include malnutrition, spinal deformities, poor eye health and respiratory diseases. Additionally social and economic challenges and low literacy levels impede their ability to prepare for a better future (MOSPI 2018; UNICEF 2016; ILO 2015).

In India, the Census of 2011 reported that from the total child population of about 26 million, more than 10 million children in the age group of 5–14 years were working (main and marginal). About

75% of these working children belonged to the age group of 10–14 years, while 25% were from the age group of 5–9 years (MOSPI 2018, p. 52). Although ILO (2017) reports that child labour numbers in India are declining, there is speculation that the phenomenon has simply become invisible. UNICEF (2016b) reports that growing awareness amongst buyers, changes in legislation and their enforcement and international pressure have moved children from formal factory settings to homes. Therefore, the decline can be attributed to the undocumented child labourers who continue to work informally or within the confines of the home. They do domestic work at their own homes (to free their parents to engage in paid labour); work as domestic helps for others; engage in agriculture labour such as cotton growing and tea-picking; and work in informal cottage industries/workshops for lock making, embroidery, stone quarrying, brick making, beedi rolling and rag picking, amongst others. Traditional-gendered roles dictate the work of girls who perform domestic and home-based cottage industry activities. Whereas boys primarily work as wage labourers at places such as unregulated food joints, motor repair workshops, small-scale factories/workshops and others.

4.3 Setting the Scene: Filling Gaps in Knowledge

The current chapter is a continuation of a body of research work (which includes papers, a master's thesis and a doctoral thesis) that I have undertaken since 2003 to highlight the social, cultural and cognitive aspects that influence the decision of working for children. Through a comprehensive review of reports and journal articles on child labour covering different disciplines (historical, theoretical, development and health economics, public policy, sociology and anthropology) and issues such as causes, implications, cost-benefit analysis and policies, I identified a number of gaps in the literature (Mitra 2014, pp. 30–36). Firstly, the voices of child labourers were missing. Childhood studies argue that understanding what a child thinks about his or her situation is crucial for any decision that is taken for them (Schildkrout 2002; Nieuwenhueys 1996).

However, my fieldwork revealed that the decision of working depended on a family's social, economic and cultural poverty and not on the child's will (Mitra 2014, p. 188). In India, where caste and traditional norms guide day-to-day life and poverty is rampant, children belonging to the most socially, structurally, culturally and economically disadvantaged groups considered that their work was the only viable option for the survival of their family (Mitra 2014, pp. 212–213). By documenting the perspectives of the children who are at the centre of this issue, and exploring the narratives that influence a family's decision to send a child for work, I aim to add to the existing body of knowledge on child labour. Furthermore, exploring the discourses that facilitate the child's acceptance of this decision, further contribute to a multidimensional understanding of the child labour issue. This is in line with what the ILO report states that one of the ways by which we can achieve the elimination of worst forms of child labour by 2025 is by "understanding and addressing family reliance on children's labour" (ILO 2017, p. 13).

The second aim of this chapter is to fill an evidence gap for mapping the extent of child labour in the unregulated beedi industry and capture the lived experiences and voices of the young beedi rollers. Beedi-making in India is a prime example of a home-based activity with a high incidence of undocumented child labour (Dube and Mohandoss 2013). Beedi, known as a poor man's cigarette as it is sold cheap, constitutes almost 48% of tobacco consumption in the country. A change in factory regulations during the 1960s led to a decline in factory-based beedi production, and the activity moved to the house of the workers (Dube and Mohandoss 2013). As a result, this traditional agroforest industry became strongly embedded in the informal sector of the country. The industry employs an estimated 6–8.5 million workers (guess estimates have been cited in various studies which include Singh et al. (2017), TII (2017), Mishra (2014) and Srinivasan and Ilango (2012)), and majority of them are below the poverty line (Ghatak 2017). These studies also estimate that about 90% to 95% workers are women and children who have no protections from unions or country's labour regulations. Current data is missing, but a health study in 2009 estimated that more than 1.7 million children were working as beedi rollers.[2]

4.4 Methodology

When I began my research on the issue of child labour, I found another gap in methodology. Many emerging scholars criticised the majority of child labour studies as they lacked the use of participatory techniques to document the perspectives of children (Liebel 2004, p. 34). However, in the last 15 years, a number of studies have started to use a bottom-up approach that provides a space for children to voice their opinions and in turn, understand them. In order to add to this emerging body of literature, I developed a participatory fieldwork plan in the state of West Bengal (Kolkata and Purulia districts). I chose these locations on the basis of expert interviews held with government officials and staff of non-governmental organisations in Delhi. I tapped into existing familial networks in these locations that helped me to connect with local officials, school administration and beedi-worker union members. From 2009 to 2011, I conducted fieldwork in two blocks of 4.5 months. In each phase, I spent 1 month in Kolkata and 3.5 months in the Purulia district. In this first phase, I worked as teacher at a National Child Labour Project[3] (NCLP) school in an indigenous community in Purulia town, for 3.5 months. In the second phase, I did another 1-month visit to Kolkata and spent the rest of the time at the school as well as in Jhalda city and Singhbajar village, where the primary economic activities are beedi-making and silk weaving, respectively.

In Jhalda, I conducted key informant interviews with three union members and observed the daily work life of six girls between the age of 11 and 17, three women and their families. I chose the snowball sampling method to find respondents wherein one respondent connected me to another. After informing the respondents about the intention of the study

[2] http://www.zeenews.com/news578951.html.

[3] National Child Labour Project is an initiative by the Government of India which provides a sequential approach to rehabilitate working children into mainstream schools. Former (and current) child workers are supported to attend non-formal bridge schools where a mix of age and ability appropriate skills is taught. Literacy, numeracy and vocational training is provided along with a mid-day meal, a monthly stipend of about US$2.5 and health care.

and seeking parental consent, I maintained a field diary[4] of their daily activities, conversations, dwellings and physical surroundings. Furthermore, I conducted semi-structured interviews with three primary school teachers working in and around Purulia town, the Additional District Magistrate and Director of the Department of Labour in Purulia. Apart from this sample, I engaged in informal conversations with several domestic helpers and children working at various locations such as railway platforms, markets, roadside food stalls, coal warehouses, stone quarries, grocery stores and brick kilns. Similarly, I conducted semi-structured conversations with several family and community members and employers, teachers and social workers to understand the social and cultural thought processes. All these conversations were recorded daily into the field diary. Each conversation was manually coded, and themes and discourses were identified and analysed.

4.5 Beedi Rolling in Jhalda

There are 400 villages in the Jhalda city (Block 1) where beedi rolling is the primary economic activity. Dried tendu leaves are cut to fit a designated mould, filled with dried tobacco flakes, rolled and tied with a thread to form a thin cigarette called beedi. The beedi-making companies in Jhalda bring the tendu leaves from Daltonganj (Bihar) and Keonjhar (Orissa) and supply it to the contractors. These contractors use subcontractors to find labour and then provide the leaves to the beedi rollers.

About 430 to 600 grams of leaves are used to make 1000 beedis in a span of 12 hours. The rollers are paid about Rs. 68 (less than US$1) for every 1000 beedis, a rate which has risen from Rs. 46 (less than US$1) which was paid in 2010. An amount of Rs. 4.90 (about US$ 0.06 cents) is deducted from Rs. 68 as a contribution to the provident fund/pension

[4] While travelling through the rural fieldwork locations in West Bengal, I came to understand that my urban clothing and use of phones, camera and recording devices served as distractions and put people on guard. Therefore, I changed my attire and stopped using devices during my interactions with children and their families. Respectful conversations, regular visits and support of a known and trusted village elder, enabled me to build a rapport and collect valuable notes from the fieldwork.

fund. The company also contributes the same amount (per 1000 beedis) to the pension fund for each roller. At the time of this fieldwork, due to the presence of a workers' union in Jhalda, the pension fund rate was steady and considered highest in Jhalda. There were reports that in other cities, companies are known to pay less.

The remaining amount of Rs. 63.1 (less than US$1) was not directly paid to the roller. The contractor found several reasons to deduct varying amounts from the total. One of the ways was by manipulating the scales while weighing the leaves or the tobacco. A lower quantity of leaves or tobacco yielded a lesser number of beedis, thus providing the contractor a reason to deduct from the pay. Discarding the poor-quality beedis further reduced the final pay. After a few strategic reductions, the contractor still did not pay the worker. In majority of the cases, the contractors owned a grocery shop where they sold goods at prices higher than the market price. The workers are provided vouchers which could only be redeemed at the contractor's store. Once the vouchers had been redeemed, the remaining amount (if any) was handed over to the beedi roller/family. Therefore, after 12 hours of rolling 1000 beedis approximately, the worker received a meagre amount of about Rs. 20–30 (less than US$0.50 cents).

The exploitative conditions, labour-intensive work and low income forced families to engage every able member to make beedis. Traditionally, it was a family activity where all members, including parents, grandparents, extended family and children, got involved. Being a trans-generational occupation, children learn from their parents and pass the skill to the next generation. But men and adolescent boys do not engage in this activity anymore. Young boys go to school and then transition to working as construction workers, rickshaw pullers, day labourers or factory employees like their older siblings and fathers/uncles. Many men and boys consider beedi rolling as the last option for them.

As a result the onus of rolling beedis to supplement the family income sat with the young girls and women. Girls as young as 9 years followed the footsteps of their older sisters and mothers/aunts. Since the work can be done within the boundaries of the household, family elders considered it as the best option to keep their female family members safe. Women and girls then do not need to be out after dark nor travel long distances for work, both of which can put them at risk of being kidnapped or sexually assaulted. Despite being the primary beedi rollers, women and girls continue to not receive the payment. The wages are collected by the male patriarch of the family, thus removing the women and girls' right to have ownership of the income.

Some of the adult males that I met attended school till grade 3 or 4, but majority of the adult females in these communities had never attended school. Similarly, many young girls had never been to a school, while others had left after primary school. However there were some girls who combined schooling with beedi rolling in order to have literacy and numeracy skills while supporting the family income.

4.6 The Beedi Rollers

The child labourers and their families in the study sample were from the most economically, socially and culturally disadvantaged groups in the country. Some belonged to indigenous communities, while others were at the lowest level of the caste hierarchy. Majority of the family members had never attended a school and those who had, did not study beyond primary level. Trans-generational child labour was a dominant feature observed throughout the study sample (Mitra 2014, p. 217).

In the following sections, I will relate the stories of the children and a description of the physical spaces into broad themes. The publicly available systems or discourses which have been produced earlier in the family or the society will contribute to understanding and deconstructing the children's perspectives about their work. Phillips and Hardy state that discourses legitimise social reality and can be seen as a social construction which is self-constructing as well (2002). They occur at the cognitive level, and at the level of talks and texts (Potter 1996). The children, their families, the peers and the society produce these discourses which influence the decision of working and normalise/justify a child's labour. The idea of a culture of child labour will be explored further in the following sections.

4.7 The Stories of Child Labourers

4.7.1 Intergenerational Child Labour: Discussions with Devaki, Sushila and Charu Bala (Late 30s)

"Our parents rolled beedis, and we are doing the same. For people like us, this is the way of life. When we were growing up, we were rolling beedis to increase our parents' income, and now we are doing the same to support our husbands and children. The boys here do not want to roll beedis; even we do not want them to toil like us. We want them to study and leave the village for a better future. Our girls will follow a similar path like us. We were married off when we were 14 or 15 years of age. We bore children when we were 15 or 16. We never went to school, but would like our daughters to study for some years. However, they will eventually quit school as they have to do household chores or beedi rolling. The older daughters must be married off too. In our communities, if a daughter has not been married by the age of 15 or 16, she is considered to have surpassed the marriageable age. Then it is hard to find a groom. Even if we find one, they ask for a huge dowry to compensate for the increased age of the girl. Hence, we prefer that the girls are married off younger. But a girl's beedi-rolling abilities are in great demand in some families. The higher the number of beedis a girl can roll, the lower the amount of dowry her parents need to pay. Learning beedi rolling then becomes an asset for us. So we teach our daughters to excel in rolling beedis" (Fig. 4.2).

4.7.2 Zoya (13 Years)

"I left school last year because it had no use for me. There was just one teacher who taught in the two schools of Belladi and Deondra, which are close to us. He could not do much as the school building was crumbling and he neither had assistance nor books to teach us. As a result he was absent for days and weeks and sometimes months. While I was studying there, the school remained closed for 6–7 months. Even the mid-day meals which are provided by all the government schools, was missing. My father decided that walking for a kilometre to a school where there was

Fig. 4.2 Devaki, Sushila and Charu Bala rolling beedis, Jhalda. ©Dakhinamitra

no learning or meals, was a waste of time. Since then, I have been rolling beedis all day. When I used to study, I made about 300–400 beedis, but now with all the time in the hand, I can roll up to 800 a day. At times, I help in household chores as I do not have any other younger sisters. I have one older sister who is married now and have four brothers. Three of my brothers are younger than me, and they go to school as they do not have to roll beedis. When they turn 13 or 14 years of age, they would seek work in the factories or leave the village like the other boys. Our eldest brother has gone to become an apprentice to our uncle who is a tailor in Jamshedpur. Once he learns tailoring, he will send us money to ease our financial burdens. My mother also rolls beedis when she gets some time off from household chores. My father is a rickshaw puller and took a loan of Rs. 80000 (about US$ 1125) for my elder sister's wedding. He must repay this amount soon or else the interest rates would keep getting higher. So I have to help my father repay this loan. Sometimes I wish that

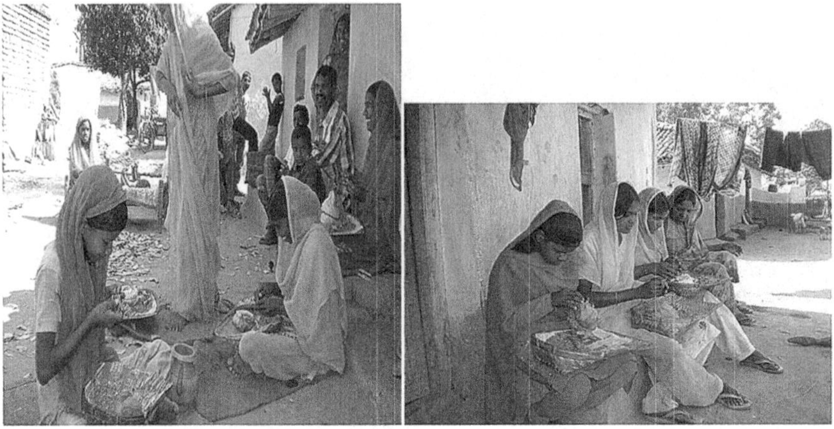

Fig. 4.3 Zoya and her friends rolling Beedi, Jhalda. ©Dakhinamitra

I could also work in the plastic bag factory, which is close to the village, and where all the older boys of our village work. In that way I can earn more money to help my family. But my father says that it is unsafe for a girl to go far from the village and work in a factory with male workers. Therefore from morning to evening I must roll beedis" (Fig. 4.3).

4.7.3 Pinky (12 Years)

"I have never been to a school because studying was never an option for me. All I know is that I have to roll beedis to support my family. I cannot remember when I started, but I think I have always rolled beedis. Few of my friends go to school and roll beedis as well. But they can afford to do so as their brothers live in big cities, earn good money and send back to their parents. I do not have any older brother. I only have 3 more sisters. One is older than me and the other two are younger. My father had to sell a part of his land to get my older sister married. Marrying at the right age (14–15) is hard for girls like us as our parents do not have enough savings and may have to sell their possessions/land or take a loan. I do not want that to happen. So I must work hard each day to help my parents to save. My younger sisters have to miss school as they do all household chores like cooking, cleaning and washing. That way, my mother and I can concentrate fully on beedi rolling. My father works at the factory, but he suffers from poor health. His income is not steady. Father also deals with the beedi contractor. He says that the contractor is constantly tricking us; hence I do not know the exact amount of money that I earn. However, it does not matter as father knows the best about family finances. Just before important festivals, we travel to our relatives or they come to visit us. Extended family members help each other to roll a large number of beedis. This boosts our income and we are able to celebrate the festivals as per our liking. I feel for people like us, this is the only option. Look around, most of my other friends are doing the same work. So I do not mind it either. In fact I feel happy that I am able to help my parents. But I worry about the future of my family once I am married off. My younger sisters do not know much about beedi rolling. I hope my father gets a proper medical treatment for his illness and goes regularly to work. But he says he does not have enough money for medicines. I do not know what the future holds for us. It is uncertain."

The stories of children provide a deep insight into the way they think about the notions of gender, caste/class divisions, rights of children and education. But before we deconstruct the stories, there is a need to understand the characteristics of the physical spaces occupied by the respondents. This will reveal discourses of distinction wherein the respondents differentiate their lives from the rest of the society and the structural barriers.

4.8 Living Conditions

Pierre Bourdieu states that human beings occupy a position in social and physical space. They are "topos" which means they exist in a site where action is taking place. The position they occupy in the social space is often synchronised with the physical space, and there are distinctions between smart areas and working areas in a geographical location. With location, things such as temporary or permanent and extent and size of space occupied by a person further determine social positions of human beings (Bourdieu 2000 cited in Mitra 2014, p. 146). The child labourers and their families as well as these communities belonged to the lowest strata of the society and occupied the lowest position in the physical hierarchy as well.

Fig. 4.4 Stagnant water, garbage and children washing dishes, Bauri Para, Purulia. ©Dakhinamitra

The fieldwork locations were characterised by narrow lanes with open drains on both sides. Open areas were treated as garbage dump sites which were a breeding ground for insects and diseases. A small rain-fed and stagnant waterbody was usually around the locality which was used for washing clothes and cleaning utensils (Fig. 4.4). There were no toilets or bathrooms inside the houses; therefore open defecation and bathing around wells, hand pumps and other waterbodies in the area were common. In each locality there were one or two public water taps which supplied clean water twice a day, and people queued up to fill their drinking water. Electricity supply was minimal with most houses relying on one or two bulbs. Having a refrigerator or a television was uncommon in these localities. If any family had domestic animals such as cows, goats, pigs and chicken, they were allowed to freely roam in the locality, which contributed to the unhygienic conditions (due to animal excreta) and stench in the lanes.

The houses were just enough to accommodate six to seven family members sleeping side by side, together. In one corner of the house, there would be clay stove next to a small window, serving as the kitchen. The small houses were stacked next to one another. The houses were so close to each other that the notion of privacy did not exist. In some cases, the way to one house was through another house. It was common for three to four families to share one courtyard which was a place for socialising, discussions and doing small activities like feeding the child or sorting out vegetables/food grains or even lighting the clay stove. Neighbours would help each other carry out small tasks, and the proximity led to the formation of a close-knit unit which acted as a social control unit as well. The unsaid norm was that all material possessions were shared with immediate neighbours. For example, if there was one television in the locality, all neighbours would get together to watch it. If someone was entertaining guests, then things such as utensils, chairs and other household items were borrowed from neighbours (Fig. 4.5).

Fig. 4.5 Houses stacked one after the other, Bauri Para, Purulia. ©Dakhinamitra

Fig. 4.6 Open drains, livestock and garbage along the lanes, Bauri Para, Purulia. ©Dakhinamitra

The physical surroundings faced structural neglect from government departments and policymakers. The city municipal cleaners and garbage collectors did not service or clean these neighbourhoods. Community members contributed and hired a cleaner two or three times a year to clean the garbage and the drains. The murky waterbodies and the open garbage dumps which included human waste as well as dirt from filthy drains, were an incubator of deadly insects/germs causing malaria, dengue and typhoid. But the people residing here have accepted this space and have lived there for at least two generations (Fig. 4.6).

Similarly, the school buildings in these areas faced structural neglect and lacked infrastructure to support education. In one of the schools, there were two classrooms, which were mosquito infested, were dark and had a limited supply of electricity. Each classroom had children sitting from two grades with one teacher attending to about 15 to 20 children.

Fig. 4.7 NCLP classroom in Bauri Para, Purulia. ©Dakhinamitra

This school served the mid-day meals, but it did not match the stipulated menu that was prescribed by the government scheme. There was one toilet, but only the teachers used it, while the children had to go out in the open field or back alleys if they needed. These localities also did not receive many "outsiders" except for census officials, occasional visits from teachers and people looking for cheap labour (Fig. 4.7).

The localities and school buildings in more affluent areas of Purulia town and Jhalda city were completely opposite to the above-mentioned spaces. They were well serviced by city cleaners and had access to electricity, water and sanitation. The school buildings had quality teachers, learning resources and good infrastructure to support children.

In terms of diet, these families consumed rice and potatoes on most days and could not afford more nutritious food items such as fruits, milk, meat and fish. If the parents or children worked as domestic help, they would be happy to eat leftovers from their employers. Many children said they wore second-hand clothes and only had one or two fancy set of clothes. In addition to this, I observed that a number of children did not wear slippers or shoes which was often a safety hazard and led to accidents. They complained about the lack of spare time to play as they had to spend most of the time in doing household chores or working. The children understood that their localities, habits and resources were in stark contrast to those of the more affluent parts of the city. These differences were internalised by the children and shaped their identity. They often mentioned that their childhood was different from the lives of "lucky" children from higher castes and classes of the society.

4.9 Deconstructing the Stories

A discourse can be defined as…

> …a group of statements which provide a language for talking about a topic and a way of producing a particular kind of knowledge about a topic. Thus the term refers both to the production of knowledge through language and representation and the way that knowledge is institutionalised, shaping social practices and setting new practices into play. ((du Gay 1996: 43) cited in Ainsworth 2001, p. 3)

There are a number of recurring themes that emerge from the talks of the older women and the young girls which are part of the larger discourses in India. Firstly, there is a clear acceptance of gender-based divisions which has roots in the patriarchal social norms. Secondly, there is an understanding about the low social and economic status which can be traced down to caste and class divisions in the country. Thirdly, despite being highly resilient, the children's sense of agency or their ability to make a choice is non-existent. And lastly, the absence of the discourse that education is useful and can be beneficial for the future.

4.9.1 Gender

In the unorganised rural sector of India, a number of studies have identified that women are engaged usually as the unpaid family worker or casual/wage labourer (Singh et al. 2017; Srinivasan and Ilango 2012; Dasgupta and Sudarshan 2011; FAO, IFAD, and ILO 2010). The labour of the girl child is said to be completely invisible (Mishra 2014). As the economic power in the household was with the men, a woman's/girl's entity was always identified in association with the man in the house. Even if they earned, the money was collected by the main male member in the house which is either the father or the husband or an older brother (Desai 1994). Through the conversations of the older women, it was evident that their identity was in relation to the support they provided to the men and children in their family.

Additionally, India's gender inequality is reflected in literacy levels. Girls have to do household chores if the mother has to work or girls schooling can be stopped if there are no economic returns (Sundaram and Vanneman 2008). In the discussions with the older women, they accept the fact that boys need to study and look towards their future, whereas the education of girls is optional as their ultimate goal is marriage. Zoya's younger brothers were allowed to go to the same school which was deemed unfit for her by her father. Furthermore, Zoya's brothers did not stay at home to do housework; and she had to help her mother instead. However Pinky's younger sisters had to skip school to do household work.

The idea of having a son who will ease financial burdens was strongly observed across the families. A number of families that I met had four or more children. The mother of Abedun said that she had one boy and three girls. As a result, her husband decided that they needed another child, in the hope for a son who would share the financial burden with him; and she conceived again. She felt lucky that she had another son at that time; otherwise she would have had to probably conceive again for a son. This and a number of other conversations confirmed the research (Kosgi et al. 2011; Paul et al. 2017) that majority of the women in these families lacked control over their bodies and had little or no say in reproductive decisions.

4.9.2 Caste and Class

All the respondents, including the union members and the government officials talked about the low socio-economic status of the workers and their communities. Burra explains poverty as “the denial of opportunities and choices most basic to human development—to lead a long, healthy, creative life to enjoy a decent standard of living, freedom, dignity, self-esteem and respect of others” (Burra 2001, p. 481). Unregulated wages and exploitation by employers kept the incomes low. Combined with low social status, poor literacy rates, illnesses and limited access to health, water, sanitation and electricity, these families faced multidimensional poverty.[5]

This was exacerbated by intergenerational child labour which meant that most parents started working when they were children. Studies confirm that there is a significant relationship between a parent's child labour incidence and years of schooling, and those of their children, thus raising the probability of intergernational child labour (Emerson and Souza 2002, p. 20). Illnesses and untimely death of children or adults were common. Yet, money earned was saved for running the household or repaying debts or for the dowry during the wedding of a daughter and not for treating illnesses. Thus the cycle of poverty continued and children as well as their parents accepted the fate that the poor have to suffer.

Every strategy these families took revolved around survival. The phrase that “time is money” was frequently brought up in conversations and focus-group discussions, and children felt it was their duty to help the family economically. Reena, a 13-year-old girl, said that if she does not work, she will be a burden for her family of 7 who have very limited resources. She had to either do housework or roll beedis and going to school was never an option.

This resonates with the idea of culture of poverty, which Oscar Lewis (1959) explains is a set of practices typical to the poor that guides their daily actions. He asserts that groups of people, who share ideas and follow similar practices to deal with the problems of poverty, have a way of life catering typically to the poor. Similarly, two other ethnographic studies by Paul E. Willis (1977) and William F. Whyte (1943) argue that

[5] http://hdr.undp.org/en/content/measuring-multidimensional-poverty-leaving-no-one-behind.

children of working classes differentiated themselves from the other classes and the school system and would tend to take up working-class jobs (cited in Mitra 2014, p. 175). They have to overcome economic, cultural and social difficulties in order to break out of their class:

> During my fieldwork, the time for Christmas celebrations came up. I was working at the NCLP school at that time and decided to treat the students with some fruits and cake to make the day. I informed them at the beginning of the class that Santa Claus would pay them a visit by the end of the class (I had arranged for a cousin to bring the goodies for the children). The children assured me, that Santa Claus does not know about their existence and they were not lucky enough to get a visit or presents from him. Field-notes: 23rd Dec. 2010, Bauri Para School, Purulia

4.9.3 Children's Agency

The girls' stories demonstrate that they depend on their parents as the wages were being paid to the parents. This was true for most of the children (except some street children who I met in Kolkata and who were very independent). The beedi-rolling girls, the domestic helpers and the food stall apprentices worked long hours, but had no control over the money they earned. In most cases, they did not choose their work, but followed what their siblings and peers were doing. These children viewed the lack of control on their choice and earnings, as a norm and duty towards the family. Their parents did the same and they were following the footsteps. This view is deep-seated because children consider their parents in a position of power which prescribes them the duties of obedience (Levison 2000). Such thinking is evident in the story of Pinky who thinks she does not need to know anything about the payments for her labour as her father is the household head.

Powerlessness of the girl child is reflected in the discussions around child marriage as well. They had little or no power in making the decision about their marriage or giving birth to babies at a young age. A number of girls believed that their parents knew the best for them and would marry them off to the right person.

Children felt powerless even when they interacted with their employers. Some of them knew that they were being exploited, but did not have the courage or power to challenge the employers. Shefuna said that the contractor was bound to reject 100 to 200 beedis while counting. This affected the wage and added a financial pressure on her, especially on the days when she would only be able to roll about 600 beedis. Additionally, the entire community knew about the exploitation through the shop vouchers, but Shefuna said nobody can do anything to change it as even the union members are corrupt and involved.

4.9.4 Education

Many children expressed their wish to study and do something different. But they had no say in the decision of going to school. Majority of the parents could not read or write, but they still wanted their children to study. However, considering the inefficiency of the school system and the costs entailed to support secondary education, many children had to drop out. All the conversations reflected that in its current state, schools and education were a waste of time and money. There were no immediate returns from attending school; hence it was seen as nonprofitable. But earning, which was a short-term benefit of working, seemed more practical for the family. The intention of the National Child Labour Project and Right to Education Act (RTE)[6] is to support children to continue school and transition to higher grades. But the success of the NCLP and the RTE Act heavily depends on the school infrastructure and the teachers. Corruption, teacher absenteeism, unavailability of funds and educational resources and dilapidated school buildings forced parents to reject the use of education and embrace the work of children.

Shefuna's father said that they cannot help their children study as they have never attended a school.

> We do not have means to pay for tuition and extra coaching to compensate for the poor quality of education. It is the task of the teachers and the gov-

[6] Right to Education Act states that all children between the age of 6 and 14 years have the right to free and compulsory education in India.

ernment. But they are apathetic to our children's educational progress. If our children become educated, they would compete with the children of the teachers and that is dangerous. Then who would clean their homes, plough their fields and do all the menial tasks of the society? Our children are hence destined to work and not study. Field-notes: 18th Jan. 2011, Beedi rollers' village, Jhalda

4.10 Discussion

The stories and discourses above are an instrumental part of the children's socialisation. They construct and rationalise the social reality of working for the children. The child participants in this study belonged to the lowest section of the society which was considered different at multiple levels from the other sections. A distinction is observed in their physical spaces, living conditions and socio-economic status. The lack of basic amenities and school infrastructure management for these communities reflect structural neglect, which is also different from the other parts of the city. Most of the children in the study cohort had internalised this distinction. The discourses of distinction therefore influence the decision of working for these children and can be seen to produce a culture of child labour.

The societal discourses of caste hierarchies, cultural practices, traditional norms, gender biases and efficacy of schooling further impede children's right to exercise their choice or influence decisions. None of the children interviewed had heard of the United Nations Convention on the Rights of the Child. They were also not aware of legislations passed by the Indian government, such as the Child Labour Ban (2008) or Prohibition of Child Marriage Act (2006), which could protect them from exploitation. As a result they exhibited a sense of powerlessness and vulnerability.

Work then was a moral duty and provided the children an opportunity to support their families. They felt pride in their ability to work and demonstrated high levels of resilience to hardships such as deaths, illnesses and family separation by means of marriage or migration at a young age. They were actively involved in the daily conversations of survival which happened among their peers and family members. I would argue that such discourses further contribute to the culture of child labour.

To conclude, this chapter provides a unique insight into the lived experiences of child labourers and the perspectives of their family members and the society. It demonstrates that child labour is not just an economic response to hardships. It is also about the social and cognitive level where discourses shape the decision of sending a child to work. In this way, the culture of child labour is generated, perpetuated and transferred from one generation to another. As a result, children and their families continue to remain at the lowest levels of the social, cultural and economic hierarchies in India.

4.11 Recommendations

A number of strategies are being developed around the world to eliminate child labour. It is being increasingly recognised that a multidimensional approach is needed to combat the issue of child labour. Education is seen as the means to levelling the playing field (UNICEF 2016a). By introducing practical educational initiatives which include basic literacy and numeracy courses combined with vocational trainings, the efficacy of education can be increased. Cash transfer programmes are becoming popular around the developing countries as well. For instance, there is emerging evidence that the concept of school stipend for girls which has been introduced in West Bengal (the Kanyashree Prakalpa conditional cash transfer programme) is serving as a deterrent to child marriage and enabling girls to complete their education (Nandy and Nandi 2019; Sen and Dutta 2018). Corruption-free implementation of regulations and policies and equal access to good quality school infrastructure are needed. Additionally, behaviour change mass media campaigns to break caste barriers that lend to the broad acceptance of child labour must be promoted. Finally, policies and legislations must act as a deterrent for employers who exploit vulnerable children and families. Without such a multi-pronged approach, the culture of child labour will continue to prevail and be an omnipresent intergenerational reality.

References

Ainsworth, S. 2001. *Discourse analysis as social construction: Towards greater integration of approaches and methods*. In Second International Conference on Critical Management Studies, Manchester.

Burra, N. 2001. Cultural stereotypes and household behaviour: Girl child labour in India. *Economic and Political Weekly*, 481–488.

Dasgupta, S., and R. Sudarshan. 2011. Issues in labour market inequality and women's participation in India's National Rural Employment Guarantee Programme.

Desai, S. 1994. *Gender inequalities and demographic behavior. India*,16. New York.

Dube, Y., and G. Mohandoss. 2013. A study on child labour in Indian Beedi industry. National Commission for Protection of Child Rights.

Emerson, Patrick M., and André Portela Souza. 2002. Is there a Child Labour Trap? Inter-Generational Persistance of Child Labour in Brazil. Working Paper No. 02-W14. Vanderbilt University, Nashville.

FAO, IFAD, and ILO. 2010. Gender dimensions of agricultural and rural employment: Differentiated pathways out of poverty. Status, trends and gaps.

Ghatak, A. 2017. *Ground realities of beedi workers in West Bengal*. New Delhi: Center for Health and Social Justice.

International Labour Organization. 2015. World report on child labour 2015: paving the way to decent work for young people. International Labour Organization. Geneva

———. 2017. *Global estimates of child labour: Results and trends, 2012–2016*.

Kosgi, S., N.V. Hegde, S. Rao, S.B. Undaru, and N. Pai. 2011. Women reproductive rights in India: Prospective future. Online Journal of Health and Allied Sciences 10 (1): 1–5.

Lewis, Oscar. 1959. Five families. Mexican case studies in the culture of poverty. 3. print. New York: Basic Books.

Levison, D. 2000. Children as economic agents. *Feminist Economics* 6 (1): 125–134.

Liebel, M. 2004. *A will of their own: Cross-cultural perspectives on working children*. Zed Books.

Mishra, D.K. 2014. Nimble fingers on beedis: Problems of girl child labour in Sambalpur and Jharsuguda. *Indian Journal of Gender Studies* 21 (1): 135–144.

Mitra, Dakhina. 2014. The habitus of working among child labourers in the districts of Purulia and Kolkata in West Bengal, India: Der Arbeitshabitus Unter Kinderarbeitern in Den Bezirken Purulia und Kolkata in Westbengalen, Indien. Freiburg: Albert-Ludwigs Universität.

MOSPI. 2018. Children in India 2018–A Statistical Appraisal. New Delhi: Social Statistics Division, Central Statistics Office. Ministry of Statistics and Programme Implementation Government of India, Delhi.

Nandy, S., and A. Nandi. 2019. Kanyashree Prakalpa, A stepping stone towards empowerment of women: An analytical view. http://admin.iaasouthbengalbranch.org/journal/19_Article4.pdf

Nieuwenhuys, O. 1994. *Children's lifeworlds: Gender, welfare, and labour in the developing world*. Psychology Press.

Paul, M., B. Essén, S. Sariola, S. Iyengar, S. Soni, and M. Klingberg Allvin. 2017. Negotiating collective and individual agency: A qualitative study of young women's reproductive health in Rural India. *Qualitative Health Research* 27 (3): 311–324.

Potter, J. 1996. *Representing reality: Discourse, rhetoric and social construction*. Sage.

Phillips, N., and C. Hardy. 2002. *Discourse analysis: Investigating processes of social construction* (Vol. 50). Sage Publications.

Schildkrout, E. 2002. Age and gender in hausa society socio-economic roles of children in urban kano. *Childhood* 9 (3): 342–368.

Sen, A., and A. Dutta. 2018. West Bengal's successful Kanyashree Prakalpa programme needs more push from state and beneficiaries, EPW (Online), 53 (17). https://www.epw.in/engage/article/West-Bengal-Successful-Kanyashree-Prakalpa-Programme-Needs-More-Push-From-State-and-Beneficiaries. Accessed 28 April 2018.

Singh, M.M., M. Amiri, and S. Sabbarwal. 2017. Socio-economic, health and working conditions of child beedi rollers in beedi industry. *Journal of Social Science Studies* 5 (1): 239.

Srinivasan, S., and P. Ilango. 2012. A study on the socio-economic conditions of female beedi workers at Khajamalai, in Trichirapalli, Tamil Nadu.

Sundaram, A., and R. Vanneman. 2008. Gender differentials in literacy in India: The intriguing relationship with women's labor force participation. *World Development* 36 (1): 128–143.

TII. 2017. *Tobacco in India: Importance & policy challenges*. Second Edition. Delhi: The Tobacco Institute of India.

UNICEF. 2016a. The state of the world's children 2016: A fair chance for every child. New York: UNICEF.
———. 2016b. Child labour in India. http://unicef.in/whatwedo/21/child-labour. Accessed 13 Aug 2019.
Whyte, William Foote. 2006, 1943. Street corner society. The social structure of an Italian slum. 4. ed., [Nachdr.]. Chicago [u.a.]: University of Chicago Press.
Willis, Paul E. 2003, 1977. Learning to labour. How working class kids get working class jobs. Repr. Aldershot [etc.]: Ashgate. http://www.worldcat.org/oclc/71629526.

5

Income Shocks and Child Labor: Evidence for the Rural Dominican Republic

Eva Rodríguez Cuevas and Lorena Vieira Costa

5.1 Introduction

Child labor is a social problem of great relevance in the world. According to the International Labour Organization (ILO) and the International Programme on the Elimination of Child Labour (IPEC), 168 million children work around the world (ILO-IPEC 2013). Among them, more than half perform hazardous work. Asia and the Pacific have the highest incidence of child labor (almost 79 million or 9.2% of the child population). In Latin America and the Caribbean, there are 13 million children (8.8%) in this situation (ILO-IPEC 2013).

Although traditionally child labor is considered a consequence of poverty (Canagarajah and Coulombe 1999; Brown et al. 2001), recent literature on the subject has pointed to multiple determinants of poverty. Among these, transitional aspects such as negative income shocks experienced, particularly among the most vulnerable families, may guide the family's choice for child labor. Thus, faced with an eventuality that

E. R. Cuevas (✉) • L. V. Costa
Federal University of Viçosa (UFV), Viçosa, Brazil

A. Posso (ed.), *Child Labor in the Developing World*,
https://doi.org/10.1007/978-981-15-3106-4_5

increases the vulnerability of the family and the absence of complete markets to assure these families in the presence of such shocks, the choice for child labor could be a response.

The study of the relationship between negative income shocks and schooling and child labor, as well as how asset ownership or access to credit helps mitigate the effects of these shocks, is one of the most discussed issues in the current economic literature on this subject.

Several authors (Bandara et al. 2015; Smith et al. 2002) have emphasized the importance of negative shocks on the probability of child entering the labor force and the reduction of schooling, in addition to the positive effect of assets for child labor. Funkhouser (1999) found that school attendance declined in Costa Rica when families suffered a negative shock in their income in the early 1980s. Similarly, Duryea (1998) analyzes the impact of negative income shocks on schooling in Brazil, finding that they increase the likelihood of the child entering the work force and dropping out of school. Fallon and Lucas (2002) and Frankenberg and Smith (2003) address the impact of economic shocks on household welfare in Mexico, Indonesia and East Asia. Their results indicate that families that suffer from income shocks show an intensification of school dropout rates.

In general, there appears to exist evidences that income shocks are significant in explaining households' behavior in the labor market and in the allocation of children's time, since infants can be used as insurance against unanticipated shocks in income (Cain 1982). In this context, the hypothesis that the possession of economic assets (which can be used as insurance or loan guarantees) could constitute an important way of mitigating the effects of these shocks arises. Jacoby and Skoufias (1997) report that in India children living in households with a reduced number of durable goods are more likely to fail at school. On the other hand, Beegle et al. (2006) point out that transient income shocks lead to an increase in child labor and that the presence of domestic assets or properties attenuated the effects of these shocks in Tanzania for 1995. Brown et al. (2001) identify a link between child labor and the possession of economic assets in households in Latin America.

The lack of coordination in the labor and credit markets can explain the emergence of child labor, as it can arise due to parents' inability to face the family crisis, sacrificing investment in children's human capital (Dessy and Pallage 2001; Dumas 2013). Baland and Robinson (2000) and Dehejia and Gatti (2005) conclude that children are used to compensate for negative shocks at home in the absence of household goods that serve as collateral in the credit market. According to Bandara et al. (2015), access to credit has attenuated the impacts of income shocks on child hunger in Tanzania, in 2011.

Child labor has a high social cost, in addition to reducing future levels of growth and economic development of the country. This is especially important in rural areas of developing countries, where households are more prone to negative shocks and have fewer tools available to mitigate them (Kruger et al. 2007). According to Kassouf (2007), the factors that explain child labor in the rural area are related to the low educational infrastructure in these areas, as well as the greater ease of the child being absorbed in rural informal activities that usually require low qualification.

The Dominican Republic provides an interesting scenario for the evaluation of this issue for a number of reasons. It is a middle-income country, in the process of development, and dependent on services and remittances. The gross domestic product (GDP) has grown in the last decade at an annual rate of 5.60% and with a GDP per capita of US$6300, on average. Also, the Human Development Index (HDI) in 2015 was 0.722, placing the country in a high category of human development. However, poverty is an urgent problem: 30.50% of the population lives below the monetary poverty line and 6.50% in extreme poverty. Similarly, inequalities in Dominican society are a challenge, since 10% of the richest population receives about 46.80% of the country's income, being the Gini coefficient of 0.468 for 2016. On the other hand, social spending is equivalent to 15.90% of GDP, of which only 4% is invested in education. In this way, the low investment in human capital (health, education or recreation and sports) keeps people in a trap that restricts the full development of their abilities, having a high social cost, in addition to reducing future levels of economic growth and development of the country (Orraca 2014).

In the rural Dominican Republic, child labor persists. About 15.99% of the population between 5 and 17 years of age worked in 2010. From these children and adolescents, 74.70% are male and 25.30% female (ONE 2010). Although this is an important issue for the Dominican Republic, few studies have provided empirical evidence on this topic. In a descriptive analysis, Guzmán and Cruz (2009) conclude that individual and family characteristics have a strong influence on the school attendance of Dominican children in 2008. On the other hand, Lozano (2012) and Soto and Taveras (2015) attest the existence of a trade-off between school and child labor at the secondary and elementary levels. ILO-IPEC (2002) and ILO-BID (2008) make a descriptive diagnosis of Dominican child labor, emphasizing the problem of sexual and commercial exploitation. Likewise, UCW (2014) examines the economic and social determinants of child labor, concluding that age, gender, orphanhood and household structure are important variables.

So far, there is no research that considers the interrelationship between school attendance and child labor in the Dominican Republic or even research that sees the importance of income shocks (frequent in developing countries) on the allocation of time for these children. In addition, this study is particularly important for rural areas where families usually face restrictions on important markets and child labor is frequent (though underreported). Thus, this work aims to contribute to the literature that investigates contexts in which income shocks and market failures can lead to the employment of children, as well as to provide the Dominican Republic with subsidies for understanding the behavior of families in situations of vulnerability and then promote ways to ensure the human capital accumulation of their children.

Specifically, this study seeks to characterize child labor in rural areas of Dominican Republic in 2010, to analyze the impacts of negative income shocks (loss of harvest) on the participation of children in the labor market and in school and to evaluate the effect of the presence of economic assets in front of a shock on the intra-family decision of children's time allocation between study and work.

After this introduction, the econometric model and the data sources of the work will be presented. In the third section, the characterization and the first results of the econometric model will be presented. The final exposures of the study will be presented in Sect. 5.5.

5.2 Market Imperfections and Child Labor

This subsection presents an economic model that considers the relation between the assets, the credit restrictions of the families and the choice between work and school for children. This model is based on the existence of market imperfections. Among the most widely used models to study the relationship between market imperfections and children's time allocation, we find Ranjan (1999) with adaptations made by Jafarey and Lahiri (2002).

The model presented here is that developed by Kruger et al. (2007) and Bandara et al. (2015), which is based on the work of Jafarey and Lahiri (2002). In it, the family decision is modeled between work and study of the child considering the level of income and assets of the parents: parents' behavior regarding intra-family decision-making, access to credit and the possibility of imperfections and market coordination failures. In this model, it is considered an economy in which parents make all the relevant decisions, including the ones about the schooling of the children and their participation in the job market. It is assumed, for simplicity, that a father and a son form the family. In this context, the utility of consumption and development of the human capital of the child is:

$$U(c, h) = \frac{c^{\sigma}}{\sigma} + \alpha h \tag{5.1}$$

Where c is the household consumption and h is the human capital of the child. σ is the elasticity of substitution, and α is a constant parameter with $0 < \sigma > 1$ and $\alpha > 0$. The model develops three situations: (a) families without assets, (b) families with assets and (c) families with assets and access to credit.

Model of families without assets. In this, the father fully participates in the job market as a resultant revenue $f(l_p, \theta_{t-1})$:

$$f(l_p, \theta_{t-1}) = w_p l_p + \lambda \theta_{t-1} + \tau \phi_p \tag{5.2}$$

Where w_p and l_p are the wage and labor of the parents. θ_{t-1} is a random transient shock at $t-1$, and ϕ_p are characteristics of families, such as parent education and so on. λ and τ are constant parameters. It is assumed that the child divides his time between working (with salary w_c) and school. The human capital of children is $h = \beta e^{\sigma}{}_c$, where ß is the technological component. The e_c is the time of the child to the school (investment in human capital), according to $e_c + l_c = t_c$, where l_c is the time allocated to work and t_c is the total amount of time of the child. Initially, it is assumed that families do not have assets or free access to credit. The problem of families is given by:

$$\max_{c,e}\left\{\frac{c^{\sigma}}{\sigma}+\alpha\beta e_c^{\sigma}\right\} \tag{5.3}$$

Subject to budget constraint:

$$c = w_c\left(1-e_c\right)+w_p l_p+\lambda\theta_{t-1}+\tau\phi_p \tag{5.4}$$

Defining λ as a multiplier of income restriction, the first-order conditions for c and e are:

$$c^{\sigma-1} = \lambda \tag{5.5}$$

$$\alpha\beta\sigma e^{\sigma-1} = \lambda w_c \tag{5.6}$$

The second-order condition of Eq. (5.5) characterizes the decision of families to send the child to school or work. If $\alpha\beta\sigma e^{\sigma-1} > c^{\sigma-1}w_c$, the marginal value of a unit of time invested in the child's human capital is greater, then the family will send the child to school. On the other hand, if $\alpha\beta\sigma e^{\sigma-1} < c^{\sigma-1}w_c$, the father will send the child to work. If $e^{\sigma-1} = c^{\sigma-1}w_c$, the family will be indifferent between the two options.

It is assumed that the relation between the wages of the father and the child is constant, so the first-order solution to the maximization problem is given by:

$$l_c = \delta + \varphi X_p + \lambda \theta_{t-1} + \tau \phi p + \eta e_c + \varepsilon \quad (5.7)$$

Where X_p is the parent's income per job and ε is the error term. δ are the fixed effects of the family. According to Eq. (5.7), child labor could be affected by the parent's income and the children's time destined for the development of their human capital. Bandara et al. (2015) note that parental income could be affected by income shocks, so in the absence of economic assets, child labor will be the only insurance against shocks in an imperfect credit market environment. It is expected that the higher the father's income, the greater the investment in human capital and the shorter hours of child labor. Income shocks, on the other hand, would increase child labor. So we expected that φ, $\eta < 0$ when $\lambda > 0$.

Model for families with assets. It is now assumed that families have economic assets. The holding of assets could exhibit effects of substituting wealth and child labor, depending on the asset's ability to generate income. For families with assets, the budget constraint is:

$$c = w_c(1 - e_c) + w_p l_p + \lambda \theta_{t-1} + \tau \phi_p + (1 - r)a - a_{t-1} \quad (5.8)$$

Where r is the interest rate and α are the family assets at time t. Regardless of whether the assets are monetary or not, they are sold or used to meet consumer needs in the event of a collision. Assets in the current period are considered as a function of the assets of the previous period if the growth rate is constant. Thus, the first-order condition of families is given by:

$$l_c = \rho + \varphi X_p + \lambda \theta_{t-1} + \tau \phi_p + \eta e_c + \mu a + u \quad (5.9)$$

Where ρ is the fixed effects term, μ is a constant parameter and u is the error term. A higher level of assets is expected to reduce child labor ($\mu < 0$) since parents could use the assets to minimize the effects of shocks on household consumption.

Families with assets and access to credit. Here Bandara et al. (2015) relax the presumption of nonaccess to credit, to investigate whether this access is capable of reducing child labor. With this relaxation, the budget constraint of the home is:

$$c = w_c(1 - e_c) + w_p l_p + \lambda\theta_{t-1} + \tau\phi_p + (1 - r)a - a_{t-1} + b - (1 - r)b_{t-1} \quad (5.10)$$

Where b is the loan at an interest rate r. It should be noted that the model allows households with access to credit to maintain their assets. The solution of the family problem is given by:

$$l_c = \phi + \varphi X_p + \lambda\theta_{t-1} + \tau\phi_p + \eta e_c + \mu a + \vartheta b + \omega \quad (5.11)$$

Where ϕ is the fixed effects term, ϑ is a constant parameter and ω is the error term. Models such as Bandara et al. (2015) allow us to study the relation between economic assets, child labor and the credit market. There is empirical and theoretical evidence that emphasizes the role of household assets in child labor decision-making, noting that they provide households with the means to manage uncertainty and, consequently, children's work is not necessary for such purposes. In addition, households with assets have more access to capital markets or can finance the formation of the child's human capital without a formal loan (Brown et al. 2001).

5.3 Empirical Strategy

We try to model two family decisions: school attendance and child labor. As both decisions are taken simultaneously within the family, the empirical strategy adopted is based on the bivariate probit method, which considers the simultaneities between decisions.[1] For modeling, it is assumed that family decisions are made through a comparison of utilities: the child attends school if this is the option that provides the family with more utility, as well as compares utilities to decide on child labor. In this

[1] This econometric model was also used in the works of Cerdas (2003); Sapelli and Torche (2004); Cacciamali, Tatei and Batista (2010); and Mesquita (2011) with similar purposes.

case, the latent variable Y_1^* refers to the utility gain from the child's work and Y_2^* to the utility of the option related to attendance at school. These two decisions can be expressed as:

$$\begin{aligned} &Y_{1i}^* = \beta_1 X_{1i} + \varepsilon_{1i} \\ &Y_{2i}^* = \beta_2 X_{2i} + \varepsilon_{2i} \\ &Y_{1i} = 1 \text{ se} Y_{1i}^* > 0; \qquad Y_{1i} = 0 \text{ otherwise} \\ &Y_{2i} = 1 \text{ se} Y_{2i}^* > 0; \qquad Y_{2i} = 0 \text{ otherwise} \end{aligned} \tag{5.12}$$

Where X_i represents a vector of explanatory variables referring to the characteristics of children, family and environment, which affect the two decisions (work and study). The simultaneous choice of these alternatives implies four different and mutually exclusive results: the child only studies (Y_{1i} = 1 and Y_{2i} = 0), studies and works (Y_{1i} = 1 and Y_{2i} = 1), only works (Y_{1i} = 0 and Y_{2i} = 1) or neither (Y_{1i} = 0 and Y_{2i} = 0). It is assumed that the random errors have mean 0, homoscedastic variance and joint distribution $(\varepsilon_1, \varepsilon_2) \sim DNB(0, 0, 1, 1, \rho)$ and $Cov(\varepsilon_1, \varepsilon_2) = \rho$ (following a standard normal distribution, with correlation among them represented by ρ), indicating the possibility that unobserved factors affecting one decision also affect the other. In addition to the coefficients of interest, the bivariate probit provides an estimate of the predicted probability of the four combinations described (Cameron and Trivedi 2005).

In this work, income losses were defined as the loss of crops of rural families and, as assets, the presence of goods worth more than US$520. Duryea, Lam and Levison (2007) represent the negative income shocks as the loss of the householder's job in urban area; Beegle et al. (2006) also use crop loss in rural areas; and Bandara et al. (2015) consider the presence of pests in crops and the death of a family member.

To define the presence of assets in the household, Bandara et al. (2015) and Dumas (2013) consider the value of land; Beegle et al. (2006) suggest a range of the value of the economic assets of the family, such as radio, bicycles, fans and so on. To examine the role of shocks and the presence of economic assets among rural families, each equation (study or work) was specified as follows:

$$Y_{ji} = \beta_0 + \beta_1 \text{Shock}_i + \beta_2 \text{assets}_i + \beta_3 (\text{shock} * \text{assets})_i + \beta_4 X_i + \varepsilon_i \quad (5.13)$$

Where Y_{ji} assumes a value of 1 if the child studied or worked in 2010; *shock* is a dummy that indicates the occurrence of crop loss in the rural domicile; *assets* is also a dummy that represents the presence of household goods (goods worth over $520) in rural households; *shock*assets* is an interaction between shock and assets that provides the role of assets in the presence of a negative shock in the family; X_i are variables of control including individual, family and environmental characteristics; and ε_i is the error term.

The empirical strategy adopted in this chapter is based on the hypothesis that the shocks suffered by the families are exogenous. Crop loss can be considered as an exogenous factor, since it relates to the phenomena of nature, independently of community, family and individual factors. However, to explain the decision between study and employment of children, control of unobserved heterogeneity should be important. This is because there may be unobserved personal and family characteristics responsible for affecting the decision between study and child labor. If this is the case, and if these unobservable characteristics are related to the explanatory variables included, our specification would suffer from bias of omitted variable. Panel data could provide means of controlling this problem. However, there is no panel data available for the Dominican Republic.

Thus, it is believed that the results achieved with the empirical strategy of this work, if not causal, approximate the maximum of such relations. In addition, to consider the fact that households located in certain areas may have correlated behaviors, the estimates include dummies by macroregions and clusters by regions in the regressions. Therefore, the exogenous characteristics of families related to their location are expected to be captured.

5.3.1 Database

The microdata of the *Encuesta Nacional de Hogares de Propósitos Multiples* (ENHOGAR) 2010, prepared by the National Statistics Office of the Dominican Republic, are used for the 31 states of the country. The year's choice is because there has been an additional research with aspects regarding women's health, education and child labor. The sample is composed of 3326 children between 5 and 17 years of age who live in the Dominican rural area, offering a considerable range of socioeconomic information about households and children.

5.4 Results

5.4.1 Child Labor in the Rural Dominican Republic

In the Dominican Republic, 21.96% of adults believe that it is reasonable for children to work as long as it does not interfere with their schooling and does not cause physical and mental harm. In addition, 61.22% of them confirmed that they had worked as children or helped their parents. This makes it possible to perceive the normalization of child labor and that most Dominicans do not see child labor as a social problem.

Among the children interviewed in the rural area, 24.96% confirmed that they were responsible for some kind of domestic work at home. In addition, 15.99% of them had performed some type of work in the last 7 days of the research reference. It is important to note that the percentage of children who study and work is 18% and children who neither study nor work add up to 4.50%. On the other hand, 2% of children only work.

The children's responsible said that the main reasons for allowing them to work are to complement the family income (22.85%), to take advantage of their time (7.62%), to acquire skills (6.95%), to help in the family business (7.95%) and to fulfil their desire to work and earn their own money (13.25%).

Working is more common among male children (75.98%). However, it is important to remember that house tasks (housework), where girls usually have more presence, are not considered in the estimates. In Latin America, as well as in the world, girls and women work in less visible forms of work and therefore subject to underreporting, such as work at home or other people's houses.

In the Dominican Republic, attendance at school and at work is closely related to the level of household income. Children in poorer families are more likely to work (52.10% of those who work belong to the poorer class). However, the fact that 1.65% of working children belong to families in the richest class points out the existence of other factors that influence this phenomenon.

As the data show, children's working hours in rural areas are on average 13 hours a week. Among the interviewed children, 81.59% answered that they work during the day, 3.59% in the evening and 7.96% in both. The main working conditions are unpaid family worker (34.32%), employee (17.32%), self-employed worker (13.88%), domestic worker with compensation (6.24%), boss (3.43%) and domestic workers without remuneration (1.72%).

When asked about payment in cash, only 53.35% confirmed receipt. From those who answered affirmatively, this payment was made daily (20.79%), weekly (40.17%), every 15 days (10.67%) and monthly (6.46%). It should be emphasized that the average remuneration is US$12.50 per week, with the payment always higher for male children. Regarding the destination of the money received by the children, 18.88% of them said they keep the total earned in the work, 25.59% said they shared with their parents and 7.64% passed on all the money to their parents.

Finally, from the working children, 35.50% and 11.95% answered that they work with the purpose of helping the parents and generating or supplementing the income of the family, respectively. Similarly, 0.18% said they work to help pay a family debt. This may be an indication that a negative income shock in Dominican households may lead to a change in the allocation of children's time.

5.4.2 Income Shocks, Assets and Their Impacts on Work and Early Childhood Education

The following are the results estimated by bivariate probit using Bootstrap and considering clusters[2] per microregion for estimates of standard errors. The first specification, without controls, aims to show the effects associated with the three variables of interest (*Assets, Shock* e *Assets***Shock*). The inclusion of controls, later, allows identifying the mechanisms by which the effects of these three variables are manifested.

The presence of household assets is statistically significant, related both to the probability of work (reducing it) and of study (raising it). Likewise, Bandara et al. (2015) point out that in Tanzania the presence of assets is associated with lower child labor and an increase in schooling, also showing that families with economic assets will have easier access to the financial market, in the face of some adversity at home.

The occurrence of a negative income shock in the family is only statistically related to the probability of child labor. Shocks, on the other hand, are not significantly associated with the decision for children to study. This is in line with the finding by Duryea, Lam and Levison (2007) for Brazil, who find that negative shocks significantly impact the probability of the child entering the labor market. On the other hand, the absence of a significant effect of shocks on the probability of child placement in school may be an indication that the child's time does not seem to compete with his or her time in school, as Ravallion and Wodon (2000) suggest. The shock may be allocating the child to the job market, but not by taking time off from school. Moreover, the interaction between the occurrence of a shock and the presence of assets in the households (variable *assets***shock*) was not significant neither for study nor for work of the child.

Thus, assets are indeed important in this decision-making process, raising the likelihood of children's study and reducing their work. Shocks

[2] Cluster analysis aims to group sample elements according to some measure of similarity (social, geographical, economic and so on). Such grouping is performed so that the variability within the groups is the smallest possible, while the variability between the groups is maximized.

raise the likelihood of child labor, but the assets do not seem to contribute to softening the negative effect.

The value of the coefficient ρ (rho), which measures the correlation between the error terms of the two equations, was −0.174 for this specification, significant at the 5% level (p-value equal to 0.048), indicating that there is interdependence between the children's decisions to work and study. Since this coefficient is negative, the unobserved factors not included in the model contribute to increase the probability of work and reduce the probability of study and vice versa.

In order to verify the consistency of the estimates, as well as to investigate the mechanisms by which the effects indicated in Table 5.1 are manifested, Table 5.2 shows additional specifications, including important controls.

Regarding the main variables of interest, it is verified that the fact that the rural household has assets continues to statistically increase the probability of school attendance of children and adolescents. Assets, however, do not appear to be significantly related to child labor, when other variables are controlled. Thus, the beneficial effect of assets on the reduction of child labor may actually be due to other factors, such as characteristics of families and children.

Table 5.1 Impact of the variables of interest on the decision of child labor and school attendance (Dominican Republic)

	Study			Work		
Variables	Coeff.	Std. Err.	Sign.	Coeff.	Std. Err.	Sign.
Assets	0.450	0.083	***	−0.136	0.068	*
Shock	0.000	0.103	ns	0.302	0.087	***
Assets*Shock	−0.092	0.146	ns	0.111	0.112	ns
Constant	1.282	0.058	***	−1.057	0.053	***
Obs.	3326					
Athrho	−0.176	0.049				
Rho	−0.174	0.048				
Wald chi2	12.859					
Prob>chi2	0.000					

Source: Research results

Notes: Robust standard deviations to heteroskedasticity. Single (*), double (**) and triple (***) asterisks denote significance at 1%, 5% and 10%, respectively; ns indicates nonsignificance

Table 5.2 Impact of the variables on the incidence of child labor and school attendance (Dominican Republic)

	Study			Work		
Variables	Coeff.	Std. Err.	Sign.	Coeff.	Std. Err.	Sign.
Assets	0.335	0.077	***	−0.055	0.094	ns
Shock	0.033	0.173	ns	0.211	0.101	*
Assets*Shock	−0.111	0.192	ns	0.132	0.124	ns
Age	−0.072	0.014	***	0.105	0.009	***
Child's gender	0.000	0.064	ns	0.736	0.072	***
Householder's gender	0.032	0.093	ns	0.023	0.093	ns
Marital status	−0.035	0.163	ns	−0.082	0.098	ns
Mother's schooling	0.036	0.009	***	−0.028	0.013	*
House size	0.042	0.056	ns	0.038	0.020	*
Members from 0 to 4 years of age	−0.292	0.085	**	−0.020	0.055	ns
Transfer	0.224	0.067	**	−0.079	0.055	ns
Water	0.122	0.052	*	−0.115	0.124	ns
Sewer	0.030	0.097	ns	−0.227	0.112	*
The mother emigrated	0.068	0.157	ns	0.104	0.103	ns
Parents emigrated	−0.344	0.166	*	−0.064	0.166	ns
North	0.065	0.114	ns	0.386	0.045	***
East	−0.093	0.168	ns	0.404	0.073	***
South	0.145	0.183	ns	0.532	0.235	*
Constant	1.678	0.365	***	−3.002	0.204	***
No. of obs.	3326					
Athrho	−0.079	0.054				
Rho	−0.078	0.054				
Wald chi2	1.988					
Prob>chi2	0.016					

Source: Research results

Notes: Robust standard deviations to heteroskedasticity. Single (*), double (**) and triple (***) asterisks denote significance at 1%, 5% and 10%, respectively; ns indicates nonsignificance

The occurrence of a negative income shock continues to increase the probability of the child entering the labor market, which is not significant for the study. Thus, even when controlling for important location variables and characteristics of children, adolescents and their families, shocks seem to be the important means of increasing the probability of child labor. There is, according to these results, some evidence that shocks cause children to combine both tasks (study and work), increasing workload without reducing school attendance. Again, the interaction between the occurrence of a shock and the presence of assets among the households (variable *Assets*∗*Shock*) was not significant for the probability of study nor child labor. Thus, there are indications that the assets are not able to reduce the effects of shocks in the rural area.

Regarding the control variables, it is noted that the child's age increases the probability of work (and reduces the probability of forming human capital). That is, as the child's age progresses, the likelihood of attending the job market and dropping out of school increases. One of the reasons behind this result is the fact that education in the Dominican Republic is compulsory only in elementary and secondary school (ages 4 to 14 years). Sapelli and Torche (2004) show that, for Ecuador, the probability of working for boys and girls is higher as age increases. They assume that, at an older age, the family's opportunity cost to keep the child in school increases, emphasizing that it has a greater "substitutive" implication between the two decisions (study and work).

Likewise, the fact that the child is male enhances his chances of attending the job market. However, it is noted that gender was not significant to explain the study decision; this can be explained, in part, by the compulsory education in the Dominican Republic. The child's gender was also not significant in the decision to study in different African countries, Peru and Ecuador (Sapelli and Torche 2004). On the other hand, in Costa Rica, Cerdas (2003) finds that the fact that the child is male increases the chances of attending the labor market in rural areas.

In relation to the mother's schooling, this reduces the probability of the child's allocation at work while raising attendance at school. The fact that the mother's schooling is associated with this beneficial effect on the children may be related both to the higher level of income of the mother, which weakens the child's need for supplementation of the income, and to the awareness about the care with the children that results from the mother's knowledge and education (Emerson and Souza 2002).

The results also show that the fact that the family benefits from a transfer program[3] raises the chances of the children being allocated to school,

[3] The transfer programs analyzed are aimed to encourage education, food and health in children and in beneficiary families.

although it does not alter the opportunity to work. This is because the transfer programs analyzed have no direct actions to reduce the work of the child, but rather to increase school attendance. Cardoso and Souza (2004) show that, for Brazil, income transfer programs do not have significant effects on the incidence of child labor, but rather on education, since there is a change in the time allocated in the activities (school and work), considering that the benefits paid by the programs are insufficient to encourage the abandonment of the labor market.

It turns out that each new member in the family raises the child's likelihood to combine work and study. This result corroborates the finding of Araújo (2010) and Emerson and Souza (2002) for Brazil, who point out that in larger families, boys and girls are more likely to enter the labor market. Another interesting result is that the greater the number of siblings younger than 4 years of age in the child's home, the lower the probability of studying the child and not significantly altering their work. Sapelli and Torche (2004) point out that, for Ecuador, in the case of the siblings, the main behavior is likely to be that in which the child stays at home to take care of his younger siblings.

As for the water and sewage service at home, access to these items raises the probability of school attendance (decreasing the chance of work). Improvements in sanitation and better infection control may also be more beneficial for girls than for boys, because girls are more susceptible to infectious diseases, as well as working more on water and housework (Drevenstedt and Eileen 2008).

Migration of parents reduces school attendance, but not the work of boys and girls. Nurwita and Rinaldi (2009), in a study for Indonesia, point out that the effects of migration are also felt among children, increasing labor and decreasing human capital. Likewise, Mesquita (2011) shows that the children of migrants study less in Brazil.

The fact that the household is located in the South region increases the probability of attending school (this region is the most beneficiary of transfer programs, whose basic condition is to send the child to school). On the other hand, living in the eastern and northern regions of the Dominican Republic increases children's chances of working, when compared to children living in other regions. This result is expected, since most Dominican children do jobs related to agriculture, manufacturing and services (tourism, hotels, restaurant and so on), activities that are more developed in these regions (East and North).

Finally, the coefficient ρ (rho), which measures the correlation between the error terms of the two equations, was −0.078, significant at the 5% level (p-value equal to 0.054), indicating that there is interdependence between work and study of children. Again, the fact that this coefficient is negative indicates that the unobserved factors not included in the model contribute to the increase in the probability of work and reduction in the probability of study and vice versa.

In order to observe if shocks and assets act differently between boys and girls, these estimates were made separately for each of these cases.[4] In these regressions, it is noted that the presence of household goods continues to increase the chance of schooling for both boys and girls. The incidence of negative income shocks, in turn, raises the likelihood of sending boys to work, but not girls. Although treatment between boys and girls is expected to be different, girls were expected to be more disadvantaged when the family faced extreme circumstances, as suggested by Duflo (2012). With respect to the interaction of assets with shocks, this is still not significant in any case.

Two models were also considered in regard to two age groups (5 to 10 years and 11 to 17 years[5]), which had results very similar to those presented in Tables 5.2 and 5.3. Assets increase the probability of studying for the two age groups analyzed, but does not change the decision about work. In addition, negative shocks decrease the probability of study for those aged 11 to 17 years. The interaction between assets and shocks (variable *Assets∗Shock*) was significant at the 1% level only for the range of 5 to 10 years, reducing its likelihood of studying. Its negative sign and lower magnitude than the asset coefficient indicate that shocks weaken the effect of assets on the probability of studying.

In Table 5.3, the impacts of the marginal changes in the explanatory variables on the four probabilities of interest are the following: neither study nor work, only work, work and study and only study. The marginal effects correspond to changes in the estimated probability given a

[4] See table in the annex.

[5] See table in the annex.

variation of one percentage point in the explanatory variable.[6] In the case of dummy explanatory variables, the marginal effects correspond to a discrete variation from 0 to 1.

Table 5.3 shows that the presence of assets in the household decreases by 2.9 and 0.56 percentage points (p.p.) the chances of the child neither studying nor working and only working, respectively. On the other hand, they increase 3.99 p.p. the chances that children will only study. Similarly, negative income shocks increase by 3.91 p.p. the probability of working and studying. The interaction between assets and shock was not significant. The results show that Dominican boys and girls tend to combine work and study in the face of a negative shock in the presence of assets and decrease the human capital formation of children.

Among the most interesting variables, it is worth noting that the fact that the householder is female reduces by 13.46 p.p. the chance of the child only to study and increases by 13.47 p.p. the probability of the child to study and to work. The mother's years of study decrease the child's likelihood of working (0.09 percentage points), working and studying (0.46 percentage points) and neither studying nor working (0.29 percentage points). At the same time, the mother's schooling increases by 0.84 p.p. the chances of just studying.

The number of members aged from 0 to 4 years in the family increases the likelihood of neither studying nor working (2.63 p.p.) and increases the chances of only working by 0.41 p.p. The fact that the family belongs to some transfer program reduces by 1.91 p.p. the probability of neither studying nor working and 0.42 p.p. of only working and increases by 3.44 p.p. the probability of studying.

Finally, residing in the North increases by 7.15 p.p. the probability to study and work and reduces by 6.47 p.p. the likelihood of only working. Similarly, living in the eastern region increases by 7.26 p.p. the probability of working and studying and decreases by 8.22 p.p. the probability of just working. On the other hand, living in the South increases by 9.94 p.p. the likelihood of working and studying.

[6] It is important to emphasize that the signal of the marginal effects is the same of the estimated coefficients, thus not interfering in the interpretation.

Table 5.3 Marginal effects of variables on child labor decision and school attendance (Dominican Republic)

	No activities			Work only			Work and study			Study only		
Variables	Coeff.	Std. Err.	Sign.	Coeff.	Std. Err.	Sign.	Coeff.	Std. Err.	Sign.	Coeff.	Std. Err.	Sign.
Assets	−2.929	0.009	**	−0.559	0.002	***	−0.508	0.018	ns	3.997	0.016	*
Shock	−0.544	0.015	ns	0.201	0.003	ns	3.914	0.018	*	−3.571	0.029	ns
Assets*Shock	0.837	0.017	ns	0.319	0.004	ns	2.244	0.021	ns	−3.400	0.036	ns
Age	0.519	0.001	***	0.230	0.000	***	1.810	0.002	***	−2.559	0.003	***
Child's gender	−0.871	0.006	ns	0.869	0.003	**	13.465	0.017	***	−13.463	0.018	***
Householder's gender	−0.318	0.008	ns	−0.021	0.002	ns	0.469	0.017	ns	−0.130	0.022	ns
Marital status	0.412	0.014	ns	−0.045	0.003	ns	−1.558	0.019	ns	1.192	0.023	ns
Mother's education	−0.293	0.001	***	−0.087	0.000	***	−0.461	0.002	*	0.841	0.003	**
House size	−0.424	0.005	ns	−0.017	0.001	ns	0.766	0.003	**	−0.324	0.008	ns
Members from 0 to 4 years	2.634	0.009	**	0.408	0.002	*	−0.796	0.010	ns	−2.246	0.015	ns
Transfer	−1.913	0.006	**	−0.425	0.001	***	−1.110	0.010	ns	3.448	0.010	***
Water	−0.952	0.004	*	−0.316	0.002	ns	−1.931	0.022	ns	3.200	0.027	ns
Sewer	0.002	0.009	ns	−0.312	0.002	ns	−4.102	0.021	*	4.412	0.025	*
The mother emigrated	−0.732	0.014	ns	0.022	0.003	ns	1.995	0.019	ns	−1.284	0.022	ns
Parents emigrated	3.156	0.013	*	0.434	0.003	ns	−1.675	0.031	ns	−1.914	0.035	ns
North	−1.039	0.009	ns	0.359	0.002	ns	7.152	0.009	***	−6.472	0.014	***
East	0.353	0.014	ns	0.615	0.004	ns	7.256	0.013	***	−8.224	0.029	**
South	−1.925	0.013	ns	0.414	0.006	ns	9.949	0.046	*	−8.438	0.063	ns

Source: Research results

Notes: Robust standard deviations to heteroskedasticity. Single (*), double (**) and triple (***) asterisks denote significance at 1%, 5% and 10%, respectively; ns indicates nonsignificance

5.5 Conclusion

The results suggest that economic assets at home improve the human capital formation of children and adolescents and concomitantly reduce their probability of work, regardless of gender and age. In respect to the negative income shocks suffered by the families, it is observed that, regardless of the characteristics of the regions, families and children, these do not affect the schooling of boys and girls. However, negative income shocks were relevant to increasing child labor. The intensity of this effect is related in a different way to age and sex, being more damaging and accentuated in the age group from 11 to 17 years and for the male children rather than for the female children. On the other hand, the empirical results do not seem to indicate significant effects of the interaction between shocks and assets on human capital development and child labor. Roughly, the results show that shocks lead Dominican children to combine study and work.

In general, increased schooling raises human capital, and furthermore the participation of children in the labor market does not help the economic development of the Dominican Republic. The results of this study suggest that policies to combat child labor and to develop human capital in rural areas should not be limited to fighting poverty. This study points to the need to consider the possession of household goods, access to credit, microcredit and the generation of equal opportunities or tools for families in rural areas to cope with economic crises. It is also necessary to consider the degree of vulnerability to shocks that different families have. In addition, it is important to generate public policies that raise awareness in Dominican society about the impact of child labor on children's education, health and future income levels.

As limitations of this research, it is mentioned that the database for child labor in the Dominican Republic is only available for 1 year (2010). Given this, we cannot compare and analyze the dynamic behavior of families nor even control unobserved factors that can affect the decision of households regarding school and child labor. In addition to purely economic assets—such as the possession of household goods—other means can be important mitigators of shocks, such as access to credit or a bank account. These limitations are based on suggestions for future research and improvement of this study.

Annex

Table 5.4 Description of the variables in the bivariate probit model

	Variables	Description
Endogenous variables	Study	It assumes a value of 1 if the child is enrolled in school
	Work	It assumes a value of 1 if the child worked in the market
Exogenous variables		
Economic assets	Assets	It assumes a value of 1 if the household has goods worth more than US$520
Suffered shocks	Crop loss	It assumes a value of 1 if the household suffered crop loss due to crop failure or fire
Assets*Shock	Assets*Shock	Interactive variable resultant of the multiplication of active variables and shocks
Child's characteristics	Age	Child's age in years
	Child's gender	It assumes a value of 1 if the child is male
Domicile characteristics	Householder's gender	It assumes a value of 1 if the householder is female
	Householder's marital status	It assumes a value of 1 if the householder is single or separated
	Mother's schooling	Indicates the mother's schooling in years of study
	House size	Total number of members in the household
	Members from 0 to 4 years of age	Number of members aged from 0 to 4 years at home
	Transfer	It assumes a value of 1 if the household receives some type of monetary transfer from the government
Basic services	Water	It assumes a value of 1 if the household has water service
	Sewage	It assumes a value of 1 if the household has a sewage system
Migration	Mother emigrated	It assumes a value of 1 if the mother of the child has emigrated
	Parents emigrated	It assumes a value of 1 if the child was left behind (father and mother emigrated)
Macro-regions	North	It assumes a value of 1 if the child lives in the North
	East	It assumes a value of 1 if the child lives in the East
	South	It assumes a value of 1 if the child lives in the South

Source: National Statistics Office (2010)

Table 5.5 Descriptive statistics of the main explanatory variables of the model (Dominican Republic, 2010)

Variables	Obs.	Mean	Std. Dev.	Min	Max
Study	3326	0.934	0.248	0	1
Work	3326	0.155	0.362	0	1
Assets	3326	0.618	0.486	0	1
Shock	3326	0.302	0.459	0	1
Assets*Shock	3326	0.180	0.384	0	1
Age	3326	10.083	3.583	5	17
Child's gender	3326	0.525	0.499	0	1
Household's gender	3326	0.296	0.457	0	1
Marital status	3326	0.237	0.425	0	1
Mother's schooling	3326	7.889	3.587	0	16
Domicile size	3326	5.359	1.842	1	13
Members from 0 to 4 years	3326	0.410	0.685	0	5
Transference	3326	0.379	0.485	0	1
Water	3326	0.288	0.453	0	1
Sewer	3326	0.322	0.467	0	1
Mother emigrated	3326	0.126	0.332	0	1
Parents emigrated	3326	0.071	0.257	0	1
North	3326	0.381	0.486	0	1
East	3326	0.304	0.460	0	1
South	3326	0.233	0.423	0	1

Source: Research results

Table 5.6 Impact of variables on child labor decision and school attendance, by sex of the children (Dominican Republic)

	Study						Work					
	Boy			Girl			Boy			Girl		
Variables	Coeff.	Std. Err.	Sign.	Coeff.	Std. Err.	Sign.	Coeff.	Std. Err.	Sign.	Coeff.	Std. Err.	Sign.
Assets	0.420	0.085	***	0.275	0.123	*	0.034	0.098	ns	−0.183	0.174	ns
Shock	−0.060	0.316	ns	0.172	0.107	ns	0.231	0.104	*	0.196	0.178	ns
Assets*Shock	−0.119	0.310	ns	−0.140	0.216	ns	0.086	0.124	ns	0.184	0.218	ns
Age	−0.083	0.020	***	−0.060	0.019	**	0.126	0.013	***	0.067	0.009	***
Householder's gender	0.008	0.137	ns	0.092	0.142	ns	0.158	0.120	ns	−0.278	0.189	ns
Marital status	0.074	0.119	ns	−0.179	0.243	ns	−0.213	0.076	**	0.182	0.222	ns
Mother's education	0.034	0.021	ns	0.041	0.013	**	−0.036	0.016	*	−0.008	0.015	ns
House size	0.023	0.042	ns	0.066	0.086	ns	0.012	0.021	ns	0.078	0.031	*
Members from 0 to 4 years	−0.232	0.108	*	−0.358	0.099	***	−0.002	0.049	ns	−0.026	0.091	ns
Transfer	0.201	0.123	ns	0.292	0.102	**	−0.048	0.045	ns	−0.168	0.175	ns
Water	0.126	0.123	ns	0.124	0.105	ns	−0.170	0.116	ns	−0.033	0.173	ns
Sewer	−0.052	0.101	ns	0.124	0.144	ns	−0.165	0.125	ns	−0.359	0.145	*
The mother emigrated	0.044	0.352	ns	0.097	0.388	ns	0.182	0.157	ns	−0.115	0.668	ns
Parents emigrated	0.012	0.370	ns	−0.658	0.445	ns	0.063	0.216	ns	−0.415	1.999	ns
North	−0.030	0.175	ns	0.136	0.083	ns	0.458	0.065	***	0.218	0.137	ns
East	−0.242	0.154	ns	0.051	0.212	ns	0.401	0.091	***	0.378	0.061	***
South	0.141	0.308	ns	0.138	0.279	ns	0.634	0.294	*	0.305	0.141	*
Constant	1.970	0.403	***	1.343	0.471	**	−2.471	0.226	***	−2.634	0.253	***
Obs.	1747		1579									
Athrho	−0.181	0.048	0.106	0.138								
Rho	−0.179	0.047	0.106	0.137								
Wald chi2	11.862		0.829									
Prob>chi2	0.001		0.363									

Source: Research results

Notes: Robust standard deviations to heteroskedasticity. Single (*), double (**) and triple (***) asterisks denote significance at 1%, 5% and 10%, respectively; ns indicates nonsignificance

Table 5.7 Impact of variables on child labor decision and school attendance, by age group (Dominican Republic)

	Study						Work					
	5 to 10			11 to 17			5 to 10			11 to 17		
Variables	Coeff.	Std. Err.	Sign.	Coeff.	Std. Err.	Sign.	Coeff.	Std. Err.	Sign.	Coeff.	Std. Err.	Sign.
Assets	0.511	0.123	***	0.220	0.117	*	−0.136	0.181	ns	0.001	0.081	ns
Shock	0.524	0.230	*	−0.299	0.152	*	0.189	0.166	ns	0.248	0.082	**
Assets*Shock	−0.901	0.338	**	0.354	0.167	*	0.232	0.225	ns	0.052	0.131	ns
Age	0.199	0.054	***	−0.243	0.022	***	0.140	0.030	***	0.093	0.011	***
Child's gender	0.056	0.095	ns	−0.084	0.074	ns	0.508	0.092	***	0.879	0.074	***
Householder's gender	−0.115	0.129	ns	0.066	0.158	ns	−0.072	0.149	ns	0.079	0.054	ns
Marital status	−0.039	0.217	ns	0.005	0.231	ns	−0.001	0.145	ns	−0.118	0.084	ns
Mother's education	0.039	0.021	*	0.038	0.011	**	−0.033	0.018	*	−0.025	0.013	*
House size	0.050	0.050	ns	0.033	0.068	ns	0.035	0.018	*	0.037	0.023	ns
Members from 0 to 4 years	−0.203	0.098	*	−0.336	0.113	**	−0.025	0.084	ns	−0.004	0.051	ns
Transfer	0.127	0.103	ns	0.232	0.112	*	−0.108	0.141	ns	−0.081	0.048	*
Water	0.113	0.088	ns	0.137	0.073	*	−0.114	0.141	ns	−0.110	0.151	ns
Sewer	−0.092	0.088	ns	0.152	0.140	ns	−0.259	0.124	*	−0.227	0.120	*
The mother emigrated	0.246	2.060	ns	−0.180	0.173	ns	0.001	0.224	ns	0.149	0.149	ns
Parents emigrated	−0.161	2.057	ns	−0.489	0.189	*	−0.169	0.386	ns	0.058	0.196	ns
North	0.090	0.904	ns	0.215	0.077	**	1.101	0.083	***	0.183	0.063	**
East	−0.344	0.160	*	0.145	0.154	ns	1.042	0.114	***	0.241	0.046	***
South	0.023	0.137	ns	0.358	0.284	ns	1.169	0.161	***	0.362	0.351	ns
Constant	−0.361	0.667	ns	4.192	0.527	***	−3.644	0.346	***	−2.824	0.204	***

(continued)

Table 5.7 (continued)

	Study						Work					
	5 to 10			11 to 17			5 to 10			11 to 17		
Variables	Coeff.	Std. Err.	Sign.	Coeff.	Std. Err.	Sign.	Coeff.	Std. Err.	Sign.	Coeff.	Std. Err.	Sign.
Observations	1608			1718								
Athrho	0.001	0.170		−0.114	0.058							
Rho	0.001	0.170		−0.113	0.058							
Wald chi2	0.000			3.544								
Prob>chi2	0.996			0.060								

Source: Research results

Notes: Robust standard deviations to heteroskedasticity. Single (∗), double (∗∗) and triple (∗∗∗) asterisks denote significance at 1%, 5% and 10%, respectively; ns indicates nonsignificance

References

Araújo, A.A. 2010. O Programa Bolsa-Família e o Trabalho Infantil no Brasil. Tese (Doutorado em Economia Aplicada). Universidade Federal de Viçosa (UFV), Viçosa, MG.

Baland, J., and J.A. Robinson. 2000. Is child labor inefficient? *Journal of Political Economy* 108 (4): 663–679.

Bandara, A., R. Dehejia, and S. Lavie-Rouse. 2015. The impact of income and non-income shocks on child labor: Evidence from a panel survey of Tanzania. *World Development* 67 (1): 218–237.

Banco Central De La República Dominicana (BCRD): Database 2016. http://www.bancentral.gov.do/estadisticas_economicas. Accessed 1 May 2017.

Beegle, K., R. Dehejia, and R. Gatti. 2006. Child labor and agricultural shocks. *Journal of Development Economics* 81 (1): 80–96.

Brown, D.K., A.V. Deardorff, and R.M. Stern. 2001. Child labor: Theory, evidence and policy. *Research Seminar in International Economics* 474 (617): 2–78.

Cain, M. 1982. Perspectives on family and fertility in developing countries. *Population Studies: A Journal of Demography* 36 (2): 37–41.

Cameron, C., and P. Trivedi. 2005. *Microeconometrics, methods and applications*. New York: Cambridge University Press.

Canagarajah, S. and H. Coulombe. 1999. Child labor and schooling in Ghana. *World Bank Economic and Sector Work (ESW)* 1 (1): 1–39.

Cardoso, E., and A. Souza. 2004. *The impact of cash transfers on child labor and school attendance in Brazil*. Working Papers, v. 407. Nashville: Vanderbilt University.

Cacciamali, M.C., F. Tatei, and N.F. Batista. 2010. Impactos do Programa Bolsa Família Federal sobre o Trabalho Infantil e a Frequência Escolar. *R. Econ. Contemp. Rio deJaneiro* 14 (2): 269–301.

Cerdas, A. 2003. Deserción escolar y trabajo infantil en Costa Rica Ana. Pontifica Universidad Caotolica de Chile (Dissertation).

Dehejia, R.H., and R. Gatti. 2005. Child labor: The role of income variability and credit constraints across countries. *Economic Development and Cultural Change* 53 (4): 913–932.

Dessy, S.E., and S. Pallage. 2001. Child labor and coordination failures. *Journal of Development Economics* 65 (2): 469–476.

Drevenstedt, G., and M. Eileen. 2008. The rise and fall of excess male infant mortality. *Journal of Economic Literature* 50 (6): 5016–5021.

Duflo, E. 2012. Women empowerment and economic development. *Journal of Economic Literature* 50 (4): 1051–1079.

Dumas, C. 2013. Market imperfections and child labor. *World Development* 42 (1): 127–142.

Duryea, S. 1998. *Children's advancement through school in Brazil: The role of transitory shocks to household income*. Working Paper #376. Washington, DC: Inter-American Development Bank.

Duryea, S., D. Lam, and D. Levison. 2007. Effects of economic shocks on children's employment and schooling in Brazil. *Journal of Development Economics* 84 (1): 188–214.

Emerson, P.M., and A.P. Souza. 2002. *Bargaining over sons and daughters: Child Labor, School Attendance and Intra-Household Gender Bias in Brazil.* Working Paper No. 02-W13. Nashville: Department of Economics Vanderbilt University.

Fallon, P.R., and R.E.B. Lucas. 2002. The impact of financial crises on labor markets, household incomes, and poverty: A review of evidence. *The International Bank for Reconstruction and Development* 17 (1): 21–45.

Frankenberg, E., and J.P. Smith. 2003. Economic shocks, wealth and welfare. *The Journal of Human Resources* 38 (2): 280–321.

Funkhouser, E. 1999. Cyclical economic conditions and school attendance in Costa Rica. *Economics of Education Review* 14 (1): 31–50.

Guzmán, R.M., and C. Cruz. 2009. Niños, Niñas y Adolescentes Fuera del Sistema Educativo en República Dominicana. Foro Socioeducativo de la República Dominicana. Proyecto Un foro para la Mejora de la Educación Dominicana.

ILO-BID—International Labor Office (ILO); Banco Intermaricano Desarrollo (BID). 2008. Diagnóstico de Situación del Trabajo Infantil y Sus Peores formas en República Dominicana.

ILO-IPEC—International Labour Office (ILO); International Programme on the Elimination of Child Labour (IPEC). 2002. Un Estudio Exploratorio sobre el Trabajo Infantil Doméstico en Hogares de Terceros en República Dominicana.

———. 2013. Marking Progress Against Child Labor.

Jafarey, S., and S. Lahiri. 2002. Will trade sanctions reduce child labour? The role of credit markets. *Journal of Development Economics* 68 (1): 137–156.

Kassouf, A.L. 2007. O que conhecemos sobre o trabalho infantil? *Nova Economia* 17 (2): 323–350.

Kruger, D., R. Rodrigo Soares, M. Berthelon. 2007. Household choices of child labor and schooling: A simple model with application to Brazil. ForschungsinstitutzurZukunft der Arbeit Institute for the Study of Labor. Discussion.

Lozano, J.M.. 2012. Determinantes de la Deserción y Repitencia Escolar de los Hogares en Condiciones de Pobreza en la República Dominicana. Universidad Católica de Santo Domingo (UCSD). Dominican Republic.

Mesquita, S.P.D.E. 2011. Migração Familiar e Trabalho Infantil no Brasil Urbano. Dissertação (Mestrado em Economia). Universidade Federal da Paraíba, João Pessoa, Pernambuco.

Nurwita, E., and R. Rinaldi. 2009. Poverty as child labor internal migration's determinant. *Journal of Indonesian Economy and Business* 24 (3): 347–362.

ONE—National Statical Office: Survey 2010. Available in 2010.

ONE—Oficina Nacional de Estadísticas (ONE): Data Base of 2017. 2010. http://one.gob.do/Estadisticas/208/medioambiente. Accessed 9 May 2017.

Orraca, P. 2014. El Trabajo Infantil en México y sus Causas. *Revista Problemas del Desarrollo* 45 (178): 113–137.

Ranjan, P. 1999. An economic analysis of child labor. *Economics Letters* 64 (1): 99–105.

Ravallion, M., and Q. Wodon. 2000. Does child labor displace schooling ? Evidence on behavioural responses to an enrollment subsidy. *The Economic* 110 (1): 158–175.

Sapelli, C., and A. Torche. 2004. Deserción Escolar y Oferta de Trabajo de los Jóvenes: ¿Dos Caras de un mismo proceso de decisión?, Documento de Trabalho, Pontificia Universidad Católica de Chile, Instituto de Economía.

Smith, J.P., et al. 2002. Wages, employment and economic shocks: Evidence from Indonesia. *Journal of Population Economics* 15 (1): 161–193.

Soto, P., and A. Taveras. 2015. Deserción Escolar y Trabajo Infantil. Un estudio sobre los determinantes de ambas decisiones en la República Dominicana. Universidad Iberoamericana (UNIBE). Dominican Republic.

UCW—Understanding Children's Work (UCW). 2014. Entendiendo el trabajo infantil y el empleo juvenil en la República Dominicana.

WBD—World Bank Data (WBD): Data Base of 2016. http://data.worldbank.org/. Accessed 1 May 2017.

6

Heterogeneous Effects of Migration on Child Welfare: Empirical Evidence from Viet Nam

Peter J. Morgan and Trinh Q. Long

6.1 Introduction

There are many studies on the impact of migration on left-behind children in the context of domestic rural-to-urban or international migration. The major issue regarding migration is that its total effect on left-behind children is a priori unknown. Theoretically, the effects could be either positive or negative. While migration may improve the family's disposable income at home (Ellis 2003), migration of adult family members may result in an increase in child labor, especially household work,

The views expressed in this chapter are the views of the author and do not necessarily reflect the views or policies of ADBI, ADB, its Board of Directors, or the governments they represent. ADBI does not guarantee the accuracy of the data included in this chapter and accepts no responsibility for any consequences of their use. Terminology used may not necessarily be consistent with ADB official terms.

P. J. Morgan • T. Q. Long (✉)
Research Department, Asian Development Bank Institute, Tokyo, Japan
e-mail: pmorgan@adbi.org; ltrinh@adbi.org

A. Posso (ed.), *Child Labor in the Developing World*,
https://doi.org/10.1007/978-981-15-3106-4_6

to compensate for the lack of adult labor, and, ultimately, may cause a reduction in children's total schooling or more restricted access to schooling. Empirical evidence has supported both views. For example, Antman (2012) found a statistically significant positive effect of (Mexican) parental US migration on educational attainment for girls. However, Antman (2012) could not find any effects of the absence of fathers on children's educational outcomes. McKenzie and Rapoport (2011) found evidence of a significant negative effect of migration of parents from Mexico to the US on children's school attendance and attainment. Furthermore, they also found that the absence of a parent results in the loss of parental attention and supervision over their children, which leads to poorer school performance. Meyerhoefer and Chen (2011) and Wen and Lin (2012) found that Chinese children whose parents had migrated to urban areas were worse off in terms of school enrollment and years of schooling than those whose parents had not migrated. However, as far as we know, there is little understanding of how children's welfare is affected by the different aspects of migration such as the type of migration (seasonal or permanent), the motives for migration (e.g., shock-induced migration), and the size and direction of remittances. The literature is also meager on how the effect of migration differs depending on the context and community in which the migrant's family lives. For example, if children are looked after by poorly educated grandparents who are unable to perform the roles of the parents in their absence, their welfare may be reduced (Biao 2007). This warrants further studies on the heterogeneous effects of migration on children's welfare.

This study examines whether the effect of parental migration on children's school performance is positive or negative and investigates whether there are differences in the impact of migration on child welfare due to factors such as migration motives, migration types, and home family context (including the child's gender). To achieve this, we use data collected from the Viet Nam Access to Resources Household Survey (VARHS) in 2012 and 2014 to examine how migration has impacted the welfare of children and young people living in rural Viet Nam. The VARHS is jointly managed by the Department of Economics of the University of

Copenhagen, Denmark, and two institutes in Viet Nam: the Central Institute for Economic Management (Ministry of Planning and Investment) and the Institute for Labor Studies and Social Affairs (Ministry of Labor, War Invalids and Social Affairs). In each survey wave, the sample included about 3700 rural households. Besides the core parts of the questionnaire, which include questions similar to those in the World Bank's Living Standard Measurement Survey questionnaire (Brandt and Tarp 2017), the questionnaire also has questions aimed at collecting information on economic shocks, vulnerability, and migration (including reasons for migration, type of migration, and remittances).

In this chapter, we follow the literature in modeling child welfare as a function of a household's characteristics (especially those of the household head), such as education level, age and migration indicators, and individual characteristics (age, gender). We use several welfare measures, including school attendance and child labor (i.e., engagement in agricultural production, household enterprise production, and wage employment). The variable indicating whether there is a household member that has migrated is the variable of interest. We use several migration indicators to distinguish the effects of different kinds of migration, as well as remittances. It's possible that there are some unobservable factors either at the household level or the individual level that influence both the migration decision and child welfare. This will make the estimates biased. To mitigate this issue, we use the child fixed-effects estimator to estimate the impact of parental migration. The main advantage of the fixed-effects estimator is that it can control for all time-invariant variables, both observed and unobserved. We simultaneously model the decisions regarding child schooling, child labor, and household income.

This chapter is structured as follows. We review the literature on child well-being and the effect of migration on it in Sect. 6.2. The empirical approach is presented in Sect. 6.3, followed by a brief data introduction and some descriptive analysis in Sect. 6.4. Section 6.5 reports our empirical results. Section 6.6 provides some concluding remarks and policy implications.

6.2 Literature Review: Migration and Effects on Child Well-Being

6.2.1 Migration and Child Well-Being

Migration is an important household livelihood strategy. There has been an increasing trend toward migration in developing countries. Migration can have profound impacts on child welfare through several channels. First, migration can increase household income through remittances (McKenzie and Sasin 2007). Increased income can result in an increase in household spending on the health and education of children, as well as reducing child work, since a higher income can release children from the need to work. Children can spend more time on education and less time on work. However, if remittances reduce work incentives for recipients (Farrington and Slater 2006; Sahn and Alderman 1996), the welfare-enhancing effects of remittances may not be realized. Second, migration could influence child well-being through the reallocation of labor among those left behind. It's possible that the left-behind children may have to perform household work and even work that used to be performed by those who have migrated. Taking on the work previously done by household members who have migrated may reduce the time children can allocate to education and thus cause poor performance and possibly lead to dropping out of school.

So far, empirical evidence on the impact of migration on child well-being has been inconclusive on these issues. Numerous empirical studies find poverty-reducing effects of migration and remittances (e.g., Adams and Page 2005; Taylor et al. 2005; Acosta et al. 2007). Citing findings in Guatemala, Pakistan, and Mexico, the UNDP-HDRO (2009) noted that families with migrants appear to be more likely to send their children to school, using cash from remittances to pay fees and other costs. Several studies find that migration and remittances help children increase education and reduce child labor (e.g., Yang 2008; Antman 2012; Alcaraz et al. 2012; Binci and Giannelli 2012). Migration is also found to improve the health and nutrition of children (Hildebrandt et al. 2005; Macours and Vakis 2010; Antón 2010). Nevertheless, there are a number of studies that find negative effects of parental migration on children's education (e.g., McKenzie and Rapoport 2011; Lahaie et al. 2009; Giannelli and Mangiavacchi 2010; Robles and Oropesa 2011; Zhang et al. 2014) and on children's health (Cameron and Lim 2007; Gibson et al. 2011; De Brauw and Mu 2011). Several studies, such as McKenzie and Rapoport (2011), Kiros and White (2004), Giannelli and Mangiavacchi (2010), and Wang (2014), found that children in migrating households have a lower educational attainment than those in nonmigrating households. In Kiros and White (2004), children in Ethiopia with migrant mothers were found to have less immunization coverage than children whose mothers had not migrated. Hence, the existing empirical studies show a wide diversity of empirical results, which calls for more empirical studies to enable a better understanding of the effect of parental absence, especially temporary absence for work, on children's outcomes.

6.2.2 Child Well-Being and Migration Studies in Viet Nam

A number of studies have examined child education and child labor in Viet Nam. However, most recent research has focused on investigating these issues separately. Some studies, such as Edmonds and Turk (2002); Edmonds (2005); Edmonds and Pavcnik (2005); O'Donnell et al. (2005); and Beegle et al. (2009), have investigated the effects of child labor on child education or health. Beegle et al. (2009) use panel data from the Viet Nam Living Standard Surveys 1993–1994 and 1997–1998 and find that there were significantly negative impacts on children's school enrollment and grade attainment.

Some previous literature has examined the patterns of migration and the effect of migration on household welfare in Viet Nam. Nguyen et al. (2008) showed that the emigration rate seems to be higher among those with higher education levels or among households engaged in wage employment. Nguyen, Raabe, and Grote (2015) and Gröger and Zylberberg (2016) found that migration is viewed as a risk-coping strategy of rural households. Regarding the effect of migration and remittances on household welfare, De Brauw and Harigaya (2007) showed that, during the 1990s, household expenditures among migrant-sending households were 5.2 percentage points higher than those of households without any migrants. Nguyen et al. (2011) estimated the impact of work migration and nonwork migration on some household welfare indicators, including income, expenditures, poverty, and inequality, in Viet Nam using the Viet Nam Household Living Standards Surveys 2004 and 2006. They found that both types of migration have a positive impact on the expenditures of migrant-sending households. Furthermore, they found that nonwork migration contributes significantly to poverty reduction, while the effect of work migration is much smaller.

Using the Viet Nam Household Living Standards Surveys 1992–1993 and 1997–1998, Binci and Giannelli (2012) found that internal remittances increased the school attendance and reduced the child work among children aged 6–15 years in Viet Nam. Booth and Tamura (2009) showed that parental absence caused sons (but not daughters) to do more paid work outside the household, while the effects of parental absence on children's school attendance and household education expenditure were found to be negligible and not statistically significant. Nguyen and Vu (2016) used data from the Young Lives surveys 2007 and 2009 to investigate the effect of parental migration on the time use of children aged 5–8. They showed that children whose parents are absent tend to spend less time on home study and more time on leisure and playing. They also found that children whose mothers are absent spend more time on home study but also spend more time on housework than children whose fathers are absent.

Our study differs from previous research in several aspects. First, we not only examined the effect of child work on child education, but we also investigated the impacts of migration, migration types, and remittances on child work and child education. This is an extension of Le and Homel's (2015) study, which does not examine the role of migration on child work. Second, similar to Le and Homel (2015), we model the decision to work and to go to school simultaneously since there are unobservable factors that simultaneously affect child labor and child education. This distinguishes our study from that of Nguyen and Vu (2016), which examines the effect of parental absence on children's time allocation separately. Third, we also conjecture that migration does not affect the child education decision directly but rather indirectly through household income and the child work decision. Using simultaneous equation econometric modeling, we jointly estimate the effect of migration and type of migration on household income and child work decision and ultimately the effects of household income and the child work decision on child education. Furthermore, we also exploit the nature of our panel data to control for individual fixed effects in our estimations. This is a further extension of Le and Homel's (2015) study, which used only cross-sectional data.

6.3 Empirical Strategy

6.3.1 Estimation Equations

6.3.1.1 Child Education Decision

Our first equation is the child education decision.

$$\text{edu}_{it} = \theta_{01}\text{Migration}_{it}^{0} + \theta_{1}\text{work}_{it} + X'_{1it}\beta + u_{1it} \tag{6.1}$$

where edu_{it} is a binary variable that takes the value of one if child i attends school at time t (t = 2002 and 2004) and zero otherwise; work_{it} is child i's time spent working (i.e., the share of working days in a year, equal to the ratio of total equivalent of 8-hour working days to 365 days); and X'_{1it} is a vector of control variables including child's age, gender, and household characteristics such as per capita income, family size, share of children under 18 and retired adults; household head's education, gender, and age; province where child i lives; and year dummies. Migration_{it} is a binary variable that takes the value of one if child i lives in a migrant-sending household and zero otherwise.

6.3.1.2 Child Labor Decision

In the first equation, work_{it} determines whether a child goes to school or not. This variable in turn is determined in Eq. (6.2) as follows:

$$\text{work}_{it} = \alpha_{0} + \alpha_{01}\text{Migration}_{it}^{0} + X'_{2it}\alpha_{2} + u_{3it} \tag{6.2}$$

where work_{it} is the same as in Eq. (6.1). Similar to Eq. (6.1), Migration_{it} is a binary variable that takes the value of one if child *i* lives in a migrant-sending household and zero otherwise, and X'_{2it} is a vector of control variables. Our X'_{2it} is similar to X'_{1it}, except that we include a dummy variable that indicates whether or not the child's household experienced at least one shock in the previous year.[1] The previous literature on child education includes this type of variable directly in the education outcome equation. However, we conjecture that the child education decision is not directly affected by household shock but rather by their time use (i.e., the time allocated to work) and by family income. In fact, when we include this variable in our first equation, it does not have a statistically significant effect on child education. This variable could be viewed as an "instrumental variable" for the endogenous variable work_{it}. Our parameter of interest in this specification is α_{01}.

6.3.1.3 Household Income

As mentioned above, the pathway through which migration has effects on child education is through income and the child labor decision. We model the household income per capita as follows:

$$\text{Inc}_{it} = \gamma_0 + \gamma_{01}\text{Migration}^0_{it} + X'_{3it}\beta + u_{5it} \tag{6.3}$$

where Inc_{it} is the per capita income of the household to which child *i* belongs. Migration^0_{it} is either a dummy variable as in Eqs. (6.1) and (6.2) or a set of alternative variables as described below. X'_{3it} is the vector of control variables including only household characteristics and provincial and year dummies.

[1] The types of shock include flood, drought, pest infestation and crop diseases, avian flu, price shocks, job losses, land loss, crime, and other family shocks (death or illness of a household member). To check for robustness, we use another shock variable, which takes the value of one if the household experiences shocks including only flood, drought, pest infestation and crop diseases, avian flu, and price shocks and zero otherwise. The results are not qualitatively different. The results are available upon request.

6.3.1.4 Endogeneity of Migration Variable

Although the migration decision of other household members and the left-behind child's decision to go to school and their labor may be independent,[2] they may potentially be correlated with factors at the household level that we are not able to observe. To mitigate this issue, we included the inverse Mills ratio in all estimation equations, which are calculated from a probit estimation equation as follows:

$$\Pr\left(\text{Migration}_{it} = 1\right) = \delta_{it}\text{MigrantDis}_{dt} + X_{1it}^{'}\delta + u_{1it} \tag{6.4}$$

in which Migration_{it} is our migration variable defined earlier. MigrantDis_{dt} is the share of migrants in the total population of the district where child *i* lives. This variable acts as the identification variable in our estimation. In fact, the prevalence of migrants at the district level may affect the migration decision of members of child *i*'s family, but it may not affect child education and child labor at the household level.

6.3.2 Effect of Different Types of Migration on Child Education and Labor

We further explore the effects of different types of migration on children education and labor. For the child education decision, we estimate the following equation:

$$\begin{aligned}\text{edu}_{it} &= \theta_{01}\text{Work}M_{it} + \theta_{02}\text{Edu}M_{it} + \theta_{03}\text{Oth}M_{it} \\ &+ \theta_{1}\text{work}_{it} + X'_{1it}\beta + u_{2it}\end{aligned} \tag{6.5}$$

where $\text{Work}M_{it}$ is a dummy variable that takes the value of one if child *i* lives in a household with at least one person who migrates to work and zero otherwise at time *t*; $\text{Edu}M_{it}$ is a dummy variable that takes the value of one if child *i* lives in a household with at least one person who migrates

[2] The migration decision of a household member may indirectly affect a child's education and labor through household income.

to study and zero otherwise at time t; and OthM_{it} is a dummy variable that takes the value of one if child i lives in a household with at least one person who migrates for other purposes, including marriage or family reunification, and zero otherwise at time t. Alternatively, instead of using binary values for each of the variables WorkM_{it}, EduM_{it}, and OthM_{it}, we use the share of each type of migration in the total number of family members.

Similarly, the child labor decision and household income can also be rewritten as follows:

$$\text{work}_{it} = \alpha_0 + \alpha_{01}\text{Work}M_{it} + \alpha_{02}\text{Edu}M_{it} + \alpha_{03}\text{Oth}M_{it} + X'_{2it}\alpha_2 + u_{3it} \tag{6.6}$$

$$\text{Inc}_{it} = \gamma_0 + \gamma_{01}\text{Work}M_{it} + \gamma_{02}\text{Edu}M_{it} + \gamma_{03}\text{Oth}M_{it} + X'_{3it}\beta + u_{5it} \tag{6.7}$$

We further examine the role of remittances by estimating the following equations:

$$\text{edu}_{it} = \theta_0^1\text{RemitIn}_{it} + \theta_0^2\text{RemitOut}_{it} + \theta_1\text{work}_{it} + X'_{1it}\beta + u_{1it} \tag{6.8}$$

$$\text{work}_{it} = \alpha_0 + \alpha_0^1\text{RemitIn}_{it} + \alpha_0^2\text{RemitOut}_{it} + X'_{2it}\alpha_2 + u_{3it} \tag{6.9}$$

$$\text{Inc}_{it} = \gamma_0 + \gamma_0^1\text{RemitIn}_{it} + \gamma_0^2\text{RemitOut}_{it} + X'_{3it}\beta + u_{5it} \tag{6.10}$$

where RemitIn$_{it}$ is the share of total remittance that child i's household received in his/her household's total income at time t and RemitOut$_{it}$ is the share of total remittance that child i's household sent out to their migrant members in total household income.

6.3.3 Estimation Strategy

In this chapter, we use several approaches to examine the effect of migration on child well-being:

1. We estimate separately two child outcome equations. For education Eqs. (6.1, 6.5, and 6.8), we use a probit estimator and include various control variables indicating migration and the inverse Mills ratio calculated from Eq. (6.4). Due to the nature of the dependent variable, Tobit estimation is used to estimate the child labor decision in Eqs. 6.2, 6.6, and 6.9.
2. We jointly estimate two equations regarding child education and child labor and assume that per capita income is exogenous to both child education and child labor decisions as indicated in Fig. 6.1.
3. We jointly estimate equations relating to child education, child labor decisions, and per capita income as in Fig. 6.2.

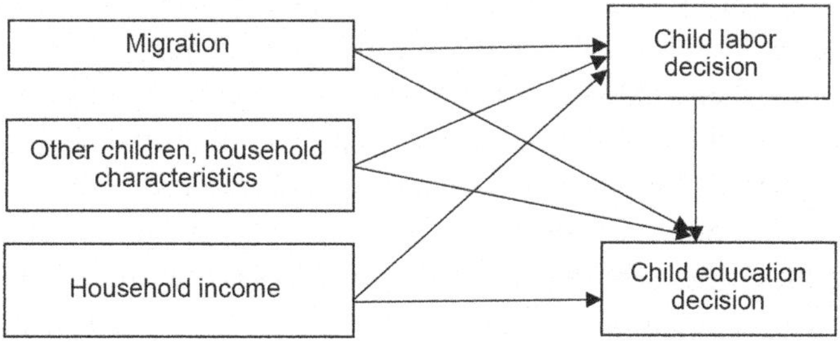

Fig. 6.1 Simultaneous Equation Model 1. Source: Authors' compilation

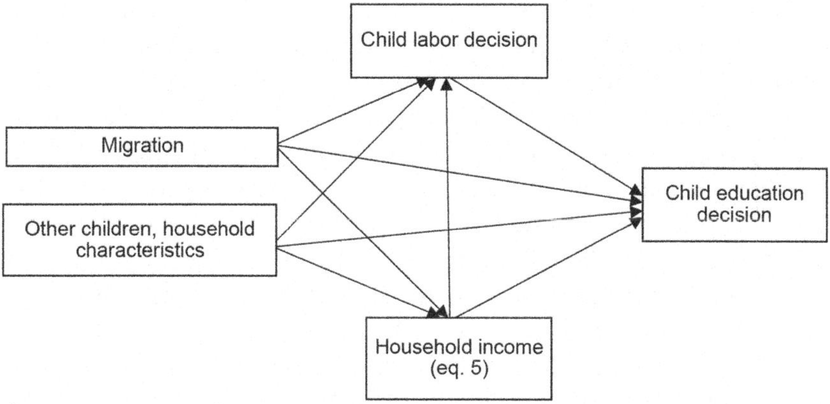

Fig. 6.2 Simultaneous Equation Model 2. Source: Authors' compilation

6.4 Data and Descriptive Statistics

In this study, we use data from the Viet Nam Agricultural Rural Household Survey, which is jointly managed by the Department of Economics of the University of Copenhagen, Denmark, and two institutes in Viet Nam, the Central Institute for Economic Management (Ministry of Planning and Investment) and the Institute for Labor Studies and Social Affairs (Ministry of Labor, Invalid, and Social Affairs), in the 2006, 2008, 2010, 2012, 2014, and 2016 (currently under embargo) waves. The initial sample size (collected in 2006) is 2300 rural households in 12 provinces (Dak Lak, Dak Nong, Dien Bien, Ha Tay, Khanh Hoa, Lai Chau, Lam Dong, Lao Cai, Long An, Nghe An, Phu Tho, and Quang Nam). It is a representative sample of rural areas in these provinces in 2006. The sample size increased to 3200 in 2008 and 2010 and then to about 3700 rural households in 2012 and 2014 to ensure better representativeness of the rural population in these provinces. The core part of the survey instrument is quite similar to that used for the World Bank's Living Standard Measurement Survey, which has detailed information on household demographics, household production, and household members' education, health, occupation, and so on. Moreover, the survey instrument has separate modules relating to economic shocks and vulnerability. In 2012, a migration module with information on reasons for migration, type of migration, and remittances was introduced.

For the purpose of this study, we limit our sample to children who live in households whose head is either their mother or father. (There are some children who live in households whose household head is their grandparent, which makes it difficult for us to identify the child's parents among the household members when there are several related families living in the same house and registered as a single household.) To maintain the panel nature of our data, the children in our sample are those whose ages ranged from 6 to 16 in 2012 and consequently from 8 to 18 in 2014. Finally, we have about 5154 children in our sample (i.e., about 2577 children in each year), living in 1459 households in each year. Among these children, our sample includes 1370 children living in households that do not have other siblings in the sample. The other 3784 children live in households with at least one sibling in the sample.

In our sample, 12.0% of the children live in households with at least one member who has migrated (10.4% in 2012 and 13.7% in 2014). Among migrants, 31% migrated to work or seek jobs (in both 2012 and 2014) and 42% of migrants in 2012 and 52% of migrants in 2014, respectively, migrated for education purposes. The remaining migrants migrated for other purposes such as family unification and marriage.

Table 6.1 presents a descriptive analysis of our sample.

6.5 Empirical Results

6.5.1 Child Education and Labor: Single-Equation Approach

Table 6.2 reports the effects of migration on child education (columns 1 and 2) and child labor decision (columns 4, 5, and 6). In columns 2, 4, and 5, we include the inverse Mills ratio, calculated from probit Eq. (6.4), which examines the probability of living in a household with migrants, to control for the endogeneity bias that may arise due to the potential endogeneity of the migration decision.[3] In column 5, we follow the methodology of Mundlak (1978) and Chamberlain (1984) by including the mean of time-varying covariates in our specification to estimate a quasi-fixed-effects Tobit regression. The results in column 1 indicate that living in a household with migrants is positively correlated with a child's decision to go to school, but this correlation is not statistically significant. However, we find that the more days a child works, the lower the probability of attending school. Children living in households with a higher per capita income, a more educated household head, a younger household head, and a smaller family size seem to have a higher probability of going to school than other children. Living in households where the father is the household head also improves a child's school attendance. We also find that most of the coefficients in column 2 are not much different from those in column 1, indicating that the potential bias of

[3] Please refer to Appendix for our probit estimation results regarding the probability of a child living in a household with migrants.

Table 6.1 Descriptive statistics

	Whole sample		Migrated households		Nonmigrated households	
	Mean	Sta. dev.	Mean	Sta. dev.	Mean	Sta. dev.
% go to school	84.0%		87.0%		84.0%	
Total working days per year	22.97	38.97	23.23	37.67	22.93	39.15
Age	12.32	3.29	13.3	3.22	12.19	3.28
Male (%)	51.0%		50.0%		51.0%	
Income per capita ('000 VND)	15,113	21,688	17,353	25,497	14,807	21,098
Family size	5.48	1.78	5.62	1.79	5.46	1.78
Experienced shock in the last year	52.0%	0.5	50.0%	0.5	52.0%	0.5
Under 18 years old (%)	51.0%	0.14	44.0%	0.15	52.0%	0.13
Retired people (%)	3.0%	0.08	4.0%	0.09	3.0%	0.08
Household head age	41.24	7.19	45.29	6.56	40.69	7.1
Household head is male	92%		92%	0.26	92%	0.27
Household head education level	5.64	4.11	6.68	4.03	5.5	4.1
No. of family members migrated	0.14	0.41	1.16	0.47		
Share of migrants	3.0%	0.08	22.0%	0.09		
Work migration	1.0%	0.05	7.0%	0.12		
Migration for education purpose	1.0%	0.05	10.0%	0.11		
Migration for other purposes	1.0%	0.04	5.0%	0.1		
Total remittances ('000 VND)	338.96	5445.15	2817.78	15,486.4		
Remittances share (over income)	0%	4.0%	0.03	0.1		
Total money sent ('000 VND)	842.12	4628.31	7000.46	11,625.19		
Money sent share (over income)	2.0%	0.19	14.0%	0.53		

Source: Authors' calculation

Table 6.2 Effects on child school and child labor decisions: single-equation approach

	(1)	(2)	(3)	(4)	(5)
	Education decision	Education decision	Labor decision	Labor decision	Labor decision
Living in HH with migrants	0.089	0.097	–0.003	–0.002	–0.002
	[0.090]	[0.091]	[0.005]	[0.005]	[0.005]
% working day/year	–2.382***	–2.385***			
	[0.288]	[0.288]			
Child age	0.019	0.020*	0.029***	0.029***	0.030***
	[0.012]	[0.012]	[0.001]	[0.001]	[0.001]
Child is male	–0.020	–0.022	0.001	0.001	0.001
	[0.061]	[0.061]	[0.006]	[0.006]	[0.006]
Per capita income	0.094**	0.096**	–0.001	–0.001	0.005
	[0.042]	[0.042]	[0.003]	[0.003]	[0.003]
Family size	–0.075***	–0.073***	–0.003	–0.002	–0.006**
	[0.019]	[0.020]	[0.002]	[0.002]	[0.003]
Share of family members under 18	0.103	0.040	0.003	–0.004	–0.032
	[0.266]	[0.299]	[0.020]	[0.021]	[0.026]
Share of family members retired	–0.310	–0.364	0.095***	0.091***	0.102*
	[0.371]	[0.384]	[0.034]	[0.034]	[0.055]
Household head education	0.041***	0.042***	–0.003***	–0.003***	–0.002**
	[0.009]	[0.010]	[0.001]	[0.001]	[0.001]
Household head age	–0.014***	–0.014***	–0.001	–0.001	–0.000
	[0.005]	[0.005]	[0.001]	[0.001]	[0.001]
Household head is male	0.250**	0.245**	0.007	0.007	0.006
	[0.114]	[0.114]	[0.010]	[0.010]	[0.010]
Experience shocks			0.011***	0.011***	0.011***
			[0.004]	[0.004]	[0.004]

(continued)

Table 6.2 (continued)

	(1)	(2)	(3)	(4)	(5)
	Education decision	Education decision	Labor decision	Labor decision	Labor decision
Province dummies	Yes	Yes	Yes	Yes	Yes
Year = 2014	0.046	0.048	−0.054***	−0.054***	−0.058***
	[0.044]	[0.044]	[0.003]	[0.003]	[0.004]
Inverse Mills ratio		0.042		0.004	0.003
		[0.089]		[0.005]	[0.005]
Intercept	0.593	0.479	−0.371***	−0.382***	−0.241**
	[0.557]	[0.607]	[0.043]	[0.045]	[0.094]
Number of observations	5154	5154	5154	5154	5154

Source: Authors' calculation

***, **, and * denote statistical significant at the 1%, 5%, and 10% levels, respectively

"Living in household with migrants" does not affect our estimation results. This is also confirmed by the lack of statistical significance from the inverse Mills ratio variables. The empirical results also indicate that a child's demographic characteristics such as gender and age do not affect their education decision. Per capita household does not influence children's schooling decision either. Living in a large family may reduce their chance of going to school; however, the chance of going to school is higher among those families that have more children under 18 years old. We also find that the education level of the household head has a positive and statistically significant effect on the child education decision. The chance of going to school is also higher for children who live in male-headed households, although this effect is quite weak.

Columns 3, 4, and 5 report our results regarding the child labor decision. Similar to the case of the child education decision, the empirical results show that migration does not have any effect on the total time a child spends working. The empirical results indicate that child age is positively correlated with the time spent working. However, we do not see any significant effect of child gender and per capita income on the time a child worked. While a child living in a bigger family tends to work less, he/she has to work more if living in a family with a higher share of retired members. A child who lives in a household with a household head with a higher level of education tends to work less than other children. However, if the family experienced a shock in the previous year, it increases the time the child worked. Our empirical results also suggest that the results obtained from RE Tobit regression (column 4) are not qualitative, in contrast to those obtained from quasi-FE Tobit regression (column 5).

Table 6.3 reports the effects of different types of migration and shares of remittances on child education (columns 1, 3, and 5) and child labor (columns 2, 4, and 6). We included the inverse Mills ratio in all specifications to mitigate the potential endogeneity problem. The empirical results show that a child living in a household with at least one member who has migrated for work significantly reduces the probability of going to school, while living in a household with at least one member who has migrated for education significantly increases that probability. This pattern is also observed when we use the share of each type of migrant in the total

Table 6.3 Types of migration, remittances, child education, and child labor

	(1)	(2)	(3)	(4)	(5)	(6)
	Education decision	Labor decision	Education decision	Labor decision	Education decision	Labor decision
% working day/year	–2.387***		–2.400***		–2.386***	
	[0.288]		[0.289]		[0.289]	
Work migration	–0.264*	–0.009				
	[0.139]	[0.009]				
Studying migration	0.298**	–0.005				
	[0.137]	[0.008]				
Migration for other purposes	0.147	0.004				
	[0.177]	[0.009]				
% working migrants			–1.218**	–0.031		
			[0.543]	[0.040]		
% studying migrants			1.776***	–0.004		
			[0.666]	[0.035]		
% other migrants			0.639	0.052		
			[0.779]	[0.038]		
Remittances/HH income					–0.591	0.023
					[0.703]	[0.056]
Sending money/HH income					0.088	0.002
					[0.158]	[0.007]
Child age	0.019*	0.029***	0.019*	0.029***	0.019	0.029***
	[0.012]	[0.001]	[0.012]	[0.001]	[0.012]	[0.001]
Child is male	–0.018	0.001	–0.018	0.001	–0.021	0.001
	[0.061]	[0.006]	[0.061]	[0.006]	[0.061]	[0.006]
Per capita income	0.093**	–0.001	0.092**	–0.001	0.100**	–0.001

	[0.042]	[0.003]	[0.042]	[0.003]	[0.042]	[0.003]
Family size	–0.076***	–0.002	–0.076***	–0.002	–0.074***	–0.003
	[0.019]	[0.002]	[0.019]	[0.002]	[0.019]	[0.002]
Share of family members under 18	0.138	0.000	0.158	0.002	0.078	0.004
	[0.266]	[0.020]	[0.266]	[0.020]	[0.264]	[0.019]
Share of family members retired	–0.272	0.095***	–0.248	0.095***	–0.323	0.096***
	[0.371]	[0.034]	[0.371]	[0.034]	[0.370]	[0.034]
Household head education	0.040***	–0.003***	0.040***	–0.003***	0.041***	–0.003***
	[0.009]	[0.001]	[0.009]	[0.001]	[0.009]	[0.001]
Household head age	–0.014***	–0.001	–0.014***	–0.001	–0.014***	–0.001
	[0.005]	[0.001]	[0.005]	[0.001]	[0.005]	[0.001]
Household head is male	0.258**	0.007	0.257**	0.008	0.248**	0.007
	[0.114]	[0.010]	[0.114]	[0.010]	[0.114]	[0.010]
HH experience shocks		0.011***		0.011***		0.011***
		[0.004]		[0.004]		[0.004]
Province dummies	0.000	0.000	0.000	0.000	0.000	0.000
Year = 2014	0.046	–0.054***	0.044	–0.054***	0.047	–0.054***
	[0.044]	[0.003]	[0.044]	[0.003]	[0.044]	[0.003]
Intercept	0.576	–0.369***	0.578	–0.371***	0.534	–0.373***
	[0.557]	[0.043]	[0.557]	[0.043]	[0.561]	[0.043]
Number of observations	5154	5154	5154	5154	5154	5154

Source: Authors' calculation

***, **, and * denote statistical significant at the 1%, 5%, and 10% levels, respectively

number of family members. This suggests that children living in households with working migrants tend to have to leave school and may follow other household members who have already migrated to work. However, as shown in column 5, remittances received or sent out do not affect the child education decision.

With regard to time spent on labor, we do not see a significant effect of having household members who have migrated for any purpose on a child's working time. The share of money the household receives from migrants (if any) or the share of money sent to migrants (if any) does not affect the time a child works.

6.5.2 Child Education and Labor: Simultaneous Equation Model Approach

Table 6.4 shows our estimation results using the simultaneous equation approach. In column 1, we estimated a child's school attendance and time spent working jointly, while in column 2, we considered per capita income as an endogenous variable and estimated school attendance, time worked, and per capita income simultaneously. For child education, similar to the results obtained from the single-equation approach (Table 6.2), we see that more time spent working reduces school attendance. However, the estimated coefficient is smaller in magnitude, indicating an upward bias in the effect of working time on child education when we considered child education and child labor separately. Meanwhile, other factors such as the child's own characteristics, family characteristics, and household head's characteristics have quite similar effects on child school attendance, except for the variable indicating the share of household members who were retired.

For child labor, our SEM estimation results indicated that children living in households with migrants have to spend more time working, suggesting a downward bias in the effect of migration on child labor compared with the results when we estimated child labor separately (Table 6.2). The downward pattern is also observed in the variable indicating whether the child lives in a household that experienced a shock in the previous year or not. While most other variables behave similarly to

Table 6.4 Migration, child education, child labor, and household income: simultaneous equation approach

	(1)		(2)		
	Education decision	Labor decision	Education decision	Labor decision	Family income (per capita)
Living in HH with migrants		0.002***	0.111	0.002***	0.046***
		[0.000]	[0.102]	[0.000]	[0.014]
Working time	−1.979***		−1.982***		
	[0.069]		[0.041]		
Child age	0.004	0.027***	0.009	0.027***	
	[0.125]	[0.000]	[0.129]	[0.000]	
Child is male	−0.022*	0.002	−0.019	0.002	
	[0.013]	[0.002]	[0.012]	[0.002]	
Per capita income	0.001	0.004	0.091**	0.004	
	[0.023]	[0.013]	[0.035]	[0.013]	
Family size	0.057	−0.005	−0.062***	−0.005	0.072***
	[0.070]	[0.005]	[0.007]	[0.005]	[0.003]
Share of family members under 18	1.371**	−0.029	−0.028	−0.029	−0.894***
	[0.579]	[0.076]	[0.198]	[0.076]	[0.010]
Share of family members retired	0.289	0.085	−0.262**	0.085	−0.559***
	[1.048]	[0.174]	[0.103]	[0.174]	[0.069]
Household head education	0.025*	−0.003***	0.032**	−0.003***	0.054***
	[0.014]	[0.000]	[0.013]	[0.000]	[0.005]
Household head age	−0.014***	−0.000***	−0.012***	−0.000***	0.002
	[0.004]	[0.000]	[0.004]	[0.000]	[0.003]
Household head is male	0.204***	0.006*	0.196***	0.006*	0.088**
	[0.007]	[0.003]	[0.019]	[0.003]	[0.036]
Experience shocks		0.023***		0.023***	−0.155***

Table 6.4 (continued)

	(1)		(2)		
	Education decision	Labor decision	Education decision	Labor decision	Family income (per capita)
		[0.005]		[0.005]	[0.010]
Inverse Mills ratio	0.060***	0.005***	0.021	0.005***	
	[0.010]	[0.001]	[0.022]	[0.001]	
Household head is a veteran					–0.039***
					[0.006]
Intercept	0.766	–0.265***	0.423	–0.265***	10.856***
	[1.359]	[0.013]	[1.444]	[0.013]	[0.008]
Var (time worked)		0.019***		0.019***	
		[0.000]		[0.000]	
Var (family income pc)					0.441***
					[0.049]
Number of observations	5154	5154	5154	5154	5154

Source: Authors' calculation

***, **, and * denote statistical significant at the 1%, 5%, and 10% levels, respectively.

the single-equation approach, per capita income has a significant effect on a child's time spent working. Children living in households with a higher per capita income tend to work fewer days than children living in households with lower per capita income.

Regarding household income, we find a significant effect of migration on per capita income. This implies a higher correlation between per capita income and migration. The results also indicate that a bigger family size, more educated household head, and male-headed households tend to have a higher per capita income, while households with a higher share of children aged under 18 or retired people tend to have a lower per capita income. Similarly, households that experienced a shock in the previous year also tend to have a lower per capita income.

Table 6.5 presents our estimation results using the simultaneous equation approach. We considered two alternative sets of indicators for migration: one indicating whether a child lived in a household with at least one member migrating for work, for education, or for other purposes (column 1) and another set of indicators indicating the share of remittances his/her household received (in total household income) from migrants and the share of money his/her household sent to migrants (in total household income) (column 2). Similar to column 2 in Table 6.4, we assumed per capita income to be an endogenous variable and estimated school attendance, time worked, and per capita income simultaneously.

The estimation results are interesting. Children living in households with migrants who migrated for education are more likely to attend school and work less than children who live in households without any migrants. Children who live in households with migrants who migrated to work do not significantly differ in terms of school and work time from those who live in households without any migrants. This suggests that households that send their family members to be educated in other areas tend to care about their children's education more than do other households. This is confirmed by the results we obtained when using variables indicating the share of money received from, and sent to, migrants in total household income. Children living in households that sent a higher share of their income to migrants are more likely to attend school than those who live in households that did not send money to migrants.

Table 6.5 Heterogeneous effects of migration on child education, child labor, and household income: simultaneous equation approach

	(1)			(2)		
	Education decision	Labor decision	Family income (per capita)	Education decision	Labor decision	Family income (per capita)
Working time	−1.995***			−2.034***		
	[0.044]			[0.210]		
Work migration	−0.824	0.012	−0.012			
	[1.205]	[0.023]	[0.431]			
Studying migration	1.736***	−0.048***	0.446***			
	[0.223]	[0.018]	[0.135]			
Migration for other purposes	0.486**	0.136**	0.027			
	[0.197]	[0.061]	[0.123]			
Remittances/HH income				−0.496	0.052***	0.337
				[0.426]	[0.020]	[0.767]
Sending money/HH income				0.134***	0.002	−0.480***
				[0.036]	[0.002]	[0.017]
Child age	0.009	0.027***		0.015	0.027***	
	[0.129]	[0.000]		[0.108]	[0.000]	
Child is male	−0.016	0.003		−0.020*	0.003	
	[0.012]	[0.002]		[0.011]	[0.002]	
Per capita income	0.088**	−0.008**		0.097**	−0.008**	
	[0.038]	[0.004]		[0.040]	[0.004]	
Family size	−0.064***	−0.001***	0.072***	−0.062***	−0.002***	0.075***
	[0.012]	[0.000]	[0.003]	[0.009]	[0.000]	[0.004]
Share of family members under 18	0.052	0.007	−0.878***	−0.040	0.013	−0.959***
	[0.102]	[0.016]	[0.008]	[0.160]	[0.018]	[0.001]
Share of family members retired	−0.186***	0.082***	−0.547***	−0.262**	0.085***	−0.613***

	[0.021]	[0.003]	[0.075]		[0.104]	[0.005]	[0.087]
Household head education	0.031**	−0.003***	0.054***		0.032**	−0.003***	0.055***
	[0.012]	[0.000]	[0.005]		[0.013]	[0.000]	[0.005]
Household head age	−0.012***	−0.001***	0.002		−0.011***	−0.001***	0.004*
	[0.004]	[0.000]	[0.003]		[0.004]	[0.000]	[0.002]
Household head is male	0.203***	0.008***	0.089**		0.191***	0.007***	0.081**
	[0.024]	[0.001]	[0.038]		[0.009]	[0.000]	[0.036]
Experience shocks		0.023***	−0.156***			0.023***	−0.155***
		[0.003]	[0.010]			[0.004]	[0.013]
Household head joined army			−0.038***				−0.043***
			[0.005]				[0.006]
Intercept	0.469	−0.280***	10.847***		0.341	−0.280***	10.829***
	[1.425]	[0.086]	[0.006]		[1.191]	[0.083]	[0.009]
Var (time worked)		0.019***				0.019***	
		[0.000]				[0.000]	
Var (per capita HH income)			0.440***				0.433***
			[0.050]				[0.042]
Number of observations	5154				5154		

Source: Authors' calculation

***, **, and * denote statistical significant at the 1%, 5%, and 10% levels, respectively

Meanwhile, children living in households receiving more from migrants tend to work more. As regards a household's per capita income, sending money to migrants reduced household per capita income, while receiving remittances from migrants did not increase household income.

6.6 Concluding Remarks

Using a unique data set collected in Viet Nam in 2012 and 2014, this study examines the heterogeneous effects of migration on left-behind children's education and child labor in Viet Nam. Since child education and child labor decisions are jointly determined, a simultaneous equation model approach is adopted to estimate the effect of migration on child education and child labor. Because migration not only affects a child's welfare but also household income, we further integrate household income into our system of equations. There are some major findings from our empirical results. First, migration does not appear to directly affect children's schooling decision, but might negatively affect their time spent working, which ultimately affects their schooling decision. Migration, however, may also positively affect household per capita income in some respects. Since family income has a significant effect on children's education and their working time, migration also indirectly affects child education and child labor.

We find that the total effects of migration on child education and child labor are negligible. This finding is different from other studies, including Binci and Giannelli (2012), which found that migration tends to increase school attendance and reduce child work. However, in contrast to our study, the previous literature examines the effect of migration on child education and child labor separately. Therefore, it appears to have ignored the negative relationship between child labor and child education as found in our study and in Le and Homel (2015).

Second, different types of migration have different effects on child schooling and labor. While children living in households with migrants who migrated for work are not found to be different in terms of school time from those living in households without any migrants, children living in households with migrants who migrated for education or other purposes tend to have a higher probability of attending school, although this relationship could be viewed as a correlation between migration and children's education rather than a causal effect. Third, children living in households with a higher share of inward remittances tend to work more. This may imply that such children may live in poorer households that send their household members to work in other areas and make left-behind children work more. Fourth, children living in households with education migration seem to attend school more and work less, but, at the same time, school time could be negatively affected by the income factor since households with education migration who have to send money to those migrants tend to have a lower per capita income.

The study has several limitations. First, due to the data availability, we could not provide adequate evidence on the effects of parental migration on child welfare. Parental migration may have a stronger effect on left-behind children than migration of other household members. Second, migration may have long-term effects on child outcomes. However, our data could only provide the contemporaneous effects of migration on child outcomes. These limitations are open for further studies.

Appendix: Probability of Living in a Household with a Migrant

	(1)	(2)	(3)
	Year 2012	Year 2014	Years 2012–2014
Share of migrants in total population	7.358***	5.652***	6.722***
	[1.235]	[1.169]	[0.952]
Experience shocks	0.092	0.100	0.083
	[0.088]	[0.078]	[0.061]
Child age	0.001	0.009	0.008
	[0.013]	[0.012]	[0.009]
Child is male	–0.207***	0.029	–0.077
	[0.077]	[0.069]	[0.056]
Per capita income	0.077	0.065	0.064
	[0.061]	[0.047]	[0.039]

(*continued*)

(continued)

	(1) Year 2012	(2) Year 2014	(3) Years 2012–2014
Family size	0.068***	0.077***	0.082***
	[0.025]	[0.022]	[0.018]
Share of family members under 18	-2.101***	-1.938***	-2.162***
	[0.320]	[0.285]	[0.237]
Share of family members retired	−1.246***	−1.682***	−1.546***
	[0.451]	[0.426]	[0.339]
Household head education	0.033***	0.011	0.021**
	[0.012]	[0.011]	[0.009]
Household head age	0.042***	0.028***	0.035***
	[0.006]	[0.006]	[0.005]
Household head is male	−0.378***	0.039	−0.160
	[0.143]	[0.128]	[0.103]
Number of observations	2577	2577	5154

Source: Authors' calculation

*** and ** denote statistical significant at the 1% and 5% levels, respectively

References

Acosta, P., P. Fajnzylber, and J.H. Lopez. 2007. *The impact of remittances on poverty and human capital: Evidence from Latin American household surveys*. World Bank Working Paper No. 4247.

Adams, R.H., and J. Page. 2005. Do international migration and remittances reduce poverty in developing countries? *World Development* 33 (10): 1645–1669.

Alcaraz, C., D. Chiquiar, and A. Salcedo. 2012. Remittances, schooling, and child labor in Mexico. *Journal of Development Economics* 97 (1): 156–165.

Antman, F.M. 2012. Gender, educational attainment, and the impact of parental migration on children left behind. *Journal of Population Economics* 25 (4): 1187–1214.

Antón, J.I. 2010. The impact of remittances on nutritional status of children in Ecuador. *International Migration Review* 44 (2): 269–299.

Beegle, K., R. Dehejia, and R. Gatti. 2009. Why should we care about child labor? The education, labor market, and health consequences of child labor. *Journal of Human Resources* 44 (4): 871–889.

Biao, X. 2007. How far are the left-behind left behind? A preliminary study in rural China. *Population, Space and Place* 13 (3): 179–191.

Binci, M., and G. Giannelli. 2012. *Internal vs. International Migration: Impacts of remittances on child WELLBEING in Vietnam*. Discussion Paper No. 6523. Bonn: Institute for the Study of Labor (IZA).

Booth, A.L., and Y. Tamura. 2009. *Impact of paternal temporary absence on children left behind*. CEPR Discussion Paper No. DP7440.

Brandt K., and F. Tarp, 2017. Characteristics of the VARHS data and other data sources. In F. Tarp (ed.) *Growth, structural transformation, and rural change in Viet Nam: A rising dragon on the move*, Oxford University Press.

Cameron, M., and S. Lim. 2007. *Household resources, household composition, and child nutritional outcomes*. Paper presented at the 2007 Australian Agricultural and Resource Economics Society Conference in Queenstown, 13–16 February 2007.

Chamberlain, G. 1984. Panel data. *Handbook of Econometrics* 2: 1247–1318.

De Brauw, A., and T. Harigaya. 2007. Seasonal migration and improving living standards in Vietnam. *American Journal of Agricultural Economics* 89 (2): 430–447.

De Brauw, A., and R. Mu. 2011. Migration and the overweight and underweight status of children in rural China. *Food Policy* 36 (1): 88–100.

Edmonds, E.V. 2005. Does child labor decline with improving economic status? *Journal of Human Resources* 40 (1): 77–99.

Edmonds, E.V., and N. Pavcnik. 2005. The effect of trade liberalization on child labor. *Journal of International Economics* 65 (2): 401–419.

Edmonds, E.V., and C. Turk. 2002. Child labor in transition in Vietnam (Vol. 2774). World Bank, Development Research Group, Macroeconomics and Growth.

Ellis, F. 2003. *A livelihoods approach to migration and poverty reduction*. Mimeo.

Farrington, J., and R. Slater. 2006. Introduction: Cash transfers: Panacea for poverty reduction or money down the drain? *Development Policy Review* 24 (5): 499–511.

Giannelli, G.C., and L. Mangiavacchi. 2010. Children's schooling and parental migration: Empirical evidence on the 'left-behind' generation in Albania. *Labour* 24 (s1): 76–92.

Gibson, J., D. McKenzie, and S. Stillman. 2011. The impacts of international migration on remaining household members: Omnibus results from a migration lottery program. *Review of Economics and Statistics* 93 (4): 1297–1318.

Gröger, A., and Y. Zylberberg. 2016. Internal labor migration as a shock-coping strategy: Evidence from a typhoon. *American Economic Journal: Applied Economics* 8 (2): 123–153.
Hildebrandt, N., D.J. McKenzie, G. Esquivel, and E. Schargrodsky. 2005. The effects of migration on child health in Mexico [with comments]. *Economia* 6 (1): 257–289.
Kiros, G.E., and M.J. White. 2004. Migration, community context, and child immunization in Ethiopia. *Social Science & Medicine* 59 (12): 2603–2616.
Lahaie, C., J.A. Hayes, T.M. Piper, and J. Heymann. 2009. Work and family divided across borders: The impact of parental migration on Mexican children in transnational families. *Community, Work & Family* 12 (3): 299–312.
Le, H.T., and R. Homel. 2015. The impact of child labor on children's educational performance: Evidence from rural Vietnam. *Journal of Asian Economics* 36: 1–13.
Macours, K., and R. Vakis. 2010. Seasonal migration and early childhood development. *World Development* 38 (6): 857–869.
McKenzie, D., and H. Rapoport. 2011. Can migration reduce educational attainment? Evidence from Mexico. *Journal of Population Economics* 24 (4): 1331–1358.
McKenzie, D., and M. Sasin. 2007. *Migration, remittances, poverty, and human capital: conceptual and empirical challenges*. Working Paper 4272. Washington, DC: World Bank.
Meyerhoefer, C.D., and C.J. Chen. 2011. The effect of parental labor migration on children's educational progress in rural China. *Review of Economics of the Household* 9 (3): 379–396.
Mundlak, Y. 1978. On the pooling of time series and cross section data. *Econometrica* 46 (1): 69–85.
Nguyen, V.C., and H.L. Vu. 2016. Should parents work away from or close to home? The effect of parental absence on children's time use in Vietnam. *Journal of Human Development and Capabilities* 17 (1): 110–124.
Nguyen, T.P., T.M.T. Ngo, T.N. Nguyen, and R. Oostendorp. 2008. Determinants and Impacts of Migration in Vietnam (No. 01). Development and Policies Research Center (DEPOCEN), Vietnam.
Nguyen, C.V., M. Van den Berg, and R. Lensink. 2011. The impact of work and non-work migration on household welfare, poverty and inequality. *Economics of Transition* 19 (4): 771–799.
Nguyen, L.D., K. Raabe, and U. Grote. 2015. Rural–urban migration, household vulnerability, and welfare in Vietnam. *World Development* 71: 79–93.

O'Donnell, O., F.C. Rosati, and E. Van Doorslaer. 2005. Health effects of child work: Evidence from rural Vietnam. *Journal of Population Economics* 18 (3): 437–467.

Robles, V.F., and R.S. Oropesa. 2011. International migration and the education of children: Evidence from Lima, Peru. *Population Research and Policy Review* 30 (4): 591–618.

Sahn, D.E., and H. Alderman. 1996. The effect of food subsidies on labor supply in Sri Lanka. *Economic Development and Cultural Change* 45 (1): 125–145.

Taylor, J.E., J. Mora, R. Adams, and A. López-Feldman. 2005. *Remittances, Inequality, and Poverty: Evidence from Rural Mexico*. Working Paper No. 05-003, Davis, CA: Department of Agricultural and Resource Economics, University of California.

UNIDO-HDRO. 2009. *Human development report 2009. Overcoming barriers: Human mobility and development*. New York: Palgrave Macmillan.

Wang, S.X. 2014. The effect of parental migration on the educational attainment of their left-behind children in rural China. *The BE Journal of Economic Analysis & Policy* 14 (3): 1037–1080.

Wen, M., and D. Lin. 2012. Child development in rural China: Children left behind by their migrant parents and children of nonmigrant families. *Child Development* 83 (1): 120–136.

Yang, D. 2008. International migration, remittances and household investment: Evidence from Philippine migrants' exchange rate shocks. *The Economic Journal* 118 (528): 591–630.

Zhang, H., J.R. Behrman, C.S. Fan, X. Wei, and J. Zhang. 2014. Does parental absence reduce cognitive achievements? Evidence from rural China. *Journal of Development Economics* 111: 181–195.

7

The Effect of Child Labour on Primary Education in Brazil

Roselaine Bonfim de Almeida

7.1 Introduction

For today's society, employment of children and adolescents is considered a crime. However, this has not always been the case. In Europe, at the end of the eighteenth century, the increase in child hiring was considered a sign of the company's prosperity. This showed that the company's workforce was not able to produce all the goods demanded by society and, thus, it was necessary to hire children. However, with the worsening of the working conditions of these children, in the beginning of the nineteenth century, part of the society began to struggle to reduce their working hours (Basu 1998; FYFE 2007).

The International Labour Organization (ILO) defines child labour as a "work that deprives children of their childhood, their potential and their dignity, and that is harmful to physical and mental development" (ILO

R. B. de Almeida (✉)
Federal University of Grande Dourados, Dourados, Brazil
e-mail: roselainealmeida@ufgd.edu.br

A. Posso (ed.), *Child Labor in the Developing World*,
https://doi.org/10.1007/978-981-15-3106-4_7

2019a). They also say that child labour is harmful because it is a serious violation of human rights and, also, because it deprives children and adolescents of a normal childhood since it discourages school attendance and impedes the development of the child's abilities (ILO 2019b).

According to Kassouf (2007), there is no single definition of child labour. This will depend on other factors such as the number of hours worked, the age of the child and the country's legislation, among other variables. For example, many studies consider child labour if the child worked for an hour or more during the week. However, some more specific researches may use information on housework or the economically active population of children, that is, working and looking for a job. Another important issue to consider is that the definition of child may vary by country, because while some areas consider chronological age, others may also consider social and cultural factors. The author argues that generally in child labour studies, current legislation is used to define whether the child or adolescent is in the child labour situation or not.

According to ILO estimates (2019b), in 2016 about 152 million children and adolescents between the ages of 5 and 17 were victims of child labour worldwide. Most of these children and adolescents can be found on the African continent, home to 72.1 million children in child labour situations. Second is the Asia-Pacific region (62 million), followed by the Americas (10.7 million), Europe and Central Asia (5.5 million) and the Arab states (1.2 million). Of this total, most child labour is in agriculture (71%), followed by services (17%) and industry (12%).

Child labour is also an old problem in Brazilian society. In the sixteenth century, children of indigenous origin were forced to perform various kinds of work. In the period of slavery, the children of slaves were forced to work, and at the beginning of industrialization in Brazil, at the end of the nineteenth century, child labour was also employed in factories (Brazil 2011). Over time, Brazilian society realized that child labour was a problem and that it should be tackled with urgency. However, despite efforts to combat this problem, it persists until these days (Almeida 2015).

Data from the National Household Sample Survey (PNAD) demonstrate this situation. Between 1992 and 2015, there was a reduction in child labour of 68%, or 5.7 million children and adolescents left work. Although this drop is quite significant, in 2015 there were still

2.7 million children and adolescents between 5 and 17 years of age working. A different feature of the world trend is that in Brazil there is a higher incidence of child labour in nonagricultural activities (ILO 2019b). However, although a large number of children and adolescents between the ages of 5 and 17 years work in the nonagricultural sector, when we analyse the age group from 5 to 13 years, it is observed that 64.7% worked in the agricultural sector in 2015 (PNAD 2015).

It is worth noting that regardless of whether child labour is in the agricultural or nonagricultural sector, it can have serious consequences for these children. Kassouf (2007) points out that the main socioeconomic consequences of the work of children and adolescents are on education, salary and health.

Among the studies that analysed the impact of child labour on school performance of children and adolescents, we highlight the work done by Ono (2015). The author analyses this relationship using data from PNAD between 2007 and 2011 and Prova Brasil/SAEB.[1] The aim of their study was to determine the impact of the work of children and adolescents on proficiency in Portuguese language and mathematics. Their results showed that child labour has a negative effect on academic achievement.

In this work we aim to analyse the effect that child labour has on the schooling of individuals. This result is important because education is essential for the child's development, and if such development is being hampered by child labour, new protective measures should be defined to protect these children.

To measure schooling, we will analyse how many years of studies the individuals have; in particular, we will analyse the years of studies comprised in elementary school. In Brazil, the first years of study of the individuals are grouped in elementary education. Until 2006, elementary education in Brazil represented a cycle of 8 years of study. The child who is 7 years old would be in the first grade, and, in case he or she didn't have any reprobation, he or she would have finished primary school at the age of 14. In that case, he or she would have completed through eighth grade without any delay. However, after intense debates in 2006 was stipulated,

[1] The Prova Brasil/SAEB is a test developed by the Brazilian government in order to evaluate the quality of the offered education through standardized tests and socioeconomic questionnaires.

by the law number 11,274, 9 years of elementary school. The idea is that the child could spend more time at school. Thus, the child enters the school at the age of 6 years (first year) and completes the elementary school at the age of 14 (9th year), in case of she or he doesn't have any reprobation (MEC 2009).

However, although the law was enacted in 2006, the government stipulated that the education systems would have until the end of 2009 to implement the new rules, that is, at the beginning of the 2010 school year, all schools would have to offer 9 years of education (MEC 2009).

Thus, in this chapter we will analyse the impact of child labour on the conclusion of certain years of study in elementary education. The period that we are going to analyse contemplates both before and after the implantation of the 9 years of elementary education.

7.2 Methodology

The methodology used in this article follows the work of Natenzon (2003) and Almeida and Pazello (2010). However, in their work the authors analysed the effect of preschool on the future school performance of individuals.

As well as the authors cited, the idea is to work with aggregate data for successive educational generations. We defined an educational generation as the set of 14-year-old individuals who, in the year analysed, had completed 7 years of study.[2] This means that if he or she had studied in the period that the primary education lasted 8 years, at age 14 he or she would be in the eighth grade. That is, they are individuals who by the age of 14 had already completed the seventh grade of elementary school without any reprobation.

If this individual had studied in the period in which elementary education lasted 9 years, with 7 years of study completed, he or she would be in the 7th year (which is equivalent to the sixth grade in elementary school of 8 years). When constructing this variable, we analysed the

[2] Educational generations are represented in Annex I. We will analyse 24 educational generations, covering the period from 1992 to 2015.

individual who had 7 years or more of study and 14 years old. In this way, the possibility is opened that the individual who studied in the period when the elementary school lasted 9 years may have at least 1 year of reprobation.

However, since the expansion of elementary education to the whole national territory occurred only in 2010 and most of the educational generations analysed studied during the period when elementary education still lasted 8 years, it was decided to analyse throughout the whole period of study individuals that were 14 years old and that had 7 years of study, regardless of whether they were in the sixth or seventh grade. The important thing is to know how the conclusion of these years of study is related to child labour.

7.2.1 Database

The information used in this study comes from the National Household Sample Survey, which is carried out by the Brazilian Institute of Geography and Statistics (IBGE). The research is carried out in a sample of Brazilian households and investigates several socioeconomic characteristics of the population, including demographic and social conditions, educational, work, income, housing and so on. In addition, in some years it features special searches and supplements, which are included according to the information needs.

In this work we use the microdata of the PNAD between 1985 and 2015, which will give us 24 educational generations.[3] From this data it is possible to obtain information about the individuals of each educational generation for a given year, such as whether the individual worked or not. It is also possible to obtain information on the quality of teaching in each state, among others.[4] Later, we will explain how these variables will help us identify the impact of interest.

[3] As can be seen in Annex.

[4] For the years in which there was no PNAD (1991, 1994, 2000 and 2010), we will make a simple interpolation of the data (average between the years before and after).

7.2.2 Estimation Model and Identification Strategy

As noted earlier, the methodology used in this chapter follows the work of Natenzon (2003) and Almeida and Pazello (2010). However, the model was adapted to our variables of interest.

To estimate the proposed model first, we must define our dependent variable, that is, *Y*, which is determined by the individuals of generation *g*, in state *i* and time *t*. By hypothesis, we admit that the probability of this generation, represented by *Y*, having 7 years of study completed at 14 years of age can be described by a logistic function. That is:

$$\Pr ob\left(Y_{git}=1\right)=\frac{1}{1+\exp\left(-\sum_{k=1}^{K}X_k\beta_k\right)} \tag{7.1}$$

where X_k are exogenous variables that explain this probability. By rearranging the expression above, we can obtain:

$$\ln\left(\frac{\Pr ob\left(Y_{git}=1\right)}{1-\Pr ob\left(Y_{git}=1\right)}\right)=\sum_{k=1}^{K}X_k\beta_k=\alpha+\beta_1X_1+\beta_2X_2\ldots+\beta_KX_K \tag{7.2}$$

If we assume that a good estimate of $\Pr ob\,(Y_{git}=1)$ is the proportion of individuals of generation *g*, state *i* and time *t* who have 7 years of complete studies at 14 years of age, expression (7.2) can be estimated using the ordinary least squares regression method. However, in this case, the marginal effect of the independent variables will not be given by β_k. In this case, the marginal effect is given by the derivative of Eq. (7.1) with respect to the chosen independent variable:

$$\frac{\partial \Pr ob\left(Y_{git}=1\right)}{\partial X_1}=\frac{-\exp\left(-\sum_{k=1}^{K}X_k\beta_k\right)\times\left(-\beta_1\right)}{\left(1+\exp\left(-\sum_{k=1}^{K}X_k\beta_k\right)\right)^2}=\frac{\beta_1\times\exp\left(-\sum_{k=1}^{K}X_k\beta_k\right)}{\left(1+\exp\left(-\sum_{k=1}^{K}X_k\beta_k\right)\right)^2} \tag{7.3}$$

Equation (7.3) shows the marginal effect of the independent variable X_1 on the probability of individuals having 7 years of complete studies at 14 years of age.[5]

Thus, for this study we will estimate by least squares the Eq. (7.4):

$$y = \alpha + \sum_{k=1}^{K} X_k \beta_k + \varepsilon \tag{7.4}$$

where we define that $y = \ln\left(\frac{\text{Prob}\left(Y_{git} = 1\right)}{1 - \text{Prob}\left(Y_{git} = 1\right)}\right)$. In this way, y represents a measure of the educational performance of the individuals of a generation g, in state i and in the year t.

According to Almeida and Pazello (2010), the idea is to stack different PNADs used in the study (which represent the different educational generations) and to look how this measure has evolved over time. To understand how to identify the impact of child labour on this measure of educational performance, we must open the K vector of variable X.

From the set of variables, the one of interest is that which represents the proportion of generation g in state i observed at time t, who was working when he or she was 14 years old. According to PNAD data, it is also possible to verify if this individual started working before age 14. The data analysed for year 2015, for example, showed that most individuals started working from the age of 10, although some children started working from the age of 5. Thus, in selecting the 14-year-olds working, we used the hypothesis that this variable can capture if these individuals started working younger, which would affect their school performance.

The objective is to identify the effect of this variable (child labour) using only the variation that occurs differently among the states over time. For this to be possible, the independent variables included a set of dummies for the states and another set of dummies for each of the years of the PNADs stacked. Thus, what is common for a given state, or the fixed effect of state, is captured by the variable indicative of state; on the other hand, the common movement for the states in time (common

[5] Estimates were performed using the Stata 14 program.

temporal movement) is captured by the variables indicative of year. The model identification is based on the remaining variation.

In addition, we also include in the vector *X* variables that characterize the quality of the education system of the states and the socioeconomic condition of the generations over time. They are pupils per teacher, the average schooling of elementary school teachers, the ratio of students per adult (indicates dependency), the logarithm of the average per capita family income of the generation (deflated by the IPCA—price index of September of 2015) and the proportion of the generation residing in the rural areas.[6] All these measures are obtained from the PNAD. Almeida and Pazello (2010) note that by including dummies for the states and dummies for the years of the PNADs, it is possible to capture the change in time that occurs differently between the states.

Thus, the hypothesis of this chapter is that, conditional on *X*, the variation in the proportion of 14-year-olds working, which is different among the states, is not correlated with the regression residue, that is, with changes in unobserved variables that occurred differently among states.

7.2.3 Econometric Analysis

In this section we present the econometric analyses performed in this chapter. First, we estimate the regression for the proportion of individuals from the educational generations Gg, where g ranges from 1 to 24, who had completed 7 years of study at the age 14, in each state, between 1992 and 2015.

The explanatory variable of interest is the proportion of the generation that was working. For this first econometric analysis, the variable *child labour* considers the individuals of 14 years of age that were working. Thus, for the same individual of 14 years of age is asked if he or she has 7 years of study completed. If the individual of 14 years old currently works apparently, this may have no impact on the conclusion of the 7 years of study since the individual began to study at the age of 7, and

[6] Data from the rural area of the northern states were only included in the PNAD from 2004. Thus, in order to ensure comparability, we extracted the observations regarding the rural area of the North region from the whole base.

only the years that he worked while studying would have an impact on the conclusion of the 7 years of study. However, usually these children did not start working at the age of 14, but rather before that age.[7] The idea is that these individuals of 14 years old had started to work before and this may have had consequences in his studies.

In order to strengthen our argument, we carried out a second econometric analysis where, in the creation of the *child labour* variable, we analysed the generation of 13 years old who worked and looked at the impact of this variable on the conclusion of 7 years of study when the generation had 14 years of age, that is, 1 year more. In this way, we can be sure that this generation worked for, at least, a year.

The other variables include the dummies for the states, dummies for the years of the PNADs, characteristics of the educational system and characteristics of the population of each state. In the case of these last two sets of variables, we will make a simple average of the data obtained in the years in which the generation should ideally be in the first, fourth and seventh grades of elementary education.[8] Thus, the data for the first econometric analysis includes 24 educational generations in 26[9] states, totaling 624 observations. For the second econometric analysis (generation that at 13 years old was working), we have 23 generations in 26 states, totaling 598 observations.

It is important to note that all estimated regressions are weighted by cell size (a cell is an interaction between generation, state and time). Take the first analysis as an example; we have 624 cells, 26 of which are relative to the G_1 generation, which is observed in 1992. Thus, for each state, with the 1992 PNAD data, we calculated the proportion of the G_1 generation that had 7 years of study completed. The weight used corresponds to the number of individuals observed from generation G_1 that were considered for the calculation of this proportion. The lower the number of individuals in this cell, the lower the weight of this cell. This is because

[7] In the next section, we will delve deeper into this analysis.

[8] Here we take the 8 years of elementary school as the standard.

[9] In 1988, the former state of Goiás was dismembered to build the current states of Goiás and Tocantins, the latter becoming part of the northern region. In the econometric exercises performed, the states of Goiás and Tocantins were considered as a single unit to make the analysis compatible with the data of the 1980s.

the smaller the number of individuals in the cell, the greater the error of the variable we want to measure (proportion with 7 years of study) and therefore the lower the weight we want give to this information.

7.3 Descriptive Analysis of Data

In this section we want to present some information about child labour in Brazil. As our first econometric exercise analyses the proportion of child labour when the individual was 14 years old, we will first quantify this information. Figure 7.1 shows the percentage of individuals of 14 years old who are declared to work. These data were extracted from the PNADs between 1992 and 2015. During this period, there was a significant drop in the percentage of child labour. In 1992, for example, approximately 31.64% of the individuals of 14 years old worked, while in 2015 this amount decreased to 6.33%.

Figure 7.2 shows the same information but now in absolute values. In this case, it can be observed that in 1992, for example, there were more than 1 million young people aged 14 years working in Brazil. In 2015, this amount has been reduced to just over 200,000 young people.

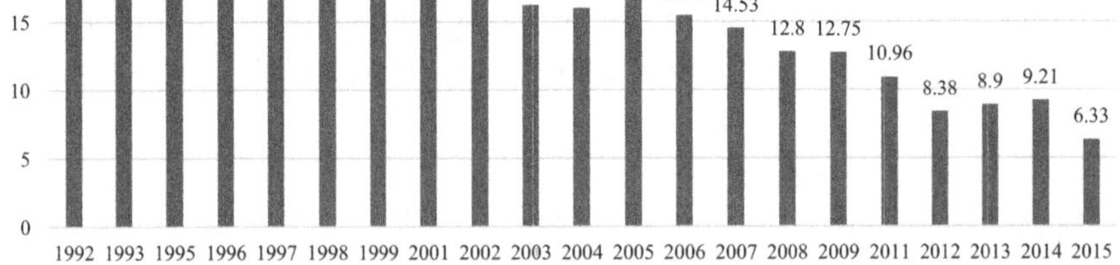

Fig. 7.1 Percentage of children of 14 years old who worked. (Source: Prepared by the author based on the PNADs from 1992 to 2015)

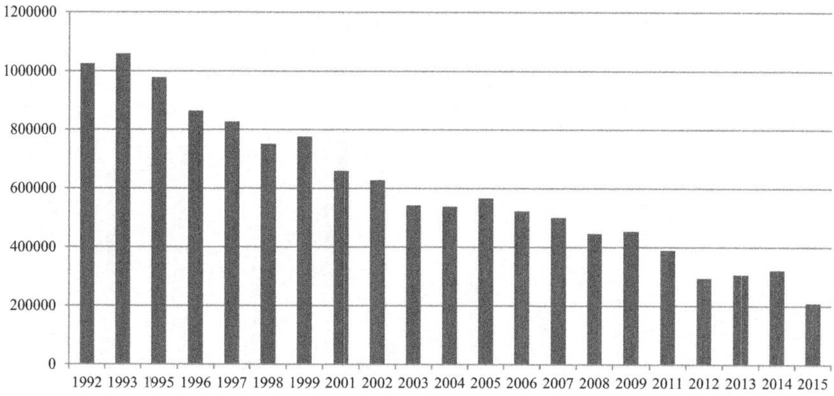

Fig. 7.2 Number of children of 14 years old working. (Source: Prepared by the author based on the PNADs from 1992 to 2015)

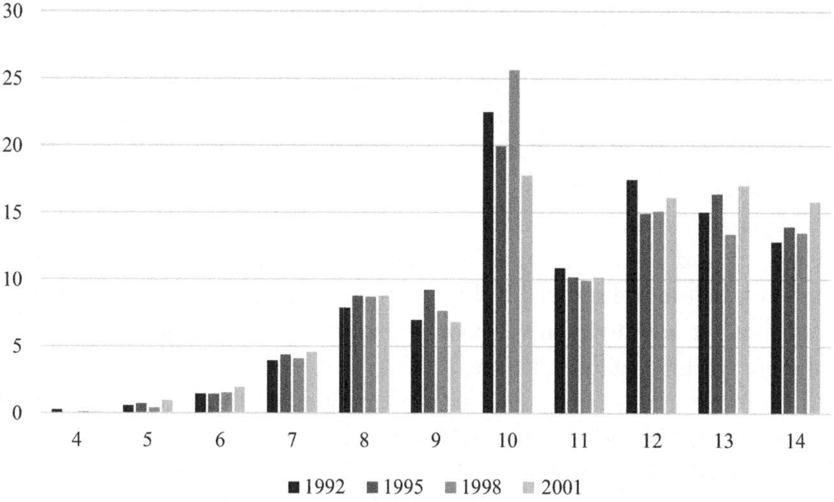

Fig. 7.3 Age at which the individuals of 14 years old begun to work, In percentage, for years 1992, 1995, 1998 and 2001 of the PNAD. (Source: Prepared by the author based on the PNADs of 1992, 1995, 1998 and 2001)

Figures 7.3 and 7.4 show the ages at which these individuals of 14 years old began to work. For each figure, a few years of the PNAD were selected for the analysis. In the two figures, it is observed that most of the young people began to work before the age of 14 years.

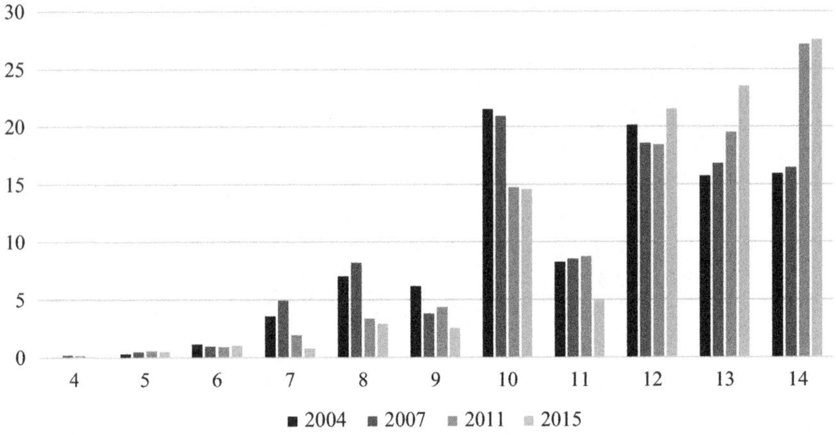

Fig. 7.4 Age at which the individuals of 14 years old began to work, in percentage, for years 2004, 2007, 2011 and 2015 of the PNAD. (Source: Prepared by the author based on the 2004, 2007, 2011 and 2015 PNADs)

For year 1992, for example, it is observed that 22.51% of the young people started working at age 10, 10.88% started working at age 11, 17.44% started working at age 12, 7.87% started working at age 8 and so on.

Although these results are not uniform, what can be observed in Figs. 7.3 and 7.4 is that in all the years most of the young people began to work before the age of 14. That is, these data corroborate our hypothesis that if the individual was working at the age of 14, he was probably already working before this age.

As our econometric exercise also analyses the proportion of child labour when the individual was 13 years old, Fig. 7.5 shows this information between the period of 1992 and 2014.

What can be observed is that over the period, there was a significant drop in the percentage of child labour. In 1992, for example, approximately 25.13% of the individuals of 13 years old worked, while in 2014 this decreased to 6.07%. To show that most of these individuals started working before the age of 13, Fig. 7.6 shows the percentage of individuals of 13 years old who reported working and who reported to begin working before the age of 13. As can be seen, Fig. 7.6 is similar to Fig. 7.5.

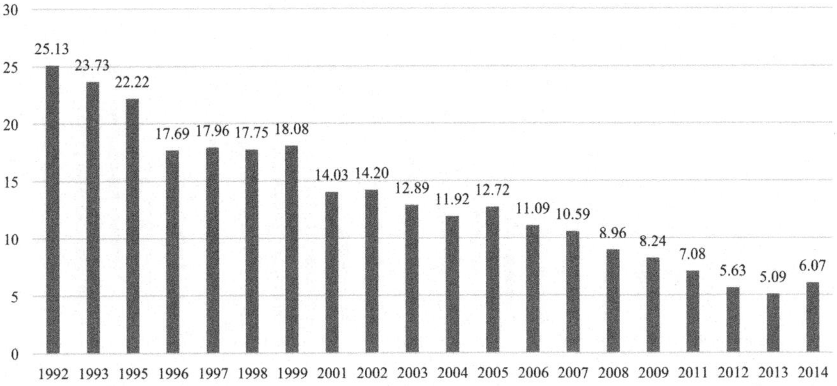

Fig. 7.5 Percentage of children of 13 years old who worked. (Source: Prepared by the author based on the PNADs from 1992 to 2014)

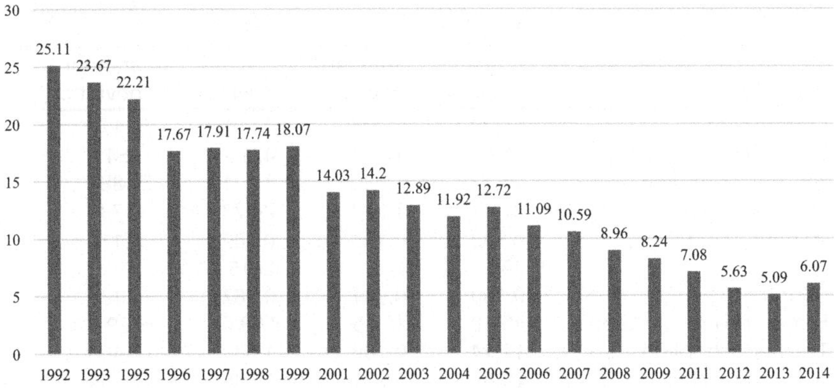

Fig. 7.6 Percentage of children of 13 years old who worked and who began to work before this age. (Source: Prepared by the author based on the PNADs from 1992 to 2014)

Figure 7.7 shows for each year, between 1992 and 2015, the average proportions of individuals who had 7 years or more of completed studies. There is a trend of growth of the average of this proportion, which in 1992 was 0.13 and in 2015 was 0.44.

Table 7.1 presents the descriptive statistics for the control variables used in the model. To simplify the analysis, we will present only the data for some selected years.

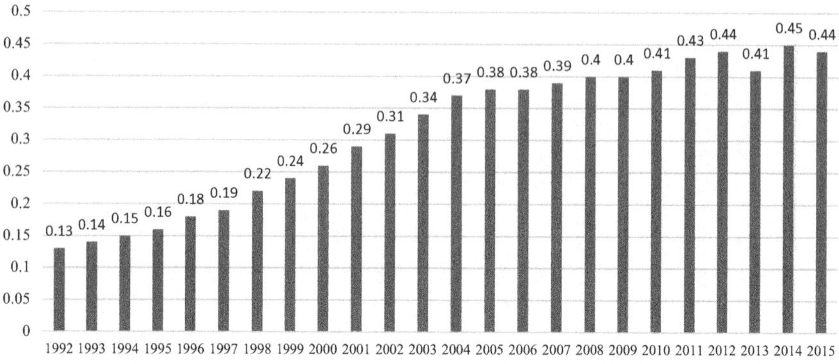

Fig. 7.7 Average proportion of individuals with 7 or more years of study completed. (Source: Prepared by the author based on the PNADs from 1992 to 2015)

Table 7.1 Descriptive statistics of control variables

	1992		1999	
Variables	Average	Standard deviation	Average	Standard deviation
Countryside	0.278	0.204	0.226	0.175
Family income per capita	362.1	146.2	421.7	154.4
Teacher' schooling	11.23	1.130	11.71	0.886
student_teacher	27.47	10.13	24.73	5.736
student_adult	0.542	0.129	0.509	0.119
	2007		2015	
Countryside	0.180	0.141	0.1627	0.135
Family income per capita	451.0	162.5	598.68	229.8
Teacher' schooling	12.74	0.709	13.85	0.463
student_teacher	20.89	3.281	19.85	2.664
student_adult	0.435	0.098	0.3126	0.067

Source: Prepared by the author based on the 1992, 1999, 2007 and 2015 PNADs

From Table 7.1, it can be observed that over the period there was an improvement in the mean value of these variables. For example, the average per capita household income increased from 362.1 *reais* to 598.68 *reais*.[10] In addition, there was an increase in the average of teacher education and a drop in the number of students per teacher.

[10] *Reais* is the currency used in Brazil.

7.4 Results

The result for the first econometric analysis can be found in Table 7.2. It is observed that our main analysis variable, that is, the proportion of the generation that at 14 years of age was working (*child labour*) had a coefficient of minus 1.154428 and a marginal effect of minus 0.0090268, which means that working reduces by 1 percentage points the probability of the individual having completed 7 years of study at the age of 14. In addition, this result is statistically significant at 1%.

Regarding the control variables, it can be observed that teachers' schooling and the ratio of students per adult are also statistically significant at 1%. These results show that increasing teacher education increases the likelihood that the individual will have 7 or more years of schooling

Table 7.2 Coefficients and marginal effects for the proportion of individuals of 14 years of age that were working and had 7 years of elementary school completed, by state, between 1992 and 2015

Variables	Coefficient	Marginal effect
Constant	−5.722466[a]	
	(0.994353)	
Child labour	−1.154428[a]	−0.0090268
	(0.3096068)	
Countryside	0.5207828	0.0040721
	(0.4439138)	
ln_family income per capita	0.1963928	0.0015357
	(0.1600318)	
Teacher' schooling	0.3724164[a]	0.002912
	(0.0319643)	
student_teacher	0.0004919	0.00000385
	(0.0043775)	
student_adult	−2.275946[a]	−0.0177963
	(0.4579103)	
Number of observations		*618*
R-squared		*0.9385*

Source: Prepared by the author
The regression is conditional on the state and year dummies
The regressions are weighted by the cell size
[a]Significant at 1%

when he or she is 14 years of age by 0.3 percentage points. In addition, the higher the ratio of students per adult, the less likely the individual is to have completed 7 or more years of schooling at 14 years of age. Another interesting result is that the higher the family income per capita, the greater the likelihood that the individual will have 7 or more years of schooling at 14 years of age. However, this result is not statistically significant at 1%.

Table 7.3 presents the same regression, but in this case, it shows the impact of *child labour* when the individuals were 13 years old on the probability of the conclusion of 7 years of elementary school.

In this case, the child labour variable had a coefficient of minus 0.9901942 and a marginal effect of minus 0.0098333, which means that working reduces the probability of the individual having completed

Table 7.3 Coefficients and marginal effects for the proportion of individuals of 13 years of age that were working and had 7 years of elementary school completed, by state, between 1993 and 2015

Variables	Coefficient	Marginal effect
Constant	−5.432895[a]	
	(1.069411)	
Child labour	−0.9901942[a]	−0.0098333
	(0.3500811)	
Countryside	0.4092675	0.0040643
	(0.4618371)	
ln_family income per capita	0.1593857	0.0015828
	(0.1692698)	
Teacher' schooling	0.3552717[a]	0.0035281
	(0.0334351)	
student_teacher	0.004213	0.0000418
	(0.0044913)	
student_adult	−2.391406[a]	−0.0237483
	(0.469237)	
Number of observations		*593*
R-squared		*0.9358*

Source: Prepared by the author
The regression is conditional on the state and year dummies
The regressions are weighted by the cell size
[a]Significant at 1%

7 years of schooling at 14 years of age by 1 percentage points. That is, we practically found the same results that we found before. In addition, this result is statistically significant at 1%.

7.5 Conclusion

In this chapter, we estimate the effect of child labour on students' school performance using an indicator that shows those who had 7 or more years of complete study at 14 years of age. The results obtained show that the work has a negative effect on the likelihood of an individual having 7 or more years of complete study.

This is not the first research that found this relationship between child labour and school performance; other authors have already found similar results. However, the differential of this work is that it considers the variables related to the quality of education in Brazil. In addition, by using a data set that varies over time, it is possible that this model is capturing changes in the educational system over time and with respect to possible changes in the states.

This result suggests that child labour is detrimental to the future of these children, since schooling is strongly related to the future income of individuals. Furthermore, our indicator looks only if that individual reached the eighth grade (when we consider 8 years of elementary school) but does not measure individuals' abilities in the contents of each grade. In Brazil, unfortunately, it is common for a student to pass the year without knowing all the basic content of the grade. That way, having reached the eighth grade does not necessarily mean that he or she knows all the content, which can further hamper his future development.

Annex: Educational generation

	1985	1986	1987	1988	1989	1990	1991	1992	1993	1994	1995	1996	1997	1998	1999
G1	1°			4°			7°	E							
G2		1°			4°			7°	E						
G3			1°			4°			7°	E					
G4				1°			4°			7°	E				
G5					1°			4°			7°	E			
G6						1°			4°			7°	E		
G7							1°			4°			7°	E	
G8								1°			4°			7°	E
G9									1°			4°			7°
G10										1°			4°		
G11											1°			4°	
G12												1°			4°
G13													1°		
G14														1°	
G15															1°
G16															
G17															
G18															
G19															
G20															
G21															
G22															
G23															
G24															

G1 = Generation of those born between July 1977 and June 1978. In 1985 this generation would have to be 7 years old and would be entering the first grade (when we consider the elementary school of 8 years) or second year (when we consider the elementary school of 9 years). For this generation, 1992 shows the proportion of individuals of 14 years old who had completed 7 or more years of elementary school; ... G24 = Generation of those born between July 2000 and June 2001. In 2008 this generation would have to be 7 years old and would be entering the first grade (when we consider the elementary school of 8 years) or second year (when we consider the elementary school of 9 years). For this generation, 2015 shows the proportion of individuals of 14 years old who had completed 7 or more years of elementary school

E = Proportion of the individuals of 14 years old who had, at least, 7 years of elementary school completed

1°, 4°, 7° = Years used of the PNAD to calculate the mean value of control variables

2000	2001	2002	2003	2004	2005	2006	2007	2008	2009	2010	2011	2012	2013	2014	2015
E															
7°	E														
	7°	E													
		7°	E												
4°			7°	E											
	4°			7°	E										
		4°			7°	E									
1°			4°			7°	E								
	1°			4°			7°	E							
		1°			4°			7°	E						
			1°			4°			7°	E					
				1°			4°			7°	E				
					1°			4°			7°	E			
						1°			4°			7°	E		
							1°			4°			7°	E	
								1°			4°			7°	E

References

Almeida, R.B., and E.T. Pazello. 2010. O efeito da pré-escola sobre o desempenho escolar futuro dos indivíduos. In *38 Encontro Nacional de Economia – ANPEC*. Salvador, Brazil: Anais do 38 Encontro Nacional de Economia – ANPEC.

Almeida, R.B. 2015. *O efeito das fiscalizações do trabalho para a redução do trabalho infantil no Brasil*. Tese de doutorado apresentada ao Programa de Pós – Graduação em Economia Aplicada da ESALQ/USP, Piracicaba.

Basu, K. 1998. *Child labor: Cause, consequences and cure, with remarks on International Labor Standards*. http://elibrary.worldbank.org/doi/pdf/10.1596/1813-9450-2027.

Brasil. 2011. Plano Nacional de Prevenção e Erradicação do Trabalho Infantil e Proteção do Adolescente Trabalhador/Comissão Nacional de Erradicação do Trabalho Infantil – 2. Ed. – Brasília: Ministério do Trabalho e Emprego. 95 p.

Fyfe, A. 2007. *The worldwide movement against child labor: Progress and future directions*. Geneva: International Labour Office (ILO). (Report) http://www.ilo.org/ipecinfo/product/viewProduct.do?productId=5168. Acesso em: 22 abr de 2013.

Internacional Labor Organization (ILO). 2019a. What is child labour. https://www.ilo.org/ipec/facts/lang%2D%2Den/index.htm.

———. 2019b. Trabalho infantil. https://www.ilo.org/brasilia/temas/trabalho-infantil/lang%2D%2Dpt/index.htm.

Kassouf, A.L. 2007. O que conhecemos sobre o trabalho infantil? *Nova Economia* 17 (2): 323–350. Belo Horizonte.

Ministério Da Educação (MEC). 2009. Ensino fundamental de nove anos: passo a passo do processo de implantação. http://portal.mec.gov.br/index.php?option=com_docman&view=download&alias=700-passoapasso9anos-pdf&Itemid=30192.

Natenzon, P.E. 2003. *Efeitos da Educação Pré-Escolar no Brasil*. Monografia apresentada ao Departamento de Economia da Faculdade de Economia, Administração e Contabilidade da Universidade de São Paulo.

Ono, I.B. 2015. O impacto do trabalho infantil no desempenho escolar. Dissertação – Escola Superior de Agricultura "Luiz de Queiroz", 144p.

Pesquisa Nacional Por Amostra De Domicílios (PNAD). 2015. Síntese de Indicadores 2015. https://biblioteca.ibge.gov.br/visualizacao/livros/liv98887.pdf.

8

Implications of Child Labour Earnings for Household Well-Being in Cameroon

Fabien Sundjo

8.1 Introduction

According to the World Bank (2006), the fraction of people living with less than a US dollar per day rose from 45% to 46% from 1990 to 2000 with most of them located in sub-Saharan Africa (SSA). Being a sub-Saharan African country, Cameroon does not in anywhere escape from this depicted poverty image. Whereas, 10 years before the middle of the 1980s, she registered a sustained annual average growth of 7% (Government of Cameroon 2003), it should however be noted that since then this has not always been the case, due to severe economic and social crises that affected the country after 1986. This crisis was caused by several factors, among which are the fall in world prices of agricultural

F. Sundjo (✉)
Department of Economics, Higher Teacher Training College,
University of Bamenda, Bamenda, Cameroon

A. Posso (ed.), *Child Labor in the Developing World*,
https://doi.org/10.1007/978-981-15-3106-4_8

products and other commodities (Epoh 2010), the depletion of income generation resource (oil) and the overvaluation of the CFA franc against the US dollar[1] (Baye 2006).

This led to the deterioration of several economic indicators as the 40% drop in per capital consumption between 1985–1986 and 1992–1993 that accompanied the fall in income (Baye 2010), the rise in external debt between 1984 and 1992 (Mbanga and Sikod 2002) and the turndown of investment in the same period from 27% to about 11% of GDP (Government of Cameroon 2003). The freeze in increments and recruitment in public services increases unemployment rates and underemployment (Baye 2010) which perpetrated poverty among households. HIV/AIDS compounded the issue by either increasing adult death rate (NIS 2008) or rendering adults economically less productive. All these further deteriorated the well-being of households in Cameroonian.

In order to augment the well-being of her citizens, Cameroon adopted the World Bank and the International Monetary Fund (IMF) Structural Adjustment Programme (SAP) which turned out to aggravate an already worst situation. Several other poverty reduction strategy plans that could fit the context of Cameroon were initiated and activated (Government of Cameroon 2003) such as the poverty reduction strategy paper (PRSP) and the 2009 growth and employment strategy paper (GESP).

Despite all these strategies, poverty remains a hard nut to crack (NIS 2008; Epoh et al. 2011). According to the 2007 Cameroon household consumption survey (CHCS), about 40% (7.1 million) of the population still live below the minimum necessary for survival. The poverty depth[2] is associated with a poverty intensity of nearly 31%, indicating a shortfall of 83,500FCFA per year for an average poor person. In this light poverty could have been eradicated by the government in 2007 if she could transfer a sum of roughly 433 billion FCFA[3] to the poor. Such a mechanism to eradicate poverty is elusive in the context where the

---

[1] Reference here is made to the 1985 exchange rates.

[2] Which measures the gap between the average annual expenditure per adult equivalent consumption of poor households and the poverty line is 12.3%.

[3] Since the 7,131,000 poor within the entire territory in 2007 corresponds to 5,211,000 when the adult equivalent scale is considered.

government had barely been coping with budgetary deficit that once led to the slashing of civil service salaries by 60%.[4]

Being aware of the impossibility for public authorities to transfer the annual shortfall of 83,500FCFA to an average poor person in each poor household, the poor households have turned to the informal sector by employing coping strategies irrespective of whether they are legal or illegal. Among these, they have considered all the members of the household as an important asset in the eradication of household poverty (Guarcello et al. 2006). Children are no longer considered as "passive objects", but as active members of the household who can influence both household conditions (Ben-Arieh 2006) and those of their own peers (Manacorda 2006).

In such a context, some parents no longer considered child labour as a delinquent activity, but as training the child with survival skills (Grootaert and Kanbur 1995) with immediate benefit in cash or kind that contribute to household well-being (Basu and Van 1998). Such convictions have increased the incidence of economically active children in Cameroon. Economic activity in children covers most of the work done by them, whether they work for the labour market or not, they are paid or not, they work part-time or full-time, and it is casual or regular and legal or illegal, and it does not include work done at home or at school. While ILO estimated the incidence of child labourto be 23.7% in 2000, in 2010 the rate was 31% according to the UNICEF statistics.

While Psacharopoulos (1997), Menon et al. (2005) and Basu and Van (1998) consider child labour resources as a vital component for household survival[5] and are sometimes used as a strategy to minimize the risk of interruption of the income stream of the household, authors like Canagarajah and Coulombe (1997) and Nielsen (1998) reject this idea. They consider child income to be too small to affect well-being as children in most cases are paid less than adult for the same task. In addition, Bhalotra and Heady (2003) showed that in Peru and Pakistan the well-being[6] improving hypothesis was not confirmed.

[4] This occurred in 1993.

[5] With this reaching 50% in some areas as noted by Cockburn 2000.

[6] Well-being was implicitly considered through poverty.

On the bases of the above background and variety of findings, it is evident that the effect of child labour on household well-being is inconclusive, suggesting that results are certainly context specific. The key question tackled in this study is: What is the effect of child labour resources on both objective and subjective household well-being in Cameroon? From this research question, the major objective of this study is to evaluate the effects of child labour resources on both objective and subjective household well-being in Cameroon. Specifically, it scrutinizes the possible influences of:

- Child labour wage on household objective well-being
- Child labour wage on household subjective well-being

In order to achieve these specific objectives, all other things being equal, we test the following hypotheses:

- Child labour wage enhances household objective well-being.
- Child labour wage enhances household subjective well-being.

The importance of such a question, in the context of Cameroon, is policy wise relevant as responses will inform us whether or not child labour is necessary for household subsistence and will enable us to start understanding why parents continue to ignore conventions against child labour. If the subsistence argument is binding, then policies that advocate the total eradication of child labour from child's rights perspective need to be reconsidered in the Cameroon context. Otherwise, child labour is more of a cultural than economic problem. If this is the case, then human rights arguments based on the enforcement of child labour laws are necessary. In addition, the deprivation theory argues that the employed can be assimilated with higher well-being, while the incentive theory asserts they have lower well-being as they may not voluntarily decide to work. Answers from the present research will reveal the maxim that matches the context of Cameroon, especially as more than half of the population is made up of the under 18 (NIS 2008).

The postulation that child labour is detrimental to children's development underpins both the theoretical literature and the policy debate. For instance, from the policy perspective, there is a general view that the worldwide returns to eliminating child labour are very large (ILO 2003). Despite the idea that child labour can contribute to household well-being, the evidence that rigorously quantifies the positive consequences of child labour on the child or household is scarce in Cameroon, partly because neither Cameroon Household Consumption Survey I nor II contained issues on child labour. However, thanks to the relatively recent CHCS III, such an investigation is possible. Revisiting this issue using the individual level data from the 2007 (CHCS III) carried out by the National Institute of Statistics (NIS) is important. The difference between the CHCS of 2007 and CHCS of 1996 and 2001 is substantial. However, with respect to our study, the striking difference relies on the observation that children from the ages of 5 to 17 were included for the first time, with the prime objective, the understanding of the phenomenon of child labour. This study will, therefore, address this research gaps in Cameroon and will set an academic springboard for future studies.

The rest of the chapter is organized as follows. Section 2 reviews the literature; Sect. 3 presents the measurement issues and model specification, while Sect. 4 highlights the estimation-related issues. Section 5 describes the data. The expected results and the dissemination strategies are presented in Sect. 6.

8.2 Literature Review

While there are remarkable empirical literatures on child labour, especially those focusing on descriptive statistic (Bequele and Boyden 1988; Addison et al. 1997; and the reference therein), they can, however, be criticized for being unable to provide adequate information on why children work. This may result from insufficient data on working and nonworking children, as well as on household and community characteristics.

These shortcomings have, however, been resolved with the advent of household survey data, which facilitates empirical investigations. Among child labour studies that exploit household surveys are Lloyd, Cigno et al. (2000), DeGraff et al. (1993), Kambhampati and Rajan (2004) and

Bonnet (1993). These authors, however, did not lay emphasis on household assets nor on household poverty which is an important problem in developing countries. For instance, Lloyd and Cigno et al. (2000) laid emphasis on household size, while DeGraff et al. (1993) focused on fertility-related issue, and Bonnet's (1993) centre of attention was the debt incurred by parents. Nonetheless, with the exception of debt incurred, household size and fertility-related issues are relatively pertinent in the developing country context. This notwithstanding, poverty has remained the most common and most substantial problem in developing countries (Ravallion and Wodon 2000; NIS 2008; Epoh et al. 2011) and could be the root of child labour.

Getting closer to address issues relating child labour to poverty are Bhalotra and Heady (2003), Yunita (2006), Sharif (1994), Basu and Tzannatos (2003) and Basu et al. (2007) who all explore the issue of poverty while focusing on household land wealth in the context of child labour. Considering the absence or smaller quantity of land as an indicator of poverty, Yunita (2006) and Bhalotra and Heady (2003) found out that the quantity of land was positively associated with child labour. Sharif's (1994) study however did not confirm this, and he argued that as the amount of household wealth (land) increases the family ceases to operate their own lands and rent them out. For Basu and Tzannatos (2003), this relation was neither positive nor negative as they observed an inverted U-shaped relation between land, wealth and child labour. Using the quantity of land as a measure of poverty does not sound pertinent in the context of our research question. This is because while a working child can contribute to household subsistence resources that can enhance household well-being, child labour resources are likely not to be enough to acquire more land.

Studies that explicitly pick up the poverty hypothesis can be classified into two main categories: those that stress that resources from child labour are vital for family survival, hence justifying child labour to be poverty driven, and those that reject this claim. In the first category, Chiwaula (2010), Okpukpara and Odurukwe (2006), Blunch and Verner (2000) and Ray (2000) all found a positive relation between poverty and child labour in Malawi, Nigeria, Ghana and Pakistan, respectively. This clearly shows as indicated by Chiwaula (2010) that the likelihood of participating in child labour increases as household consumption falls. This suggests that children work to enhance household well-being.

While in Paraguay child labour contributes to about one-third of household income, an amount definitely not negligible, in Bolivia it contributed to 13% to total household income on average (Patrinos and Psacharopoulos 1994). In the same vein, and using a survey of 110 households, Sharma and Mittar (1990) showed that child labour income in India was very substantial as they contributed above 20% in two-thirds of the households and more than 40% in one-fifth of the households. In effect, it was found out that the number of households below or on the poverty line having the minimum necessary for survival was increased when the child labour income was retrieved from household income. As such child labour income is capable of uplifting a household from below the minimum necessary for survival to this minimum or even above (Sharma and Mittar 1990).

In the same context, the self-insurance strategy was tested by Jacoby and Skoufias (1997), Jensen (2000) and Beegle et al. (2006). They confirmed the self-insurance strategy. In effect, children were all removed from schools and sent to the labour market when an unanticipated crop failure due to insect or fire accident occurred. This confirms the result of Basu and Van (1998) in which child labour contributions are necessary and substantial. In Brazil, while child labour contribution lies between 10 and 30% for approximately 50% of the sample (Kassouf 1998), in Paraguay, Myers (1989) showed that child labour income contributed at least half of the household income for 50% of the household. The question remains whether these contributions in cash or in kind effectively ameliorate household well-being.

The second category of literature regroups authors who fail to affirm that child labour resources can augment household well-being. In this direction, Grootaert and Kanbur (1995), Nielsen (1998), Bhalotra and Heady (2001), Beegle et al. (2006), Kassouf (1998) and Jensen challenge the conventional wisdom that child labour emerges from poverty. Evidence exists to which children may work just to gain independence and not because of family poverty. This is explicit in the work of Delap (1998) in urban Bangladesh as sited by Bhalotra (2000). In such a context, child labour cannot increase household income and has nothing to do with household well-being.

Most studies that find household incomes uncorrelated with child labour are confronted with some unresolved estimation issues (Ray 2000).[7] Firstly, child labour income may not contribute to household income simply because children may be paid in kind rather than in cash. This is evident in Cameroon where children work sometimes for 18 hours per day for payment in kind (LUTRENA 2003),[8] with some of them receiving 3000 CFA francs[9] per month according to the 2003 LUTRENA study. Secondly, most studies in their specification consider household income or household poverty as being exogenous. As noted by Bhalotra (2000), this can create a positive bias in the OLS coefficients. This problem can be solved if appropriate instrumental variables are used (Bhalotra 2000) or by tracking children in the same house over time (Edmonds 2007). An attempt will be made in view to resolve these problems in the present study.

8.3 Measurement Issues and Model Specification

8.3.1 Measurement Issues

Child wage to be used in the estimation is the imputed wage from child labour activity extracted from the 2007 CHCS. As child labourers, we shall consider only economically active children. Economic activity in children covers most of the work done by them, whether they work for the labour market or not, they are paid or not, they work part-time or full-time, and it is casual or regular and legal or illegal. It does not include work done at home or at school. For the interest of this study, we followed the definition of economically active children. Nevertheless, we

[7] He tried to solve this by retrieving child income from household income.

[8] A survey by the Subregional Project for the Fight against the Trafficking of Children in West and Central Africa (LUTRENA).

[9] 1 US dollar = 500 CFA F on average.

ignored unpaid work as we were interested in the effect of paid work on household well-being. This is because the 2007 CHCS explicitly posed a question based on the amount received in monetary terms by the child, if any. To capture the outcome variable of household well-being, two indicators will be used.

First, we propose to use an objective measure of well-being, in which well-being is considered as "a measure or degree of people security with the vital blessings, means of existence". This is what is referred to in the literature as economic household well-being with annual consumption expenditure per adult equivalent acting as its proxy (Slesnick 1998) and includes purchase and auto consumption.

This economic household well-being will be constructed at three stages; firstly, it is calculated at the household level. Then, in the second stage, it is normalized by dividing by the number of adult equivalence in the household so as to account for the differences in household composition. Finally, the resultant is then divided by a spatial deflator that takes into account differences in the cost of living between regions. This indicator is better than household income and permits the rating to be objective and hence adequate for comparison across individuals, households or regions.

Nevertheless, the consumption-based proxy considered by economists to be the best has been criticized by Alkire, Sen (1999), Diener and Seligman (2004), Ryff, Diener (2000) and Perry. Sen (1999) and Perry argue that it relies more on the means than on well-being itself. A life well lived is linked to personal happiness or feeling and must be evaluated based on a subjective approach (Ryan and Deci 2001). The merit of the subjective indicator is that it is multidimensional as it involves social, psychological, economic, cultural, physical and environmental dimensions. This indicator is important, as calculated annual consumption expenditure per adult equivalent might be high, while the household believes they are not better off (Sen 1999). In this light we shall add household subjective well-being indicator which is related to how individuals themselves judge their own well-being.

8.3.2 Model Specification

We depart from the general specification in the child labour literature in which child working status or hours worked is modelled as the dependent variable (Baland and Robinson 2000; Patrinos and Psacharopoulos 1994; Okpukpara and Odurukwe 2006; Sasaki and Temesgen 1999). The estimation of the relationship between household well-being (objective and subjective) and child wage will be based on the following empirical model of household well-being determination:

$$W_{cf} = X\delta + \beta CW + \varepsilon \tag{8.1}$$

where W_{cf} represents well-being which could be subjective (self-assessed well-being) or objective (captured by annual consumption expenditure per adult equivalent) during estimation. X is a vector of exogenous covariates such as individual, household, community and regional characteristics, and δ is a vector of parameters including the constant term and those of exogenous explanatory variables that correlate with W_{cf}. β is the parameter associated with the endogenous "treatment variable"[10] child labour wage (CW), while ε is the error term. In order to estimate Eq. (8.1), we propose to use an econometric technique that takes care of potential estimation issues.

8.4 Estimation Issues

Regressing Eq. (8.1) by OLS will yield biased estimates and hence err policy recommendations if endogeneity, heterogeneity and intra-household correlation problems are not considered and handled with care. Endogeneity can emerge from the likelihood that well-to-do households may have children who are well equipped calorie wise and therefore able to handle income-generating tasks in family firms or even out of home. A

[10] See Strauss and Thomas (2007).

well-fed child can participate in child labour for longer hours, and if payment is linked to the number of hours worked, they will definitely generate sufficient income. In the same vein, a working child, due to payment in kind or cash, can contribute in the amelioration of the household well-being (Basu and Van 1998; Edmonds 2007 and Manacorda 2006). This suggests a bidirectional link between household well-being and child labour wage, hence posing the problem of simultaneity.

Further, the difficulties and complexities in understanding and defining child labour and hence child wage can be another source of endogeneity. In such a case, respondents especially children are likely not to give precise values of child wage leading to measurement errors[11] that can further compound the endogeneity issues. To handle these endogeneity problems, Dammert (2005) and Duryea and Arends-Kuenning (2003) applied a mechanical approach that retrieves from household well-being any child labour income. While this approach can deal with mechanical endogeneity, Edmonds (2007) however highlights that this does not solve broader endogeneity problems.

Another estimation problem that is likely to surface is heterogeneity bias from unobserved preferences that influence the choice of current household well-being inputs (Schultz 2008; Rosenzweig and Wolpin 1980). In the household well-being production function, the issue of heterogeneity may originate from exogenous well-being factors that are not observable by a researcher but are however known to the individual household (Rosenzweig and Schultz 1983; Kabubo-Mariara et al. 2009). For instance, the observation that the family's current well-being input is a choice variable is likely to introduce heterogeneity bias in the household well-being function.

In addition, self-assessed well-being depends on respondent assessment and hence on factors specific to the individual. Further, the link between household well-being and child wage is such that poor household will differ from rich ones in several ways and disentangling these is difficult (Edmonds 2007). Finally, the amount of wage contributed by each child for household well-being will be ruled by his instincts which can be egoistic or altruistic. In this case, individual-specific covariates are intended

[11] The measurement error that causes endogeneity in this case is that linked to child labour.

to incorporate observation-specific effects (Greene 1993). As noted by Kabubo-Mariara et al. (2009) and Rosenzweig and Schultz (1983), this exogenous well-being heterogeneity definitely will produce deceptive results as well as policy inference.

Intra-household correlation is another potential problem as members belonging to the same household are more likely to be similar than non-members with regard to several measures. This does not only reduce the effective sample size but influence the standard errors of the estimates, hence rendering significance tests invalid. Arceneaux (2005) points out the need to correct the standard error by accounting for the idea that individuals within clusters share unobserved characteristics. If one fails to account for endogeneity, heterogeneity and intra-household correlation issues, in the estimations, estimates will be unreliable (Mwabu 2009; Rosenzweig and Schultz 1983). In the midst of all these, ample effort will be allocated to deal with these issues. From Eq. (8.1), to resolve these estimation problems, we propose to make use of a reduced form equation:

$$CW = Z\gamma + \xi \tag{8.2}$$

Where Z is a vector of exogenous variables that includes X covariates in Eq. (8.1) and a vector of instrumental variables. γ represents a vector of parameters including the constant term and those of exogenous explanatory variables that correlate with child wage, while ξ is the error term. The reduced form Eq. (8.2) will be run using the OLS estimator and the resultant residual, $\hat{\xi}$, predicted.

In this context, Eq. (8.1) will be augmented with the fitted residual, $\hat{\xi}$, from Eq. (8.2) and run as the two-stage least squares (2SLS). This approach will yield consistent estimates if unobserved variables are linear in $\hat{\xi}$. Nevertheless, this approach does not take care of any potential non-linear interactions of unobservable variables with the household economic well-being, hence the advantage of the control function approach over the IV technique.

Regarding the heterogeneity-related problem, we shall employ the control function approach (CFA) used for the first time by Garen (1984) in the schooling context. The standard IV approach does not eliminate the influence of the heterogeneity in all situations (Garen 1984). The IV technique produces biased and inconsistent estimates when the unobservable in the economic well-being function conditional on the instruments does not depend on the instruments (Kabubo-Mariara et al. 2009).

In this light, we employed the CFA (Garen 1984; Mwabu 2009; Baye and Fambon 2009) which is based not only on inserting the residual from the child wage reduced form equation into Eq. (8.1)[12] but equally on the insertion of the interaction of the fitted residuals with the potential endogenous variables *CW*. This will then purge any effect of the unobservable and permits child wage to be treated as an exogenous variable in the household well-being function. This gives rise to the control function in Eq. (8.3):

$$W_{cf} = X\delta + \beta CW + \lambda\hat{\xi} + \upsilon CW * \hat{\xi} + \mu. \tag{8.3}$$

λ and υ are the parameters associated with the fitted residual and the interaction term, while μ is the error term. The term $\hat{\xi}$ represents the estimated residual from the child wage treatment equation in Eq. (8.2), and $CW * \hat{\xi}$ represents the interaction term portraying the idea that the unobservable varies non-linearly with child wage. All these are control function variables because they control for any effect from unobservable factors that would otherwise bias the coefficients of the structural parameters (Ajakaiye and Mwabu 2007). As noted by Card (2001), the interaction term purges any endogeneity bias if the unobserved component is linear in the child wage residual. The non-linear indirect effect of child wage on well-being is captured by $v\hat{\xi}$.

Different estimation techniques will be used to run Eq. (8.3) depending on whether we are dealing with objective or subjective well-being. In the case of objective well-being, Eq. (8.3) is run using the OLS approach when well-being is captured by the annual consumption expenditure per adult equivalent. In the case of subjective well-being, using the popular multinomial probit or logit model fails to account for its ordinal nature, while the ordinary regression will err in the opposite direction (Greene 1993). In addition, because subjective well-being depends on

[12] As in the case of the IV approach.

respondent's assessment and hence on factors specific to the individual and can be ordered, we shall privilege an ordered response model for the estimation (Zovoina and McElvey 1975) which had its origin in biostatistics (Aitchison and Silvey 1957). It appears reasonable to use ordered probit, assuming that "very satisfied with life" is better than "not very satisfied" which is in turn better than "not just satisfied with life".

With subjective well-being, Eq. (8.3) is therefore run using an ordered probit technique. In both cases estimation of Eq. (8.3) will be done in a stepwise fashion: (1) resolving no econometric problem, (2) addressing the problem of endogeneity and (3) addressing both the endogeneity and unobserved heterogeneity biases. In the initial version, the control function variables are ignored. In the IV version, the interaction term is ignored. In the control function version, all the variables in Eq. (8.3) are included.

8.5 Presentation of Data

The data used for this analysis is the 2007 Cameroon household consumption survey (2007 CHCS) collected by the government statistics office (National Institute of Statistics). This survey covers the national territory and involves all regular[13] households and its individuals. It includes, among others, housing characteristics, socio-demographic characteristics,[14] economic activities, perception of poverty, household consumption and most importantly child labour-related data. Though two other surveys had been carried out by the NIS in 1996 and 2001, we however shall privilege the 2007 survey, not necessarily because it is the most recent survey but because (1) the number of household surveyed increased to 11,391 as opposed to 1700 and 10,992 households in 1996 and 2001, respectively; (2) it incorporates child labour–related issues not found in the other surveys; and (3) the 1996 survey had 300 nomenclature

[13] This is used in order to oppose it from collective households that include boarding, barracks, hospitals and convents.

[14] Household composition, health, education and employment of household members.

consumer products against at least twice for the 2007 survey. The advantage of this is that it incorporates nearly all items necessary for household well-being.

In addition, while most child labour studies focused on child working status partly because child labour data failed to account for child labour intensity, the 2007 CHCS gives a value added to this study as it explicitly explores the issue of child wage and hours worked. As concerned instrument, we shall use children employment rate per region which will be gotten from the Survey on Employment and the Informal Sector (SEIS) carried out in 2005.

8.6 Empirical Results

8.6.1 Descriptive Statistics

Table 8.1 reveals the relationship between subjective poverty status and child activity options. It is evident from the table that the incident of participating in the work-only option increases as a family feels she has become poorer. This is in confirmation with Basu and Van (1998) study. This may suggests that when income falls below the minimum necessary for survival the likelihood for children to work in order to augment household income which ameliorates household subjective well-being is increased. In addition as postulated by the literature (Patrinos and Psacharopoulos 1995 and Nielsen 1998), the proportion of children combining school and child labour is higher in very poor households than in rich ones. In the same vein, the proportion of children who study only is increased as the family feels they are better off, further suggesting that children are likely to be retrieved from work places when the family goes above the minimum necessary for survival.

The seminal work of Basu and Van (1998) postulates that the main reason behind child labour is poverty and that its contribution is substantial for family survival. The present data to some extent seems to confirm that child labour is poverty driven as the number of hours worked by

Table 8.1 Child activity options and household subjective poverty status

	Child activity options			
Poverty status	No activity	Study only	Work only	Work and study
Very poor	3.48	58.11	6.57	31.84
Poor	2.68	61.58	6.07	31.84
Rich	2.75	74.85	3.65	18.75
Total	2.85	65.63	5.31	26.21

Source: From the author's calculation using the CHCS 2007

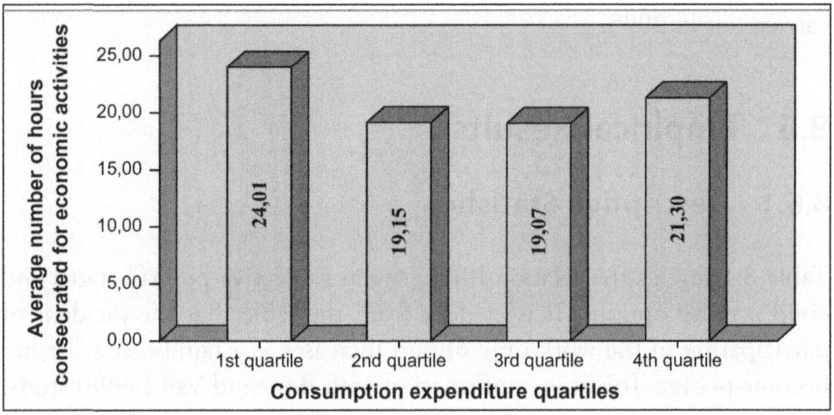

Graph 8.1 Average number of hours worked by children, age 5–17 years by household consumption expenditure quartiles. Source: From the author's calculation using the CHCS 2007

children in household located in the first quartile of consumption expenditure is the highest (24.01%) as indicated in Graph 8.1. If work performed by children generates payment in cash or in kind, then longer hours worked will certainly imply enough resources for survival for these families. Compared to other households in other quartiles, the importance of these resources is certainly vital for the household belonging to the first quartile of consumption expenditure. This might justify the longer hours worked for this category. Nevertheless, because the trend does not persist, the effect of the contribution from these longer hours worked to household well-being remains a major reason for econometric analysis.

The indicator of how much collinearity that a regression analysis can tolerate (tolerance) and the indicator of how much of the inflation of the standard error could be caused by collinearity (VIF) suggest in Table 8.2 that interrelationship among the various variables is not a cause for concern as both tolerance and VIF value pass the rule of thumb (Statistical Consulting Group)[15] of 0.1 or less and 10 or greater, respectively.[16] This suggests that resulting coefficients are free from inflated standard errors due to multicollinearity.

8.6.1.1 Household Objective Well-Being and Child Wage Results

The results of the various models are presented in Table 8.3, and their respective Chi-squared values indicate that the predicators are significant. From Table 8.3, it is evident that the size of the effect of various predicators on household well-being is not independent of the method used. For instance, the effect of child wage, child age and livestock ownership varies as we move from the OLS model to the IV model. In effect, the estimated effect of child wage on household well-being increases greatly from the OLS method to the IV technique and from the IV model to the CFA. In this light appropriate care needs to be taken to select the right model if reliable policies are to be inferred.

8.6.2 Regression Results

The coefficients associated with the reduced form child labour wage in both 3a and 3b of CFA are statistically significant with t-ratio = 4.63 and 3.03, respectively. This indicates that child wage is endogenous to well-being. From these coefficients it is evident that both the IV model and the CFA have a value added compared to the OLS method. In addition, as we move from the OLS model, the R-squared which measures how the

---

[15] Introduction to SAS UCLA: Statistical Consulting Group from http://www.ats.ucla.edu/stat/sas/notes2/ (accessed November 24, 2007).

[16] It is a call for concern if tolerance is 0.1 or less and when VIF is 10 or greater, respectively.

Table 8.2 Collinearity diagnostics test using tolerance and VIF indicators

	VIF	SQRT VIF	Tolerance	R-squared		Eigenvalue	Index
Male child	1.07	1.04	0.9305	0.0695	1	10.7805	1.0000
Child's age	1.08	1.04	0.9292	0.0708	2	0.9680	3.3372
Muslim	1.23	1.11	0.8136	0.1864	3	0.8995	3.4620
Agriculture sector work	1.74	1.32	0.5761	0.4239	4	0.7313	3.8394
Log (child's wage)	1.18	1.09	0.8485	0.1515	5	0.5820	4.3038
Female household head	1.15	1.07	0.8707	0.1293	6	0.4554	4.8656
Household age	1.25	1.12	0.7973	0.2027	7	0.4256	5.0329
Household head never gone to school	1.54	1.24	0.6478	0.3522	8	0.3422	5.6129
Household head not working	1.04	1.02	0.9631	0.0369	9	0.2844	6.1570
Household size	1.16	1.08	0.8640	0.1360	10	0.1614	8.1729
Household owns a farm	1.66	1.29	0.6035	0.3965	11	0.1507	8.4581
Income very unstable	1.04	1.02	0.9659	0.0341	12	0.0895	10.9728
Owns livestock	1.24	1.12	0.8042	0.1958	13	0.0629	13.0885
Urban areas	1.41	1.19	0.7076	0.2924	14	0.0471	15.1351
Child's employment rates	1.33	1.15	0.7532	0.2468	15	0.0154	26.4559
					16	0.0041	51.1897
Mean VIF	*1.27*						
Condition number					*51.1897*		
Det (correlation matrix)					*0.1457*		

Eigenvalues and Cond Index computed from scaled raw sscp (w/ intercept)
SQRT means square root

Table 8.3 Determinant of child wage and household objective well-being under different assumptions

	Well-being: endogenous child wage	Instrumental variable model		Control function approach	
		Instrumented child wage	Well-being	3a	3b
Child's characteristics					
Male child	−0.039	0.417	0.153	0.153	0.149
	(2.34)[b]	(16.13)[c]	(2.71)[c]	(3.46)[c]	(3.29)[c]
Child's age	0.003	0.068	0.033	0.033	0.032
	(0.67)	(12.12)[c]	(3.47)[c]	(4.30)[c]	(4.06)[c]
Muslim	0.213	0.141	0.289	0.289	0.289
	(6.02)[c]	(3.73)[c]	(6.81)[c]	(7.53)[c]	(7.52)[c]
Log (child's wage)	−0.015		−0.469	−0.469	−0.459
	(1.22)		(3.72)[c]	(4.78)[c]	(4.57)[c]
Parental characteristics (household head)					
Female	−0.013	−0.000	−0.031	−0.031	−0.030
	(0.41)	(0.01)	(0.79)	(0.95)	(0.94)
Age	0.005	0.002	0.006	0.006	0.006
	(5.41)[c]	(1.43)	(4.93)[c]	(5.93)[c]	(5.94)[c]
Never gone to school	−0.204	−0.007	−0.161	−0.161	−0.162
	(6.99)[c]	(0.14)	(4.33)[c]	(5.34)[c]	(5.36)[c]
Not working	−0.068	−0.104	−0.114	−0.114	−0.114
	(1.04)	(1.47)	(1.54)	(1.81)[a]	(1.81)[a]
Household characteristics					
Household size	0.072	0.006	0.075	0.075	0.075
	(8.12)[c]	(1.31)	(8.63)[c]	(8.27)[c]	(8.26)[c]
Income very unstable	−0.109	−0.210	−0.211	−0.211	−0.210
	(4.29)[c]	(5.96)[c]	(5.36)[c]	(6.28)[c]	(6.25)[c]
Owns livestock	−0.013	−0.194	−0.076	−0.076	−0.076
	(0.54)	(4.50)[c]	(2.10)[b]	(2.71)[c]	(2.69)[c]

(*continued*)

Table 8.3 (continued)

	Well-being: endogenous child wage	Instrumental variable model		Control function approach	
		Instrumented child wage	Well-being	3a	3b
Household owns a farm	0.060	−0.233	−0.016	−0.016	−0.014
	(1.10)	(4.15)[c]	(0.25)	(0.27)	(0.24)
Urban areas	−0.131	−0.316	−0.260	−0.260	−0.258
	(3.95)[c]	(7.81)[c]	(4.82)[c]	(5.85)[c]	(5.75)[c]
Constant	12.788	7.787	16.454	16.454	16.368
	(83.99)[c]	(62.58)[c]	(16.11)[c]	(20.69)[c]	(20.11)[c]
Control function variables					
Child's employ. rates		0.008			
		(5.60)[c]			
Child's wage residual				0.466	0.407
				(4.63)[c]	(3.03)[c]
Log (child's wage) [a]Residual					0.007
					(0.72)
Estimation statistics					
Observations	1,801,827	1,801,827	1,801,827	1,801,827	1,801,827
R-squared	0.36	0.19		0.37	0.37
F-test of excluded instruments				F(1, 2653) = 31.34	
				Prob > F = 0.0000	
Underidentification test Ho: underidentified: Kleibergen-Paap rk LM statistic				Chi-sq(1) = 25.29	
				P-val = 0.0000	

3a: Model with other controls with reduced form child wage residual
3b: Model with other controls with reduced form child wage residual interacted with child wage
Robust t statistics in parentheses
[a]Significant at 10%, [b]significant at 5% and [c]significant at 1%

independent variable explains the variation in the dependent variable is increased, further fortifying the superiority of the IV and CFA over the OLS estimator.

We employ the CFA of column 3b so as to address any heterogeneity-related issues (Mwabu 2009). The interacted term, child wage and the reduced form child wage residual, meant to purge the estimate of any effect of heterogeneity is statistically insignificant, suggesting that heterogeneity issues arising from interaction of child wage with unobserved determinants of household well-being are not a serious problem. In addition, the by-hand insertion of the residual and the interacted term into the household well-being function can greatly influence the estimates due to collinearity between the correction terms from the reduced form child wage equation and other regressors. The consequence of this is the resultant inflated standard errors of estimates from both 3a and 3b.

As expected the coefficients from the IV model are identical to those in 3a suggesting that we could interpret any of the models. Nevertheless, we privileged the results of the IV model for two reasons. Apart from accounting for endogeneity problem, the adjustment of the inflated standard errors of estimates is automatically accounted for in the IV estimator in Stata statistical package. This is not the case in 3a. While the difficulty of having completely valid instruments remains an issue in the literature, our instruments used though not strongly valid, they are, however, sufficiently strongly correlated with child wage, and the under-identification test suggests that there is no need for further instruments.

Results from the IV model justify the idea that when the household head is a female, the well-being of the household is lower compared to households headed by a male. This does not challenge conventional wisdom as it is often believed that men in a traditional society are physically stronger and hence capable of carrying out very difficult tasks to take care of the family. This is why in traditional societies widow-headed families are often regarded as needing more help than any other family. In addition families whose heads had never been to school or are not currently working have lower household well-being. These results are consistent with previous research indicating the importance of education for the family well-being (UNESCO 1994; Romer 1986; Lucas 1988; Becker 1992 and Behrman and Wolfe 1989 and the references therein).

As indicated by Cain and Mozurnder (1980), our results confirm the idea that household income instability is another important issue that can put household well-being at stake.

While several researches have indicated the significant importance of child labour resource in contributing to household well-being (Sharma and Mittar 1990; Patrinos and Psacharopoulos 1994 and Basu and Van 1998), our results seem not to confirm this in the case of Cameroon. The results show that child wage is not sufficient to augment household well-being. On the contrary it diminishes household well-being. This rejects the hypothesis of the deprivation theory, which argues that the employed can be assimilated with high well-being. Nevertheless, the results support the incentive theory which argues that workers may have lower well-being as they may not voluntarily decide to work.

This suggests that though children work for long hours as adults, what they receive as payment in cash or in kind is far less than that of adults for the same work done.[17] This is evident in Cameroon where the ILO and the Cameroon government study of 2003 showed that children work for very long hours for only 3000 CFA francs[18] per month for most of them. This sum is certainly unable to cover even the calories lost from child labour and therefore unable to improve household well-being. Another reason for this result could likely be that working children do not bring the obtained resources home for the entire household.

Though our results do not corroborate those of Sharma and Mittar (1990), they are however similar to those of Delap (1998), Bhalotra and Heady (2003) and Menon (2005). This result rejects the illusive belief of parents that child labour resources contribute to household well-being. Hence results support evidence in Delap (1998) to which children may work just to gain independence and not because of family poverty.

[17] This is evident in Cameroon where children work sometimes for 18 hours per day for 3000 CFA francs per month (LUTRENA, 2003).

[18] 1 US dollar = 500 CFA F on average.

8.6.2.1 Household Subjective Well-Being and Child Wage Results: Ordered Probit Model

Results in Table 8.4 indicate that the size of the effect of child wage on household subjective well-being is method dependent. Nevertheless, the significance of child wage residual suggests that child wage is endogenous in the household subjective well-being function. The estimates from the IV estimator therefore seem appropriate, for policy implication. In addition to test for model specification, we applied a regression equation specification error test (RESET). To implement this, we saved the predicted values from the regression in column 3, took it square and re-estimated the model with this new variable added as an extra explanatory variable. This test gave a Chi-squared statistic of 1.72 with a p-value well above conventional significance levels (p=0.1899) indicating that there is no evidence of miss-specification. This further fortifies the results for policy implications.

As in the case of objective well-being, results suggest that individuals in households where parents are females and uneducated are likely to report very poor self-assessed well-being. In addition, the more the household income is unstable, the higher the likelihood of reporting very poor well-being status. Child labour wage does not augment subjective household well-being. The result shows that the effect of child wage is insignificant. This result questions the veracity of the theoretical framework of Rosati and Rossi (2001) in which parents compare the maximum utility under the regime when the child is only working to the regime where he is only schooling and select the one that yields the highest welfare (Table 8.5).

8.7 Conclusion and Policy Implications

Investigating if child wage contributes to family well-being is vital for formulating policies to curb child labour especially when the effect is positive, as a legal ban of child labour in the context of poverty may push children out of their families into the streets. The objective of this chapter

Table 8.4 Determinant of household subjective well-being and child wage under different assumptions

	Well-being: endogenous child wage	Instrumented child wage	Well-being: exogenous child wage
	(1)	(2)	(3)
Child's characteristics			
Male child	0.036	0.417	0.178
	(0.85)	(16.13)[c]	(1.55)
Child's age	0.011	0.068	0.033
	(1.14)	(12.12)[c]	(1.68)[a]
Muslim	0.172	0.141	0.228
	(2.35)[b]	(3.73)[c]	(2.74)[c]
Log (child's wage)	−0.006		−0.340
	(0.17)		(1.36)
Parental characteristics			
Female	−0.130	−0.000	−0.143
	(1.80)[a]	(0.01)	(1.95)[a]
Age	−0.001	0.002	−0.001
	(0.36)	(1.43)	(0.26)
Never gone to school	−0.167	−0.007	−0.136
	(2.40)[b]	(0.14)	(1.90)[a]
Not working	−0.085	−0.104	−0.119
	(0.71)	(1.47)	(0.96)
Household characteristics			
Household size	0.035	0.006	0.038
	(2.64)[c]	(1.31)	(2.76)[c]
Income very unstable	−0.558	−0.210	−0.634
	(9.20)[c]	(5.96)[c]	(8.56)[c]
Owns livestock	0.097	−0.194	0.051

	(1.53)	(4.50)[c]	(0.70)
Household owns a farm	−0.139	−0.233	−0.194
	(1.44)	(4.15)[c]	(1.82)[a]
Urban residence	−0.301	−0.316	−0.396
	(4.22)[c]	(7.81)[c]	(3.92)[c]
Constant		7.787	
		(62.58)[c]	
Control function variables			
Child's employ. rates		0.008	
		(5.60)[c]	
Child's wage residual			0.342[a]
			(1.85)
Estimation statistics			
Observations	1,801,535	1,801,827	1,801,535
Prob > chi2(F)	0.0000	0.0000	0.0000
Reset test (3)	chi2(1) = 1.72: Prob > chi2 = 0.1899		
/cut1	−1.177		−3.872
/cut2	0.466		−2.227

Robust z statistics in parentheses
[a]Significant at 10%, [b]significant at 5% and [c]significant at 1%

Table 8.5 Descriptive statistics of outcome, regressor and instrumental variables

Variables name	Definition	Obs.	Weight	Mean	Std. Dev.	Min	Max
Outcome variables							
Log annual consumption expenditure per adult equivalent	Annual consumption expenditure per adult equivalent in local currency	17,550	5,999,053	13.37	0.64	7.12	16.69
Subjective well-being	= 1 if very poor, 2 if poor and 3 if rich	17,537	5,997,608	2.08	0.70	1	3
Independent variables							
Child's characteristics							
Child gender male	= 1 if male child, = 0 otherwise	17,550	5,999,053	0.50	0.50	0	1
Age of child	Age of child (year)	17,550	5,999,053	10.59	3.74	5	17
Muslim	= 1 if Muslim child, = 0 otherwise	17,550	5,999,053	0.23	0.42	0	1
Child labour	= 1 if a child has ever work, = 0 otherwise	17,550	5,999,053	0.26	0.44	0	1
Sector of activity	= 1 if working in agricultural sector, 0 = otherwise	6002	2,427,973	0.85	0.36	0	1
Log child wage	Log child annual wage in local currency	4628	1,809,404	8.77	0.87	4.12	11.93
Parental characteristics							
Household head gender	= 1 if female household head, = 0 otherwise	17,550	5,999,053	0.24	0.43	0	1
Household head age	Age of the household head (year)	17,550	5,999,053	45.76	13.33	11	95
Household head education	= 1 if household head has never gone to school, = 0 otherwise	17,485	5,979,615	0.34	0.47	0	1
Working status of household head	= 1 if the household is not working, = 0 otherwise	17,550	5,999,053	0.10	0.31	0	1

Household characteristics							
Household size	Number of household members (person)	17,550	5,999,053	7.41	4.10	1	43
Household owns a farm	= 1 if they own a farm, = 0 otherwise	17,532	5,996,374	0.75	0.43	0	1
Stability of income	= 1 if income is very unstable, = 0 otherwise	17,537	5,996,423	0.52	0.50	0	1
Livestock	= 1 if a member of the family owns livestock, = 0 otherwise	17,539	5,997,978	0.47	0.50	0	1
Community variables							
Zone	= 1 if the child lives in the urban area, = 0 otherwise	17,550	5,999,053	0.68	0.46	0	1
Instrumental variables							
Child employment rate	Child employment rate	17,550	5,999,053	42.55	20.65	8.80	75.20

was to empirically exploit the claim that child labour resources are well-being enhancing. Nevertheless, in order to avoid any unreliable policy implication, we used two indicators of well-being, and after addressing potential endogeneity and heterogeneity, we came to a conclusion that heterogeneity is not a serious issue in our data. Conscious of the fact that miss-specification can err our result, we used the RESET and found out among others that child wage does not in any way increase the well-being of the family.

Policy wise these results suggest that a legal ban of child labour is likely to be more beneficial than harmful to the families. Therefore the hypothesis postulated in the literature according to which a legal ban of child labour may on one hand push children out of their families onto the streets and on the other hand put families at starvation risk is not confirmed in the context of Cameroon. On the bases of these results, the 1992 Cameroon labour code placing a legal restriction on the employment of children needs to be reinforced. In addition, to ameliorate household well-being in the future, today's children who are tomorrow's family heads should be encouraged to go to school as household well-being significantly depend on whether the household head attended a school or not.

References

Addison, T., P. Teixeira, and T. Zwick. 1997. *Works councils and the anatomy of wages*. Center for European Economic Research.

Aitchison, J., and S. Silvey S. 1957. The generalization of probit analysis to the case of multiple responses. *Biometrika* 44 (1/2): 131–140.

Ajakaiye, O. and G. Mwabu. 2007. The demand for reproductive health services: an application of control function approach.

Arceneaux, K. 2005. Using cluster randomized field experiments to study voting behaviour. *The Annals of the American Academy of Political and Social Science* 601 (1): 169–179.

Baland, J., and J. Robinson. 2000. Is child labour inefficient? *Journal of Political Economy* 108 (4): 663–681.

Basu, K., and Z. Tzannatos. 2003. The global child labour problem: What do we know and what can we do? *World Bank Economy Review* 17 (2): 147–173.

Basu, K., and P. Van. 1998. The economics of child labour. *American Economic Review* 88 (3): 412–427.

Basu, K., S. Das, and B. Dutta. 2007. *Child labor and household wealth: Theory and empirical evidence of an inverted-U,"* CAE Working Paper #07–02.

Baye, F. 2006. Growth, redistribution and poverty changes in Cameroon: A Shapley decomposition analysis. *Journal of African Economies* 15 (4): 543–570.

———. 2010. *Exact configuration of poverty, inequality and polarization trends in the distribution of well-being in Cameroon*. AERC Research Paper 207.

Baye, F., and S. Fambon. 2009. Linking parental education, child health and economic well-being in Cameroon. Paper presented at the Centre for the Study of African Economies (CSAE) Conference, 2009 at St Catherine's College, Oxford, March 22–24.

Becker, G. 1992. Human capital and the economy. *American Philosophical Society* 136 (1): 85–92.

Beegle, K., R. Dehejia, and R. Gatti. 2006. Child labour and agricultural shocks. *Journal of Development Economics* 81: 80–96.

Behrman, J. and B. Wolfe. 1989. Does more schooling make women better nourished and healthier. *Journal of Human Resources* 24 (4): 644–663.

Ben-Arieh, A. (2006). Is the study of the "State of Our Children" changing? Revisiting after five years. *Children and Youth Services Review* 28(7): 799–811.

Bequele, A., and J. Boyden. 1988. *Combating child labour*. Geneva: ILO.

Bhalotra, S., 2000. *Is child work necessary*? Bristol Economics Discussion Papers No.03 (554), Department of Economics, University of Bristol, UK.

Bhalotra, S., and C. Heady. 2003. *Child farm labor: The wealth paradox*. University of Bristol UK, Working Paper, Bristol Economics Discussion Papers No. 03/553.

———. 2004. *Child farm labor: The wealth paradox*. The World Bank Economic Review. 17. 10.1093/wber/lhg017.

Blunch N., and D. Verner. 2000. *Revisiting the link between poverty and child labour: The Ghanaian experience*. Policy Research Working Paper No. 2488, World Bank, Washington, DC.

Bonnet, M. 1993. Child labour in Africa. *International Labour Review* 132 (3): 371–389.

Cain, M. and A. Mozurnder. 1980. *Labour market structure, child employment and reproductive behaviour in rural South Asia*. Population and Labour Policies Programme Working Paper.

Canagarajah, S., and H. Coulombe. 1997. *Child labor and schooling in Ghana*. World Bank's Policy Research Working Papers No. 1844.

Card, D. 2001. Estimating the return to schooling: Progress on some persistent econometric problems. *Econometrica* 69 (5): 1127–1160.

Chiwaula, L. (2010). Household poverty and child labor decisions in Malawi. *Research in Labor Economics* 31, 33–51. https://doi.org/10.1108/S0147-9121(2010)0000031005.

Cigno, A., F. Rosati, and Z. Tzannatos. 2000. *Child labour, nutrition and education in rural India: An economic analysis of parental choice and policy options.* Social Protection Discussion Paper, Washington, DC.

Cockburn, J. (2000). *Child labour versus education: Poverty constraints or income opportunities?* Paper presented at a Conference on Opportunities in Africa: Micro-evidence on firms and households.

Dammert, A. 2005. *Does child labour decline with household income? A non-parametric approach.* Department of Economics, Syracuse University.

DeGraff, D., R. Bilsborrow, and A. Herrin. 1993. The implications of high fertility for children's time use in the Philippines. Chapter in Lloyd, 1993: Fertility, family size, and structure: Consequences for families and children. Proceedings of a Population Council Seminar, New York.

Delap, E. 1998. *The determinants and effects of children's income generating work in urban Bangladesh*, processed.

———. 2000. Subjective well-being: The science of happiness and a proposal for a national index. *American Psychologist* 55 (1): 34–43.

Diener, E., and M. Seligman. 2004. Beyond money: Toward an economy of well-being. *Psychological Science in the Public Interest* 5 (1): 1–31.

Duryea, S., and M. Arends-Kuenning. 2003. School attendance, child labour and local labour market fluctuations in urban Brazil. *World Development* 31 (7): 1165–1178.

Edmonds, V. 2007. Child Labor IZA Discussion Paper No. 2606. Available at SSRN: https://ssrn.com/abstract=969364.

Epoh, N. 2010. *Determinants of poverty in Cameroon: A binomial and polychotomous logit analysis.* Social Science Research Network Working Paper.

Epoh, B., F. Baye, and N. Manga. 2011. *Explaining spatial and inter- temporal sources of poverty, inequality and gender disparities in Cameroon: A regression-based decomposition analysis.* Poverty and Economic Policy (PEP) Research Network, October. www.pep-net.org.

Garen, J. 1984. The returns to schooling: A selectivity bias approach with a continuous choice variable. *Econometrica* 52 (5): 1199–1218.

Government of Cameroon. 2003. The poverty reduction strategy paper. *Ministry of economic affairs, programming and regional development, Cameroon.*

Greene, W. 1993. The econometric approach to efficiency analysis. In *The Measurement of productive efficiency*, eds. H. Fried, K. Lovell, and S. Schmidt. Oxford: Oxford University Press.

Grootaert, C., and R. Kanbur. 1995. Child labour: An economic perspective. *International Labour Review* 134 (2): 187–203.

Guarcello, L., S. Lyon, and F. Rosati. 2006. *The twin challenges of child labour and youth employment in Ethiopia*. Understanding Children's Work, Working Paper.

ILO. 2003. *Labour overview Latin America and the Caribbean*. Switzerland, International Labour Office.

Jacoby, H., and E. Skoufias. 1997. Risk, financial markets and human capital in a developing country. *Review of Economic Studies* 64 (3): 311–336.

Jensen, R. 2000. Agricultural volatility and investments in children. *The American Economic Review* 90 (2): 399–404.

Kabubo-Mariara, J., G. Ndenge, and D. Mwabu. 2009. Determinants of children's nutritional status in Kenya: Evidence from demographic and health surveys. *Journal of African Economies* 18 (3): 363–387. https://doi.org/10.1093/jae/ejn024.

Kambhampati, U., and R. Rajan. 2004. Does child work decrease with parental income? The luxury axiom revisited in India. *European Journal of Development Research* 17 (1): 649–680.

Kassouf, A. 1998. *Child labour in Brazil*. Mimeograph London School of Economics and University of Sao Paulo.

Lucas, R. 1988. On the mechanics of economic development. *Journal of Monetary Economics* 22 (1): 3–42.

Manacorda, M. 2006. Child labour and the labour supply of other household members: Evidence from 1920 America. *American economic Review* 96 (5): 1788–1800.

Mbanga, G., and F. Sikod. 2002. *The impact of debt and debt-service payments on investments in Cameroon*. African Economic Research Consortium, Nairobi, Kenya.

Menon, N. 2005. *Why might credit used to finance investments increase child labour?* Brandeis Universtiy, Working Paper.

Menon, A., C. Homburg, and N. Beutin. 2005. Understanding customer value in business-to-business relationships. *Journal of Business-to-Business Marketing* 12, 1–38. https://doi.org/10.1300/J033v12n02_01.

Menon, M., F. Pareli, and F. Rosati. 2005. Estimation of the contribution of child labour to the formation of rural incomes: An application to Nepal. *Centre for Household Income, Labour, and Demographic Economics, Rome, Italy.*
Mwabu, G. 2009. The production of child health in Kenya: A structural model of birth weight. *Journal of African Economies* 18 (2): 212–260.
Myers, W. 1989. Urban working children: A comparison of four surveys from South America. *International Labour Review* 128 (3): 321–335.
Nielsen, H. 1998. *Child labour and school attendance: Two joint decisions.* Centre for Labour Market and Social Research, Aarhus, Denmark.
NIS. 2008. *Living conditions and profile of poverty in Cameroon in 2007. Themain report of the third Cameroon household's survey.* Yaoundé: National Institute of Statistics.
Okpukpara, B., and N. Odurukwe. 2006. *Incidence and determinants of child labour in Nigeria: Implications for poverty alleviation.* AERC Research Paper No. 156.
Patrinos, H. and G. Psacharopoulos. 1994. Educational performance and child labour in Paraguay. *International Journal of Educational Economics* 15 (4): 47–60.
———. 1995. *Educational performance and child labor in paraguay.* https://lst-iiep.iiep-unesco.org/cgi-bin/wwwi32.exe/[in=epidoc1.in]/?t2000=005275/(100).10.1016/0738-0593(94)E0001-5.
Psacharopoulos, G. 1997. Child labour versus educational attainment: Some evidence from Latin America. *Journal of Population Economics* 10 (4): 377–386.
Ravallion, M., and Q. Wodon. 2000. Does child labour displace schooling? Evidence on behavioural responses to an enrolment subsidy. *The Economic Journal* 110 (462): 158–175.
Ray, R. 2000. Analysis of child labour in Peru and Pakistan: A comparative study. *Journal of Population Economics* 13 (1): 3–19.
Romer, P. 1986. Increasing returns and long run growth. *Journal of Political Economy* 94 (5): 1002–1037.
Rosati, F., and M. Rossi. 2001. *Children working hours, school enrolment and human capital accumulation: Evidence from Pakistan and Nicaragua.* Understanding Children's Work Working Paper.
Rosenzweig, M., and T. Schultz. 1983. Estimating a household production function: Heterogeneity, the demand for health inputs, and their effects on birth weight. *Journal of Political Economy* 91 (5): 723–746.
Rosenzweig, M., and K. Wolpin. 1980. Testing the quantity–quality fertility model: The use of twins as a natural experiment. *Econometrica* 48 (1): 227–240.

Ryan, R., and E. Deci. 2001. On happiness and human potentials: A review of research on hedonic and eudemonic well-being. *Annual Review of Psychology* 52 (1): 141–166.

Sasaki M., and T. Temesgen. 1999. *Children in different activities: Child labour and schooling in Peru.* Draft, Word Bank, Washington, DC.

Schultz, T. 2008. Population policies, fertility, women's human capital, and child quality. In *Handbook of development economics*, ed. T.P. Schultz and J. Strauss, vol. 4. Amsterdam.

Sharif, M. 1994. Child participation, nature of work, and fertility demand: A theoretical analysis. *Indian Economic Journal* 40 (4): 30–45.

Sharma, B., and V. Mittar. 1990. *Child labour and the urban informal sector.* India: Deep and Deep Publications New Delhi.

Slesnick, D. 1998. Empirical approaches to the measurement of welfare. *Journal of Economic Literature* 36 (4): 2108–2165.

Strauss, J., and D. Thomas. 2007. Chapter 54 Health over the life course. *Handbook of development economics*. 4. 3375–3474. https://doi.org/10.1016/S1573-4471(07)04054-5.

UNESCO. 1994. *World declaration on education for all and framework for action to meet basic learning needs*. Paris: UNESCO.

World Bank. 2006. *Global monitoring report 2006*. Washington, DC: World Bank.

Yunita. 2006. *Determinants of child labour in Indonesia: The roles of family affluence, bargaining power and parents' educational attainments*. ILO-IPEC.

Zovoina, R., and W. McElvey. 1975. A statistical model for the analysis of ordinal level dependent variable. *Journal of Mathematical Sociology* 4 (1): 103–120.

9

Child Labour in a Pastoral Tribe of Jammu and Kashmir: Impact of Spatiality Within a State of Conflict

Afreen Gani Faridi

Most of the studies on child labour in India employ a legal positivist approach while determining the incidence of child labour across social groups. Even as ethnographic studies on Scheduled Tribes (STs) highlight the distinct cultural nature of their work practices, most of the analyses of child labour amongst tribes continue to rely on the universal definition of child labour prescribed within child labour legislation to determine the success or failure during its implementation. Studies on child labour in Jammu and Kashmir have been sporadic and restricted to case studies of specific regions or industry which rarely employ a cultural perspective of labour while generating empirical data. The rationale behind current child labour analysis in India assumes an environment of peace, where the praxis between formal and informal institutions is coherent and homogenous across regions. Furthermore, the debate on child labour is restricted to a utilitarian bias, which often uses poverty as a justification for child labour. Even if child labour is located within a social construct,

A. G. Faridi (✉)
Centre for the Study of Law and Governance, Jawaharlal Nehru University, New Delhi, India

A. Posso (ed.), *Child Labor in the Developing World*,
https://doi.org/10.1007/978-981-15-3106-4_9

it is condoned on the basis of tradition while engaging in an altruist assumption within such a social system.

This chapter analyses the nature of child work in the Bakkarwal tribe in Jammu and Kashmir while locating the spatial and temporal impact of conflict on the traditional work practices of the aforementioned pastoral tribe. Unlike existing literature in Jammu and Kashmir, child work is contextualised using historical, cultural and social realities for determining the efficacy of law in tackling child labour in a state ridden with violence.

9.1 Contextualising Child Work in a State of Conflict

Even with the ratification and implementation of legislations and schemes such as the Child Labour (Prohibition and Regulation) Amendment Act (2016), National Policy on Child Labour (1987) and the Right of Children to Free and Compulsory Education Act (2009), the total number of child workers in India stands at 23.8 million for persons up to 18 years of age, constituting 5% of the workforce in India (George and Panda 2015). Children of the age group 15–17 years are 13.7 million in numbers, while those between 5 and 14 years comprise 10.1 million (Census 2011). The decline in the magnitude of children engaging in work between ages 5 and 14 years in 2011 has only been from 5% in 2001 to 3.9% in 2011. However, actual figures of child labourers in India would be higher as 'migrant children and children of migrant families are unlikely to be included in full measure in the census' (George and Panda 2015).

India possesses the second largest tribal population in the world, with 8.2% of the total Indian population comprising tribes (Census 2011). Of all the social groups, the Scheduled Tribes (STs) have faced the worst brunt of child labour with an incidence of 6.7% as against an incidence of 3.9% amongst Scheduled Caste groups (Census 2011). In Jammu and Kashmir, 11.9% of the total population comprises Scheduled Tribes with over 1.49 million individuals (Census 2011). Here, the Gujjar and

Bakkarwal tribes are the two largest tribal groups in the state—comprising 65.6%and 7.5% of the population, respectively. It is pertinent that the incidence of child workers in Jammu and Kashmir was highest for Scheduled Tribes at 6.7% (Census 2011).

Since the end of colonial rule in 1947, India and Pakistan have fought four wars for control over Indian-Administered Kashmir, resulting in the emergence of a zone of conflict (hereafter categorised as the state of Jammu and Kashmir). The conflict stems from the promise of a plebiscite at the time of the erstwhile princely state's accession to India, in order to determine the will of the region's inhabitants regarding the region's sovereign status.[1] In 1989, after an election which was contested to be illegitimate and rigged, Jammu and Kashmir witnessed the rise of a popular armed movement against the Indian state leading to the deployment of more than 700,000 armed forces as a part of counter-insurgency operations by the Indian state (Duschinski et al. 2018). The implementation of legislation such as the Armed Forces (Special Powers) Act (1958) and the J&K Public Safety Act (1978)[2] has facilitated the creation of a state of siege within the region, establishing what is termed as a 'late-modern colonial occupation' (Mbembe 2003 in Duschinski et al. 2018) governed through to a 'state of exception' (Agamben 2005). The civilians face the brunt of intrastate as well as interstate hostilities over the fate of Kashmir. International and Kashmiri human rights organisations put the toll of civilian deaths at over 70,000 in Jammu and Kashmir (International People's Tribunal on Human Rights and Justice in Indian-Administered Kashmir and Association of Parents of Disappeared Persons (2015) in Duschinski, H., M. Bhan, A. Zia, and C. Manmood 2018, p.2). In 2018 alone, 61 people were killed and 250 injured in ceasefire violations numbering 2936 cases over the Line of Control and the International Border within the state, the highest in 15 years (Business Line 2019):

[1] For a detailed history of Indian-Administered Kashmir's accession to India, its impermanence and the special relationship with the Indian state constituted through Articles 370 and 35A of Indian Constitution, read Noorani (2011, 2014).

[2] The Armed Forces (Special Powers) Act empowers the state to deploy its armed forces against a civilian population with the impunity to engage and kill, even in the absence of an executive order, and protects the armed personnel by restricting judicial recourse. The J&K Public Safety Act provides for preventive detention of individuals without trial. For further reading, refer to Amnesty International (2012, and CRN 2011).

> While visions of Kashmir's alternative political futures might vary, it is clear that ethnic and religious communities in the state have suffered from the Indian government's lack of political commitment to resolve the long-standing dispute. Kashmir has repeatedly been used as a political tool to shore up nationalist sentiments in both India and Pakistan, and years of cross- border wars and conflict have rendered the lives of people across the LoC both precarious and unstable. Amid such social and political uncertainties, the government, as several chapters in this volume show, has played a critical role in further fragmenting communities and fomenting interreligious unrest and anxieties. (Bhan et al. 2018, p. 6)

It is within this governmentality that there is a need to analyse the links between how institutions and policy frameworks interact with social and economic realities to regulate child work within tribes. As the socio-economic structures in tribal communities are markedly different from that of the general populace, there is a need to analyse whether the scope and extent of labour legislation and institutional mechanisms in India are sufficient to deter child labour within distinct socio-economic groups. At the same time, locating the perspectives which shape child labour legislations become particularly pertinent to determine whether they bear the bias of a majority.

9.2 Approaching the Field

On the one hand, studies such as ones conducted by Pandit (1991), Gani and Shah (1998), Bhat and Rather (2010) and Bhat (2015) mainly focus on the predominant handicrafts industry in Kashmir for determining incidence and magnitude of child labour in Jammu and Kashmir. While providing empirical estimates of child labour, the spatially located studies on child labour focus on providing information regarding age, education, sex, health and wages of child workers. However, as the studies do not locate child labour across social groups, they leave a research gap to study child labour within tribes. On the other hand, ethnographic work on tribes (Sharma 2009) in Jammu and Kashmir studies limits themselves to a descriptive analysis of culture and tradition without linking it to child labour policies implemented by the state.

Majority of the work undertaken on child labour use a neo-classical approach which fails to analyse the prism in which work is viewed in state legislation and in the social systems where the legislation is implemented. Such an approach valorises a pecuniary view of work, while historical, social and cultural aspects of work are either stripped or obscured during analysis. Hence, the debate on child labour is restricted to a utilitarian bias, which often uses poverty as a justification for child labour. Even if child labour is located within a social construct, it is condoned using altruist assumptions of tradition within such a social system. The use of 'modern' theories and perceptions of child labour provides a monolithic of understanding work practices across spatial and temporal zones. Studies limited to such analytical tools do not reflect the dialect between the state, market and society in creating circumstances conducive to child work. Unfortunately, neo-classical frameworks have influenced labour legislation promulgated by the 'modern' state, including India, and have crystallised the definition of child labour against which work practices occurring in all societies are judged. Mainstream economics ignores the structural causes of violence organised socially and culturally to regulate capital-labour relations (Edwards 1990). Hence, causes of child labour such as displacement due to development, migration, low literacy rate, high unemployment in adults, gender discrimination, social stratification, poor implementation and ignorance of state policies (Tripathy 1991; Nika 2007) and conflict are not brought to the fore.

While engaging in this study, work was considered as an essential component which bore an enormous influence on the social life of an individual engaging in it (Marx 1976). Such a perspective stems from a Marxian analysis which pulls away the neo-classical veil from the 'hidden' abode of production to show that work if avoided under capitalism is only because of its exploitative form of organisation. Furthermore, institutions and their roles have been viewed apart from the fulfilled expectations they bear so as not to give them the permanence they might not deserve (Hahnel 2002). Using 'complementary holism' (Hahnel 2002), the chapter ascertains 'embeddedness' of law (Cotterrell 2013), and its capacity to regulate relations and structures. Additionally, institutional analysis and development framework (Abitbol and Flechas 2008) is employed to analyse state policy in a zone of conflict. This aids in establishing the 'political economy of work' (Spenser 2009) bore upon by tribal children in Jammu and Kashmir to view the impact of such customary work practices on their lives.

For an exploratory study such as the one contemplated here, the researcher engaged in both primary and secondary forms of data collection. The paper embeds child labour legislation and state policy against cultural notions of child work using a case study of a pastoral tribe in Jammu and Kashmir. The paper presents a provisional analysis of child labour legislation to analyse the implicit assumptions of 'child' and 'work' within the legal framework. Using semi-structured interviews, time use and observation methods, the researcher gathered information on education, socio-economic conditions and work practices of children from the Bakkarwal tribe. A simple random technique was used to select multiple households for this case study. While the parents acted as the primary respondents, the children were the secondary respondents.

The researcher engaged in fieldwork in three districts of Jammu and Kashmir, namely, Jammu, Reasi and Rajouri. The spatiality of the field was established after the analysis of 2011 Census data for J&K state and its districts to identify districts and specific geographical belts with a high incidence of child labour amongst the Scheduled Tribes. The researcher also used the District Aggregation of Census Data (2011) to determine the population of Bakkarwal Tribes in various districts of Jammu and Kashmir to locate the districts with a high density of tribal population. Regions with high population density were chosen for greater chances of success in contacting the tribe. The pastoral nature of the Bakkarwals makes them set up *deras* close to pastures. As these pastures lay few and far in between mountains and its foothills, the community was mostly spread over terrain only accessible by foot.

The total number of Bakkarwals in the state of J&K stood at 113,198—with Rajouri having the highest number with 36,163 members, followed by Reasi at 16,393. Furthermore, the Rajouri district recorded the highest incidence of child labour amongst Scheduled Tribes at 17.5% with a higher Work Participation Rate (WPR) in rural areas at 17.7% compared to 3.4% in urban areas. The Reasi district had 9.64% ST children working as child labourers with a similar incidence of about 9% both in urban and rural regions. In Jammu, a sizable number of Bakkarwals migrated and lived in and around urban settlements of the Jammu district (6997) with the WPR of ST children at about 4.1%, allowing for a comparative analysis of work practices of tribes living in the predominantly rural regions of Rajouri and Reasi to the predominantly urban regions of the Jammu city. Even though specific blocks and villages were narrowed down for locating the tribe members using District Level Census Data and past work undertaken by Kavita Suri on the educational status of Bakkarwal children (2016), locating the *deras* of the Bakkarwals in about 6560 square kilometres (Census 2011) of diverse terrain emerged out to be an exploratory exercise. The exercise was undertaken using the advice of state officials, who had an experience of engaging with the Bakkarwal tribe, and prominent community leaders of the tribe living in cities. While the officials and community members aided in locating the field up to the block level, it was mostly with the aid of forest guards, local community dwellers of the three districts and visual cues that the *deras* of the tribe could be accessed, especially in rural areas.

In district Jammu, the researcher surveyed 22 Bakkarwal households; in the district of Reasi, the researcher gathered data from 42 households; and in Rajouri—57. The Bakkarwal community in Jammu resided in residential areas lying at its outskirts, namely, Kargil Colony, Bathindi and Ragura Village. The regions of Gujjar Kothi, Talwara, Khari Mohalla and Neela Dab were accessed in the Reasi. The locations surveyed in the Rajouri district were Lamberi, Dolagaw and Thanamandi. The surveyed locations in Reasi and Rajouri were either rural or semiurban, while those in Jammu were urban and peri-urban.

The researcher sought information regarding three generations in the households he surveyed in all three districts. With the base as children who were primary research subjects, the first generation was composed of their grandparents, their parents were considered as the second generation and the children themselves along with their elder siblings as the third generation.

Besides the members of the Bakkarwal community, including its political leaders and its representatives in the state, officials predominantly working in the Department of Labour, members of the civil society and non-governmental organizations, and academicians from the state university who worked on issues of child labour or had engaged with the Bakkarwal tribe were interviewed as well.

9.3 The Problem of Crystallised Definitions

The phenomenon of child labour can only be understood after conceptualising a definition for it. However, as Schlemmer 2000) asserts, the task of evolving a precise definition of 'child labour' is difficult due to its dependency on the meanings of the terms 'work' and 'childhood' (Bhukuth 2008). There exists an ambiguity in the conceptualisation of a 'child' owing to multiple visualisations. As per the International Labour Organization (ILO), a person is a child until she or he has completed 15 years of age, and in this context, the ILO 138 Convention sets the minimum age for entry into any form of work or employment as 15 years (ILO 1973). On the other hand, the United Nations Children's Fund considers a child as 'an individual under the age of eighteen years based on the UN Conventions 1989 on the rights of the child (Convention on the Rights of the Child 1989), including the right to be protected from economic exploitation' (OHCHR Accessed 16th May 2019). However, child labour is defined in reference to 'children working before they reached the lawful minimum age for employment in their country, often the same as the cut-off age for compulsory attendance at school' (OHCHR Accessed 7th May 2019).

In India, distinct legislation related to children establishes distinct standards for defining 'child' as per their age (Deshta and Deshta 2000). The Child Labour (Prohibition and Regulation) Amendment Act (2016) defines a child as one who has not completed 14 years of age, while the Factories Act (1948) specifies a child as one below 15 years of age. Furthermore, the Juvenile Justice (Care and Protection) of Children Act (2015) sets the bar for defining a child at 18 years. However, 'child labour' as a term has been, conceptually and operationally, restricted to mean the employment of children that is gainful in nature, both while pursuing an education or in exclusion. The age group of children employed in productive work has been observed as ranging from 5 to 14 years of age—including both formal labour and informal labour, and the significant point is that such work affects child growth and development (Sudha and Tewari 1985). Stein and Davis (1940), and later Folks (1946), raised an essential aspect in the definition of child labour when they defined it, not in the context of labour relationship or the activity undertaken but regarding the effect of the activity on the child. According to the National Child Labor Committee of the United States (in Stein and Davis 1940), 'any work by children that interferes with their full physical development, the opportunities for a desirable minimum of education and of their needed recreation' was considered as child labour. Similarly, the Indian government in 1979 articulated that 'Child labour may be defined as employment of children in gainful occupation which are detrimental to their health and deprive them the chances of development'.

Besides the above-stated view on child labour, a group of thinkers argue for considering all out-of-school children as child labourers as they refer to the close links between child labour and education. They consider it inevitable that an out-of-school child would be drawn into supplementing family labour or managing family assets. This argument is corralled by Burra (1989) and the United Nations Development Programme (2004) (Fukuda-Parr et al. 2004) where child labourer is 'basically, a child who is deprived of the rights of education and childhood'.

Several studies have argued for assigning an economic value onto activities undertaken by children at home to broaden the definition of child labour (Knual 1988 in ILO 2007; Blunch and Verner 2000). Such an argument is made on the proposition that by narrowing the concept of child labour to that of wage employment, the interests of the girl child and her contribution to the economy are undermined (Edmonds 2009). In this regard, Khan and Ali (2005) widen the scope of child labour to include non-monetised work undertaken by children within and outside of homes, in addition to monetised work undertaken for wages inside or outside household enterprises.

Social scientists have distinguished between 'child work' or 'light work'[3] and 'child labour'. Such a distinction perceives light work to be a gradual initiation into adulthood and a stimulant in a child's development (Fyfe 1989). On the other hand, 'child work' is used to refer to such activities that do not impose a cost on a child's leisure, play or education. Such work forms a part of a child's socialisation and is devoid of any form of physical or mental exploitation. These activities do not relate to employment in the economic sense but are essential for a child's mental and physical growth, especially during their early years of development (Siddiqi 2003). On a similar vein, the World Bank (1998) had argued that 'child work' needed to be distinguished from child labour when there was no presence of the notion of exploitation as child work undertaken within the family could even contribute to his or her development.

> Not all child labour is harmful. Many working children are within a stable and nurturing environment with their parents or work under the protection of a guardian can benefit in terms of socialization and from informal education and training. (Sharma in World Bank Report 1998, p. 1008)

As seen from the above-stated definitions on child labour, much of the debates on the definition of child labour seek its crystallisation to abolish child labour through corresponding legislation. By ascribing economic value to activities undertaken by children, and considering it a form of 'child labour', one could justify its blanket ban by setting such work practices apart from the processes of production. However, as legislations choose a particular chronological age as 'the universal measure of biological and psychological maturity' (Nieuwenhuys 1996), they reject the cultural and social meanings attached to age and labour. However, before one can rely on the legislative definition of child labour based on the implicit economic value that it attributes to certain activities, or dismiss

[3] ILO describes light work in Article 7 of Convention 1383 by stating that:

> National laws or regulations may permit the employment or work of persons 13 to 15 years of age on light work which is—(a) not likely to be harmful to their health or development; and (b) not such as to prejudice their attendance at school, their participation in vocational orientation or training programmes approved by the competent authority or their capacity to benefit from the instruction received.

it for ignoring traditional notions of work, one needs to understand the implicit moral and economic values ascribed to work undertaken by children in different contexts.

As Gabarrón (1996), a Mexican psychologist, elaborates, work undertaken by children forms 'one of the most important pathways to enculturation among indigenous people' (Larsen 2003) for 'establishing socio-cultural integration and collective identity' (Larsen 2003). Traditional livelihoods and apprenticeships, as forms of knowledge transmission, are often disregarded by national legislations and projects while promoting notions of labour, education and knowledge that are 'modern' and uniform. Prevalent studies on the issue of child labour in tribes of India ignore the sociocultural perspective of labour in tribes and single-mindedly seek to provide an empirical extent of the same using the boundaries set by legislation. The study of indigenous tribes raises the need to address the peculiarities of child labour with a distinct socio-economic milieu. For tribes' folk, traditional education typically includes participating in traditional occupations (ILO 2001). Studies of tribal groups have shown that participating in traditional occupations, in the form of light work, is often more useful for furthering the interests of the tribe than the formal education system which can be more disruptive—'in social, emotional and economic terms' (Larsen 2003). Even as children of tribes work as an intrinsic process of socialising and learning while growing up, one cannot justify a blind acceptance of 'cultural' explanations given for child labour, even if they are provided by their parents, employers or the state. One cannot look at the 'cultural explanation' of child labour as a value-neutral developmental force in the growth of tribal children. While tribal customs and traditional attitudes are frequently cited as causes of child labour, such an explanation is often contradicted by the documentation that depicts changes and disruptions affecting tribal traditions (Larsen 2003).

9.4 Institutional Bias Through Collusion

India is an intermediary between a 'predatory' and a 'developmental' state (Evans 1995), where one can see the interplay between state, market and the society through state-led planning. Such planning, visible during the colonial period, extends onwards into the independent Indian state. The increase in the role of Indian capitalists during the nationalist movement in the 1930s resulted in the creation of an economic nationalism post-independence which drove state economic policy to cater to the needs of Indian business houses. This economic nationalism was characterised by the interplay of social forces, market, and the state in order to use patriarchy, caste and religion to establish a monopoly in the family-run businesses in India (Mohanty 2006; Das Gupta 2016).

The most significant aspect of this collusion affected the Indian labour regime through the institutionalisation of labour cheapening and wage depression by the Indian state at the behest of the Indian capitalist class. The collusion mentioned above shaped policy perspectives determining the nature of labour legislation in India, including ones on child labour. The Indian state facilitated the maintenance of profitability for the domestic capital, against foreign capital, by drafting labour laws that ensured a steady supply of cheap surplus labour. The second-generation economic reforms depict the state's keen interest in undertaking labour reform for the benefit of the capitalists. Since the reforms were based on the principle of 'rationalising' existing laws relating to labour (Second National Commission on Labour Report 2002 p. 6), subsequent legislation regulating work and worker relations was prioritised towards efficiency and international competitiveness through reducing labour costs (Roychowdhury 2018). While rationalisation tended to the reduction of both—physical effort in undertaking work and the cost incurred, Singh (1967 in Roychowdhury 2018) emphasised that in India, rationalisation was a means to reduce only labour costs by reorganising labour and working conditions. Such rationalisation led to an increased precarity within work, reduced the collective bargaining powers of workers and led to the withdrawal of state regulation for ensuring ethical work practices. In an inverse logic, the World Bank (2010) encouraged the drawback of labour regulations as they covered only 10% of workers, while 90% of the workers in India existed without any state protection in the unorganised sector.

A paradigmatic shift in worker-employer relations was achieved through the promulgation of the Industrial Disputes Act (1956).[4]

The Act formalised the use of social hierarchy in labour relations to benefit the capitalist class by incentivising informal employment. The 1956 Industrial Disputes Act confined the definition of a workplace to a 'factory', thus limiting the area where adjudication on labour issues would be possible and constricting the space in which the workers could practice their labour rights. It restricted the formalisation of all employer-employee relationships in India that could extend to 'private dwellings', thus excluding the labour undertaken in domestic settings of a household—including engendered child work from the ambit of the law. We witness a confluence of class power that moves the state to reinforce its dominance in the market by shaping the relationship between capital and labour through policy interventions (Das Gupta 2016). However, this influence of class power in the current relationship between capital and labour in India could not exist in the absence of social value systems emerging from India's feudal past, whose preservation by the dominant class is the very aim of the current confluence. These value systems based on the institutionalisation of class, caste and gender have led to the perpetuation of labour hierarchy through the creation of labour laws which deny legal protection to the majority of the workforce not covered under the definition of a 'worker'. As a result, the capitalist class ensures a steady supply of cheap surplus labour through the practice of wage depression and use of unpaid labour in an informal economic setup.

Consequently, it is not possible to understand the relationship between the state and the market without the context of the society in which the state lies embedded. This intimacy of the state with the market and the

[4] Roychowdhury (2018) provides a succinct analysis of the state of labour laws in the organised sector.

intensity of its intervention based on social values is not only limited to India. It has been a regular feature of a modern state as traced by Marx (1976) in his analysis of the institutional frameworks affecting labour relations during the expansion of capitalism in Europe. It is within this context that one needs to realise the 'embeddedness' of child labour legislation in India and view the value of work borne by the definitions that shape such legislations.

9.5 Abolish Not Regulate

The Constitution of independent India (1950) provided a substantive list of civil and political rights for children to ensure a safe and healthy environment for their growth and development.[5] However, one does not witness any substantive measures being undertaken by the Indian state to eradicate child labour until the 1980s. Such an attitude cannot be excused by citing a lack of awareness of the magnitude and incidence of child labour, especially in the unorganised sector. It only can be ascribed as a result of deliberate policy decisions—as major governmental reports pointed to the awareness of the issue amongst policy framers. The National Commission Report (1969), chaired by Justice P. B. Gajendragadkar, citing the Census of India (1961), reported that workers below 15 years constituted 8% of the workforce in India—a majority of whom were employed in agriculture and allied activities, whereas 'the organised sectors of the economy accounted for only a small proportion' (Ministry of Labour and Employment and Rehabilitation 1969).

Furthermore, child work in the family establishment was condoned for the benefit of tradition, and there was no attempt by the framers of

[5] The right to equality before law and protection of the law (Article 14) was available to any citizen of independent India, including children (Constitution of India 1950);

Article 15 (3) of the Indian Constitution (1950) empowered the state to formulate special laws for the welfare of children;

Article 23 of the Indian Constitution (1950) prohibits human trafficking and forced labour;

Article 24 specifically prohibits the employment of children under the age of 14 to be employed in any factory, mine or be 'engaged in any other hazardous employment' (1950).

These articles exist as a fundamental rights guaranteed to the citizens in Part III of the Indian Constitution and are justiciable in nature (1950).

the Indian Constitution to criminalise child labour in 'hazardous' settings in accordance with Article 24 (1950). In presenting its 1969 report, the National Commission on Labour attributed child labour to be an 'economic problem'. The commission condoned the existence of child labour citing that 'the economic difficulties faced by the poor and their children were real' and recommended a combination of work alongside education through 'flexible employment hours' (Gomango 2001, p. 173). The report chose to ignore the social acceptance of exploitation of poverty-stricken children and keep faith in the 'philanthropic intent' of the employers of child labourers.

Independent India's first comprehensive legislation on child labour can be ascribed to the Child Labour (Prohibition and Regulation) Act (CLPRA 1986). The Employment of Children (Amendment) Act (1978) was essentially a colonial act which failed to provide a uniform standard to deal with the practice of child labour in India. The Child Labour Act (1986) was consequential for establishing a uniform definition of a child as one who did not complete 14 years of age and banning their employment in specified occupations and processes mentioned in Schedule 3 of the 1986 Act while regulating their conditions of work in others. The law was forward-thinking in the fact that it established procedures for allowing the central government to modify and add banned occupation and processes to Schedule 3 of the Act, through the advice of a Child Labour Technical Advisory Committee mandated for this purpose.

Thirty years later, the Child Labour Amendment Act of 2016 evolved the definition of child to link it to the Right of Children to Free and Compulsory Education Act (2009) as 'a person who has not completed his fourteenth year of age or such age as may be specified in the Right of Children to Free and Compulsory Education Act 2009, whichever is more' (Government of India 2016). Furthermore, it recognises a new category of persons between 14 and 18 years of age as 'adolescents'. Section 3(1) of the 2016 Act prohibits the employment of a child, that is, a person below the age of 14, in any occupation or process, while Section 3A prohibits the employment of adolescents in any hazardous occupations or processes outlined in the stated Section. The Child Labour Amendment Act (2016) increases the penalties for the violation of the Act and includes parents or the child in the ambit (Section 14). Offences committed by the employers have been amended to make them cognisable as per law, in addition to providing procedures for compounding of the offences (Section 14A). In a significant move for securing the welfare and rehabilitation of the rescued children, the 2016 Act provides for the Child and Adolescent Rehabilitation Fund and also confers duties and puts the onus on the state government to rehabilitate the rescued child (Section 14B).

However, even after three decades since the ratification of the 1986 Child Labour Act, India has still not made any paradigmatic shift concerning its policy towards child labour even after putting the Child Labour Act (2016) into force and ratifying ILO Conventions 138 and 182 in 2017. The status quo of state policy towards child labour is evidenced by the fact that the 2016 Child Labour Amendment Act does not put a blanket ban on labour undertaken by persons under 18 years of age. It merely creates a separate regulatory and prohibitory standard for children and adolescents. The Act continues to 'regulate' and 'prohibit' child labour as recommended by the Gurupadaswamy Committee report (1979), rather than seeking to altogether abolish it as recommended by the National Commission for Protection of Child Rights—through the deletion of the word 'regulation' from the law in order to make child labour abolition non-negotiable (Mehendale 2016).[6]

Even as the 2016 legislation on child labour takes a step forward by prohibiting children from working in any occupation or process, it extends the exemption from 'family' to include 'family enterprise' (Section 3(2)). The 2016 Act allows children to work after school hours or during vacations with a caveat that such work is neither hazardous nor does it affect the child's education. The exemption is precarious as it fails to enunciate on what work would bear 'effect [on] the school education of a child' (Section 3(2)) and what age would be a minimum threshold to engage in such exempted work. The exemptions provided for in the Act go against the Fortieth Report of the Standing Committee on Labour (Government of India 2013) constituted to review the amendments to the Child Labour Amendment Bill (2012). The Committee had stated,

[6] Similarly, Article 24 of the Constitution of India (1950), which constitutes fundamental rights, prohibits children below 14 years of age from working in factories and mines and under hazardous conditions.

in its report to the Parliament, that such an exemption created a loophole for the exploitation of children. It would be difficult to keep a check on working children in their homes and ascertain whether they were helping their families or supplementing the household income. The Committee had recommended, without success, that employment of children should be prohibited in all occupations where a subordinate relationship of work and labour could be established (Government of India 2013, p. 10).

In another detrimental move, the Child Labour Act (2016) replaced the list of 18 prohibited occupations and 65 prohibited processes in Schedule 3 of the 1986 Act with a new list that governed the employment regulations for adolescents. The list was narrowed down to mines, inflammable substances or explosives and hazardous processes in the 2016 Amendment Act. Such a move restricted the definition of hazardous in contrast to the suggestion made by the Standing Committee on Labour recommending it to be widened. This could be done by using the Minimum Age Convention No. 138 to include 'all those occupations/processes that may jeopardise health, safety and morals of adolescents' as hazardous (Government of India 2013, p. 40). Conversely, the Child Labour Amendment Act (2016) in Section 3A of the Act defines 'hazardous' by referring to the Factories Act (1987) wherein the benchmark for hazardous is set for adult factory workers and the point of environmental pollution (Section 2(cb)).

A significant criticism of the current paradigm of child labour legislation emerges in its inadequacy to regulate work undertaken by children in peasant societies. Such shortcomings stem from research on child work, especially in colonies such as India, which suffer from social biases which justify child work in familial settings. By using utopian ideals of parenthood (Dandekar 1989) as cloaks for constructing a notion of child labour, any work considered as a threat to such ideals was not recognised as 'real work'. Such cognition of child labour relied on not allocating value to everyday activities performed by children, especially in rural environments. The latest Census (2011) attests to this limitation—10.1 million children (5–14 years) continue to engage in work, out of which 8.1 million reside in rural areas. It is significant to note that the major sectors of child work in rural areas remains agricultural labour (40.1%), cultivation (31.5%) and the household industry (4.6%)

(Census 2011). Furthermore, there has been an increase in the proportion of child workers in the age group of 5–9 years from 14.6% in 2001 to 24.8% in 2011 as per Census data from the respective periods, with an increase in main workers within the age group of 5–9 years from 14.2% to 25.6% for the same period (Census 2001, 2011).

Nieuwenhuys points to three categories of work, undertaken by children within the household, that are directed towards the production of socially valued goods and services yet not ascribed any economic value by such a paradigm influenced by neo-classical economics.

> The categories include-
>
> (a) activities that extract resources from the physical and social environment;
> (b) activities concerning the 'unpaid' allocation, preparation and distribution of these resources;
> (c) activities that concern the care of human beings. (Nieuwenhuys 1994, p. 16)

Even as such work is denied any value in the household, it bears economic value as 'real work' when children are replaced with workers hired from outside the household. Hence, proving that children undertaking such work within the household do engage in economic exercise. Using a Marxist perspective to analyse such work undertaken in domestic settings, modern thinkers have called out the exploitative intent of such a valuation stemming from a capitalist desire of maximising profits, especially within a feudal setting (Rey 1973 and Meillassoux 1977 in Schlemmer 2000). Legislative inputs formulated by former colonies often find inspiration in their colonial histories. Consequentially, the Indian legislative framework for child labour also continues to bear a capitalist intent while ascribing meaning to child labour. One that allows for a steady supply of cheap surplus labour to the domestic capitalist by incentivising the informal supply of labour. The Indian state's continual condoning of child labour can be witnessed in the 2015 cabinet note where it justified the exemptions proposed for the 2016 Act. It did so by hinting at the utility of children as workers and the state's interest in preserving the 'socio-economic condition and social fabric' of the country (Press Information Bureau 2015). Thus, values of work inculcated in the child labour legislation continue to follow the colonial need of maximum surplus extraction through the depression of wages.

While labour analysis in India employs the politics of class, caste and gender to view child labour in rural India, it fails to look at influences beyond a feudal-capitalist lens, as the analysis is limited to economic relations based on private ownership of modes of production (Rey 1973 in Schlemmer 2000). On the one hand, this can be understandable, as most of the rural labour relations are affected by an amalgam of feudal-capitalist bias where there is a constant tussle towards ownership of property and means of production across class, caste and gender. However, it results in an analytical constriction while engaging with societies and communities such as nomadic pastoral tribes, which predate feudal and capital structures, where much of the traditions and labour values do not stem from private ownership of property, especially that of land. Hence, it becomes imperative to challenge the status quo and analyse child work in such 'cultural' settings against 'modern' legislations (Gabarrón 1996; Larsen 2003) on two counts: one being whether such a cultural tradition of child work results in exploitation or endangerment of a child and, secondly, how a law rooted in 'modern' prerogatives deals with work undertaken in 'premodern' social-economic groups.

While bearing the above-stated constructs in mind, this endeavour analyses how institutions and policy frameworks on child labour interact with social and economic realities of the Bakkarwal tribe within which children engage in productive work.

9.6 An Introduction to the Bakkarwal Tribe

The Constitution (Jammu & Kashmir) Scheduled Tribes Order (1989) and the Constitution (Scheduled Tribes) Order (Amendment) Act (1991) notify the presence of 12 tribes in the state of Jammu and Kashmir. It was during the 2001 Census that the 12 Scheduled Tribes were enumerated officially for the first time (Suri and Raina 2016). As stated previously, the Scheduled Tribes constitute 11.9% of the total population of the state of

Jammu and Kashmir. The Scheduled Tribes are predominantly rural, as 95.3% of them reside in villages (Census 2011).

The Bakkarwal tribe is found in all three regions of the state of Jammu and Kashmir, namely, Jammu, Kashmir and Leh. The tribe, with its unique social, cultural and linguistic identity, forms the third largest tribal community in the state numbering 113,198 members. The name 'Bakkarwal' is sourced from the words 'bakra', which means a goat or a sheep, and 'wal' referring to 'one who takes care or rears' (Sharma 2009, p. 14). As signified by their name, the Bakkarwals are mostly pastoralists who rear and herd sheep and goats for livelihood; they also rear horses and *Bakkarwali* dogs for load-bearing and guarding the flock, respectively. The Bakkarwal's most valuable possession is the flock, which is referred colloquially as 'maal', a word which means 'wealth'. The tribe lives in tents or temporary shelters known as 'deras' and subsists on rice, maize, goat's milk and wild vegetables and fruits that they gather. Seasonal nomadism is a primary trait of this pastoral tribe as the practice is integral to their subsistence. Traditionally, Bakkarwals did not privately own any pastoral land that they accessed. Being nomadic, they merely set up temporary shelters, called 'Kullas', where they stopped during seasonal migrations. Hence, the idea of spatial and temporal transience is quintessential for understanding the customs and traditions of Bakkarwal tribe, as their social, political and economic setup has been historically determined by the constant need to move for securing a livelihood through pastoral nomadism. The Bakkarwals use the word 'Khanabadosh' (nomadism) for this quintessential character of their lifestyle. However, a few amongst the pastorals partially practice agriculture for subsistence and a fewer number, only 1%, have given up nomadism altogether to settle down as agriculturalists (Sharma 2009; Suri and Hooda 2014). The nomadic tribe migrates to high reaches of the Pir Panjal Range or the Zanskar Belt, of Jammu and Kashmir, during the summer months to access grazing grounds for their flock. In winters, they descend to the foothills of the Himalayas or the plains of Jammu along with their flock. As was tradition, most Bakkarwals migrate on foot, with horses carrying the loads. However, in recent times, a few wealthier Bakkarwals have taken to hiring vehicles to assist in the migration (Sharma 2009).

The Bakkarwals of Jammu and Kashmir are adherents of the Sunni sect of Islam, adhering to 'Sunnah', that is, 'the practices and customs associated with the life of Prophet Muhammad' (Sharma 2009, p. 63). Religion holds a significant influence as the tradition and culture of the tribe remains aligned with Islamic practices. Since the Bakkarwals consider their ancestors and themselves to be the followers of Prophet Muhammad, they believe the practice of nomadic pastoralism to be sanctified within Sunnah. *Khanabadoshi* and associated work practices gain religious meaning as an essential tradition in the Islamic faith. Thus, the Bakkarwal tribe was loath to look for any other way of life besides nomadism or seek any other livelihood besides pastoralism as they believed that the divinity in its practice had kept them well fed and aided in their propagation. Due to the differing needs and requirements of the nomadic lifestyle, the Bakkarwals did not find it expeditious to become a part of the formal system of education. Consequently, due to high rates of 'illiteracy',[7] the Bakkarwals tend to keep away from the legal system of the state—they do not trust a system dependant on written procedural norms and documentation which they cannot comprehend.

Kinship plays a vital role in the social organisation of the Bakkarwal tribe, with the family acting as a keystone for upholding the social, political and economic norms within the community. A Bakkarwal household is a working unit of production and sustenance, which comes into being after a male member establishes an independent establishment after marriage. The family provides the social context which moulds the social behaviours and establishes relationships, values and worldview of the community (Sharma 2009). The basic unit of social structure among the Bakkarwals is a household unit of a family which comes into existence when a male member of the community marries and establishes an independent patriarchal household consisting of about 5–6 members. Marriage mostly occurs within the Bakkarwal community or with members of the Gujjar community. The family structure of the Bakkarwals is patriarchal and patrilineal in their character. All decisions regarding the household and its sustenance are undertaken by men. Even though a household forms the basic unit of society, it is a 'dera' which forms the

[7] In the modern sense of the term being outside the formal education system endorsed by the state.

prime unit of organisation for the social, economic and political functioning of a tribe as it is central to the practice of nomadic pastoralism. A *dera* is a cluster of households that live and migrate as a single unit, whose origin can be traced to early hunter-gatherer societies that banded together for safety and survival. The division of labour among the members of the household occurs on the basis of gender and age. The division extends as a communitarian exercise for the upkeep of the dera based on customs and traditions. The tasks allocated through a division of labour can be grouped into three prime categories, namely domestic activities, pastoral activities and nomadic activities (Sharma 2009; Suri and Hooda 2014). Even though households are hugely interdependent when agglomerated into a dera, they retain independence within the group. The Bakkarwal household is a harmonious blend of independence and interdependence, aimed to optimise gains from a large pool of resources. There exists a dialectical relationship between the social and economic functions of different members of the tribe. It is within this context that one needs to understand the notions of 'work' within the Bakkarwal tribe and division of work practices amongst its members.

Customary work practices amongst the Bakkarwal tribe were divided at a household level according to gender and age. However, work bore a communitarian nature as it was taken up at the level of a *dera*. The Bakkarwal tribe, in its traditional practice of nomadic pastoralism, did not sell the labour of its individuals in the modern capitalist market in exchange for a wage but undertook work as a collective exercise at a subsistence level within the community. The concept of work and the value ascribed to it in the Bakkarwal community predates even the feudal structures, as the community did not lead a sedentary life and did not engage in the monetisation of work and property. The subsistence work undertaken by the tribe possesses similarities to hunting, foraging and food gathering that relied on a barter system for securing what could not be provided domestically.

As stated by Marx, 'within a tribe, there springs up naturally a division of labour, caused by differences of sex and age, a division that is consequently based on a purely physiological foundation' and that the aim of such a division is to expand the material wealth of the community (Marx 1867, p. 245). Thus, every social relation and customary practices within the tribe were geared for the successful undertaking of *Khanabadoshi* since whole communities were dependent on it for their survival. Spatial, temporal and social isolation from other groups, due to nomadism, did not provide alternative sources of subsistence in the case of exigencies. Unlike modern capitalism, workers in the *Bakkarwali* tribal system are an intrinsic part of the production system and own their labour. The communitarian nature of work, located at the level of dera, was based on the indigenous practice of resource optimisation between groups with common economic and social goals (Marx 1867; Galaty and Johnson 1990; Sharma 2009).

As stated earlier, Bakkarwals divide work on the basis of gender and age. While some chores have strict demarcation in their assignment to a particular gender, others allow for joint or random undertaking depending on the situation and the availability of resources. Traditionally all work for the subsistence of a dera was undertaken solely by its members. Pastoral activities form the core work practice in a dera undertaking *Khanabadoshi*. The herding of the flock to pastures and water sources is mainly performed by the male members of the community as it often involves spending extended periods away from the household, even during temporary settlements. Other arduous tasks such as shearing of the flock, repairing tools, gathering food for the flock, procuring rations and, in specific cases, ploughing and harvesting crops were limited to the domain of men. However, women assisted the men when the flock was situated in the periphery of the deras. Such work could include driving the flock into pens, milking the flock, medicating them and separating the newly born animals from their mothers. Domestic activities such as cooking, cleaning, fetching water, washing clothes, spinning wool, knitting clothes and care work involving rearing of children and looking after the elderly were relegated primarily to women. During the period of migration, the men are responsible for herding the flock and ensuring its safety during the night, while the women packed possessions onto the horses and rode them ahead of the herd to set up camp and undertake ancillary activities such as procuring water. However, some chores were performed jointly by both men and women during and after the period of migration. They include procuring firewood, pitching up and dismantling tents for the journey.

Children are initiated into gender roles of work from a young age due to the labour-intensive nature of the nomadic pastoralism. The boys start to accompany their fathers to herd the flock at an early age of 8–10 years, while girls help with household chores when even younger. The traditional lifestyle of the community did not require or provide for access to formal systems of education existing outside the community. The indigenous knowledge systems focused only on what was needed for the continuation of customary and occupational practices of the tribe, and the most efficient way of passing on such knowledge was through a 'hands-on' approach. Child work, within this isolated communitarian setup of the tribe, was not considered exploitative in nature, even if there existed a subordinate relationship between the adults and the children. The absence of exploitation was because goods and services generated from such work practices remained within the community under the collective ownership of all participants. The absence of social hierarchies affecting work and social setup within the Bakkarwal tribe, such as the caste system, allowed for homogeneity of work conditions across community members. However, one does need to keep in mind the gender disparity, especially in power relations and ownership while debating the efficacy of such work practices in ensuring the survival of the tribe.

In the process of following such customary values and practices of work, almost all of the elderly folk of the first generation were illiterate in modern school education but were well versed in religious teachings and indigenous knowledge systems to secure the survival of the household. As these elders did not think of any occupation for their children but the inheritance of their own, almost all of the current generation of adults (the second generation) did not go to school and did not look beyond patrilineal occupations unless forced by circumstance.

It might seem that one is justifying child labour within a tribe premised on the passing of traditional practices, survival of households, the embeddedness of work and protection of the 'social fabric', as is used by the Indian state in the framing of the labour legislation for regulating child work. However, this is not the case as such work practices which were bereft of exploitative relationship could only exist until the time the tribe members were wholly isolated and self-reliant. Over time, the Bakkarwal tribe has had to contend with coming out of isolation resulting in increased engagement with the modern means of production driven by the capitalist market system, which organises and exploits labour for maximising surplus value for the benefit of capital.

9.7 'Traditional' Work in a State of Conflict

It would not be possible to overstate the importance of migration and its impact on the socio-economic conditions of the Bakkarwal tribe and vice versa. The function of *Khanabadoshi* or nomadism, its presence or absence, determines the creation of distinctness between different members of the Bakkarwal communities. Thus, the emergence of conflict in Jammu and Kashmir along with commensurate state-led developmental policy in Jammu and Kashmir led to a paradigmatic shift in the fortunes and work conditions of the Bakkarwals. On the one hand, the development of motorable roads has allowed certain economically well-off groups to travel and transport of flocks through trucks using arterial roads built across mountain passes of the Himalayan range, which the Bakkarwals cross every season. On the other hand, practitioners of traditional migration, on foot and using horses, have faced increased difficulties due to conflict, political and climate change, and development practices that invariably affect their ability to access their traditional routes of migration through forests and pastoral lands. Conflict in Jammu and Kashmir, as an impediment to migratory practices within the tribe, has been established through past academic works (Casimir and Rao 1995; Suri and Hooda 2014). Since the wars of 1965 and 1971, between India and Pakistan, traditional pastoral grounds and mountain routes used by the Bakkarwals, especially those beyond the Vale of Kashmir, have been shrinking due to the translocation of Indian military and paramilitary personnel into the region of conflict. The armed forces either occupied the area or denied access to the Bakkarwals and other civilians in such contested regions. The Bakkarwals had to deal with restrictions imposed on their access to summer pastures (in the now Pakistan-occupied Kashmir) with the demarcation of the Line of Control in 1972 (Government of India 1972) and after the Kargil war in 1999. The period of the 1980s is noticeable for the rise of armed rebellion and the militarisation of the region. This period is pointed as the beginning of the economic decline amongst the Bakkarwal tribe. The Bakkarwals had to forgo a sizable number of their sheep, goats and horses to militants under duress, which the Bakkarwals use for sustenance and transport, respectively, when they moved to the upper reaches in summers. Such exchanges caused them to be suspected and branded as militant sympathisers and informants by the army. As a result, the army restricted their ability to access traditional pastoral grounds and undertake seasonal migration to and from the rich pastures in the upper reaches of the Himalayas, where militants often camped. The restricted mobility took a toll on the number of the flock and the livelihood of the community. The spatial and temporal mobility of the Bakkarwals was further diminished by the forest policies of the state government. The state demarcation and fencing of forest reserve areas resulted in forest officials impeding the entry of Bakkarwals to pastures, water sources and pathways during migration and the eviction of *Van* Bakkarwals (the forest dwellers) from their traditional lands in the higher reaches.

The emergence of private property and its centrality in political representation was quintessential in determining the identity of 'permanent residents' of Jammu and Kashmir.[8] The absence of private ownership

[8] Article 370 extends certain special provisions to the state of Jammu and Kashmir: The state is exempted from the provisions of the Constitution that deal with the administration of Indian states. This allows Jammu and Kashmir, unlike any other Indian state, to have its own Constitution within the Union of India.

Article 35A (Constitution of India 1950) allows the Constitution of Jammu & Kashmir to

1. Define 'Permanent Residents' of the State;
2. Confer Special Rights and Privileges to its Permanent Residents (and deny other the same) with respect to employment, acquisition of immovable property, settlement and scholarships or any other state aid within J&K.
3. Part-III of Constitution of Jammu and Kashmir, 1956 defines permanent residents on the basis of a. Birth and Residence and b. Acquisition of Immovable Property.

Note: The President's notification regarding the Constitution (Application to Jammu and Kashmir) Order of 2019 of August 5 resulted in the amendment of Article 370 of the Indian Constitution.

The recent the notification has taken away the special rights and privileges enjoyed by the residents of Jammu and Kashmir as mentioned above. The impact of such notification shall be far-reaching and is a site of future analysis. (The Constitution (Application to Jammu and Kashmir) Order 2019)

excludes Bakkarwals from being fairly represented in the state and shaping socio-economic policy to their benefit. Hence, the conflict acted as a tool for 'primitive accumulation' (Marx 1976) wherein traditional grazing pastures were 'enclosed' by the state in establishing military cantonments leading to the pauperisation of Bakkarwals—both politically and economically. Subsequently, the second-generation members of the tribe did not find it viable to continue owning and herding sheep in the plains. As per a survey conducted by the Tribal Research and Cultural Foundation in 2012, more than 39% Bakkarwals gave up their nomadic lifestyle due to the restrictions imposed by the militants and the security forces since the advent of the conflict. Furthermore, as per the community leaders and the members of the state administration, the marginalisation of the tribe was further accelerated due to extreme climatic factors that made the *Khanabadoshi* Bakkarwals incur economic losses from which they could not recover.

The political economy of conflict forced Bakkarwals to shift from their traditional mode of production into engaging with the market economy. Here, one witnesses the collusion of the state in extracting maximum surplus from a group which has barely any collective power of bargain due to limited political representation. The Bakkarwals derive a majority of their sustenance from selling the wool of their flock in the market. However, while engaging with the market to sell wool, the Bakkarwals had to contend with low auction rates set by the government in a period of inflation and increased competition from imported wool. Furthermore, increased costs arose from an absence of adequate medical facilities by the animal husbandry department of Jammu and Kashmir. Meat buyers exploited the Bakkarwals by quoting low rates, as they knew that the Bakkarwals had to return in a set period, thus lowering the bargaining capacity of the tribe as they had no pastures to hold their flock. The *Khanabadoshi* Bakkarwals are often forced to search for alternate sources of livelihood immediately after the loss of a flock. The flock is their sole source of economic wealth since they are mostly landless and they barely have any monetary savings in the absence of access to a formal banking system. One could say that the flock is their saving account. Similarly, the lack of access to systems of credit makes them unable to access capital for buying a new flock and restarting their livelihood.

In most cases, the Bakkarwals have moved to engage in daily wage labour as an alternative source of livelihood. Such wage labour involves construction work in urban or peri-urban areas, working in plantations and farms during the sowing and harvest seasons as farm labour and herding flock owned by persons from within the community or outside it. The community members have also taken to seeking employment from the government, especially the forest department, as daily workers employed to undertake menial tasks in offices or as guards for securing forest lands against timber smugglers and land encroachers.

9.8 Unravelling Child Work in the Bakkarwal Tribe

As stated in the above section, the members of the Bakkarwal community have been forgoing their traditional livelihood practices to enter wage work after facing competition from modern market systems. The shift has resulted in a breakdown of homogeneity within the tribe and has developed social hierarchies, with increasing disparities in ownership of private property, especially landholdings amongst tribal groups. With the changing nature of occupation and employment, children face greater vulnerability, as they along with women become tools in the hands of capital for shortening the necessary labour time for the reproduction of labour power and depressing wages by either working alongside the adult workforce or lowering the cost of subsistence by undertaking domestic work (Marx 1867). The work carried out within the community no longer bears any divine sanctity as it is pitched and valued in a market where the mode of production no longer lies in the hands of the Bakkarwal tribe. Thus, in present times, any 'traditional' undertaken by children, even under a familial setup, bears a subordinate relationship which is exploitative and hampers the growth and development of the child.

It is important to reiterate that over time certain factors, both natural and human-made, have led to a shift in occupational practices within the Bakkarwal community bringing about a shift in perceptions regarding work and education amongst children. The awareness of decreasing profits from pastoralism over time and the need to search for alternate modes of livelihood have made the whole community view formal education as an essential tool for securing their future and lifting themselves out of penury.

The following observations were made based on fieldwork regarding child work amongst the Bakkarwal tribe.

The nature and incidence of child labour amongst the Bakkarwal tribe does not figure in major studies undertaken in Jammu and Kashmir. Past studies mostly focused on the traditional handicraft sector of carpet making and practices of usury in the valley of Kashmir (Ali 1987; Gomango 2001; Bhat and Rather 2010), and bonded labour in brick kilns of Jammu where migrant workers from outside the state of Jammu and Kashmir work in conditions of slavery (Perappadan 2012).

The Bakkarwal children were most likely to engage in work, from a very young age, in households engaged in herding as a primary or even secondary source of income, due to the labour-intensive nature of work. Such engagement was witnessed in both urban and rural settlements and amongst landowners as well. Child work was divided along the lines of gender, and its intensity would increase in inverse relation to school attendance. Even as Bakkarwals sought formal school education across three districts, the decrease in access to mobile school posed a considerable deterrent for the nomadic Bakkarwal households without permanent dwellings to send their children to school. Ownership of land for setting up a permanent dwelling increased the ability of a household to provide education to the children. In households with the head of the family having high wages, more education and labour market experience, children were more likely to be at school in relation to the time spent working. It is to note that most of the child work occurred within the 'family establishment' or the community. Customary practice played a vital role in allowing for child work as most of it is done in a familial setup. However, some families did send their children to urban areas to work as domestic servants. Other families sent their children to work in orchards in and around the Kashmir Valley during the harvest season.

Structural poverty, loss of flock and death of an earning adult member of the family are the reasons for pushing children to work in either other Bakkarwal communities or as domestic and plantation workers for securing a source of income. In such conditions, it is usually the younger children who are sent to work outside the family establishment, while the older children are retained within the family to herd the flock. One witnesses a sense of 'alienation' within the tribe and an increased precarity owing to participation in such wage work. As a result, communities bereft of access to formal education and private property show an increased incidence of child workers, case in point being district Rajouri which is a hotspot with 11.6% child workers (Samantroy et al. 2016, p. 66).

The child work undertaken by the Bakkarwal children violates the provisions of the Child Labour Amendment Act (2016) on the principle that it impedes their education and plays a crucial role in supplementing the income of the family. Furthermore, customary work under the family establishment does not involve only such a household to which the child belongs, as a dera forms the principal unit of economic organisation in such a communitarian setup. Hence, the Bakkarwal child is supplementing the incomes of multiple households, directly or indirectly. Furthermore, the activities undertaken by children of both genders are hazardous and could be fatal. The traditional occupation of the Bakkarwals involves traversing difficult mountainous terrains where children are exposed to vagaries of nature. The hazards involved in herding the flock and indulging in domestic work such as fetching water include harsh weather, treacherous terrains and danger from wild animals such as bears and leopards. The children also traverse long distances along the mountainous roads during the periods of migration where accidents involving vehicles are commonplace. Moreover, working as domestic servants exposes them to physical abuse, and agrarian work can bring them in contact with pesticide and other chemicals as they handle farm produce without any protection. The children of communities dwelling in the border district of Rajouri are exposed to cross-border fire between the militaries of India and Pakistan (Suri 2014a, 2014b, 2014c, 2014d, 2014e.

The materialisation of sectarian politics in India, especially with the resurgence of ethnonational political organisations led by the *Bharatiya Janata Party*, has made the social milieu of Jammu and Kashmir volatile. One can witness the pitting of Hindu majority regions of Jammu against the Muslim majority regions from where the Bakkarwals originate. The bodies of tribal children become sites of majoritarian sectarian violence in order to reinforce social hierarchies. The coming together of the state, market and the society in reifying marginal status of the Bakkarwals was seen predominantly as members of Bakkarwal tribe were attacked during migration by vigilante 'cow protection groups'.[9] Furthermore, the children of Bakkarwals are prone to physical violence and sexual assaults; methods that have been valorised by right-wing political ideologues to deter Bakkarwals from settling in the Hindu-dominated plains of Jammu.[10] Such violence inflicted upon the bodies of Bakkarwal children is structural and seeks to regulate the hegemonic sway of a particular community; the violence originates from the state-market-society triad and permeates the spaces of work inhabited by children, thus making child work hazardous.

9.9 Efficacy of State Action in 'Regulating' Child Labour in the Bakkarwal Tribe

As observed during fieldwork across three districts of Jammu, work undertaken by children in the Bakkarwal tribe does bear an exploitative nature, even when undertaken as per the principles of customary traditions and modes of livelihood. It is against such work that state law and policies must be embedded to determine their efficacy in securing the interests of the Bakkarwal child. The legislative and executive action against child labour in Jammu and Kashmir stems from approaching the issue from two fronts, namely prohibition of child labour and enforcing compulsory schooling amongst children.

The primary policy referred by the Department of Labour of the Jammu and Kashmir government for dealing with child labour was the National Child Labour Project (NCLP) which had been approved by the Government of India in 1987. The NCLP sought to tackle the problem of child labour using a legislative action plan based on the child labour

[9] In 2017, a mob of 200 people attacked a nomadic family in Reasi, including a 9-year-old girl, as they migrated with their livestock (Khajuria 2017).

[10] In 2018, an 8-year-old girl from the Bakkarwal community was sexually assaulted and murdered in Kathua district of Jammu division (Fareed 2018).

legislation, convergence of general development programmes for the benefit of child labour and project-based action plans in areas with a high concentration of child labour (Government of India 1987).

As per the NCLP, the provisions of the Child Labour Amendment (Prohibition and Regulation) Act (2016) become the first line of defence to secure the interests of the Bakkarwal children. While Section 3(1) of the CLPRA (2016) prohibits the employment of a person below the age of 14, in any occupation or process, Section 3A of the 2016 Act prohibits the employment of adolescents in any hazardous occupations or processes outlined in the stated Section.

However, during the analysis of CLPRA (2016), it was found that the exemption clause on work undertaken in 'family enterprises' in (Section 3(2), CLPRA 2016) of the Act legitimised child work in such settings. Furthermore, Section 3A of CLPRA narrowed the definition of hazardous work, allowing for adolescent children to face greater dangers in places of employment. These same provisions, when analysed against the work practices of Bakkarwal child, depict the lack of legislative teeth to recognise and tackle exploitative work undertaken by children from within the community. Section 3(1) allows for children to engage in herding the flock owned by their family as a customary practice, as it would not consider such a pastoral activity as generating income for the family. Additionally, Section 3 of CLPRA does not provide for a legal provision to deal with cooperative work within a *dera* wherein every family can lay claim that the child is working under a familial setup. To make matters worse, Section 3(A) does not recognise the hazardous nature of various tasks that the Bakkarwal children have to undertake while following gendered norms in dealing with nomadic work within a state of conflict. These provisions render child labour undertaken by Bakkarwals, within the community as invisible before the law. Thus, the Bakkarwal children and their families do not qualify for educational and economic rehabilitation as per the convergence strategy of the Ministry of Labour for the welfare and development of children under the National Child Labour Project (2003).

The inadequacy of state policy for tackling child labour in Jammu and Kashmir can be seen from the lack of a state-specific child labour project scheme and implementation of the Integrated Child Protection Scheme.

The foremost challenge faced in the eradication of child labour was the lack of human resources in the Department of Labour, which was the nodal agency tasked with the implementation of the child labour law. There were a large number of vacancies for the post of labour officers and inspectors which were primarily tasked to undertake raids at business establishments and other sites which potentially employed children. Furthermore, inadequate infrastructure and want for technology such as vehicles and recording devices made it very challenging for the department to undertake such tasks, especially in rural areas where long distances need to be covered. Another concern afflicting the implementation of child labour law was the presence of inadequate knowledge of procedural norms both amongst the enforcement agency and judicial officers, which resulted in low conviction rates during prosecution.

The labour legislation uses a homogenous definition of child labour, one that serves the capitalistic mode of production and imposes it on a vulnerable population prone to exploitation. Such state policy actuates 'institutional bias' while claiming to eradicate child labour, both in the substantial definition of work and during its implementation to check exploitative practices of child labour in the Bakkarwal tribe. As an antithesis to child welfare, the legislative bias towards exploitative capital gains sanction from both social and legal canon.

9.10 Conclusion

The expanse of the capitalist mode of production into every aspect of social relations in the contemporary paradigm renders upon every work an economic value of exchange. Hence, while categorisation and distinctions of child work might help in distinguishing the degree of vulnerability faced by children while undertaking such work, at the end every work undertaken by children under a subordinate relation of power is tantamount to child labour. However, the neo-classical theory, in its analysis of child work, makes such relations of power affecting the child's agency to choose for themselves as invisible. It becomes erroneous to ascribe benign naivety to value systems where perceptions of work undertaken by children lay entrenched as they bear the power to affect the lives of children.

Child labour does not occur merely as a consequence of market forces. It is acted upon by the institutions of the state as well as the society. The definitions of child labour might reflect a mere economic perspective of work, but such a perspective emerges out of an institutional system that uses it for a particular end. Hence, a crystallised definition of child labour is quintessentially a monolith comprising dominant social, economic and political perspectives. Such perspectives subsume marginal value systems for formulating homogenous work practices in order to maintain its hegemony. The vulnerability of working tribal children is further acerbated due to their marginal socio-economic materiality as well as spatial inhabitation in a conflict zone. More importantly, such conditions get obscured through neo-classical explanations of child work. For Bakkarwal children, the absence of 'good work' becomes a lived reality within such capitalist spheres of production (Spenser 2009). The situation of tribal children will only worsen as their communities are forced to deal with the effects of alienation from their traditional practices brought upon by their integration into the market economy.

This endeavour restricts itself from giving policy prescriptions at this stage, but it highlights the need for future policy action based on lived realities. A utilitarian understanding of work needs to be eschewed as it fallaciously views symptoms as causation, resulting in inefficacious policy prescription. Policies for eliminating child labour would be incomplete in the absence of recommendations which tackle the structural factors which cause children to engage in work.

References

Abitbol, P., and D. Flechas 2008. Deliberative action Arenas on public policy making in conflict zones: A case study with Women's Groups in Colombia. In 5th Annual Conference of the HDCA. New Delhi.

Agamben, G. 2005. *State of exception*. Trans. Kevin Attell. Chicago: University of Chicago Press.

Ali, N. 1987. Child labour in the carpet industry of Kashmir. In *Seminar on child labour in India & the new legislation*. Srinagar: Asian Workers Development Institute.

Amnesty International 2012. INDIA: STILL A 'LAWLESS LAW': DETENTIONS UNDER THE JAMMU AND KASHMIR PUBLIC SAFETY ACT, 1978. [online] London: Amnesty International Publications. Available at: [Accessed 6 May 2020].

Approval to move official amendments to the Child Labour (Prohibition & Regulation) Amendment Bill, 2012. 2016. Pib.nic.in. http://pib.nic.in/newsite/PrintRelease.aspx?relid=121636. Accessed 18 Mar 2016.

Bhat, Bilal Ahmad. 2015. Child labour practices in Kargil (Ladakh). *Bangladesh E-Journal of Sociology* 6 (2). http://www.bangladeshsociology.org/Child%20Labour%20Practices%20in%20Kargil.pdf. Accessed 9 Sept 2015.

Bhat, B., and Tareak Rather. 2010. Child labour in Kashmiri society: A socio-human rights study. *Human Affairs* 20 (2). https://doi.org/10.2478/v10023-010-0017-9.

Bhukuth, Augendra. 2008. Defining child labour: A controversial debate. *Development in Practice* 18 (3): 385–394. https://doi.org/10.1080/09614520802030466.

Blunch, Niels-Hugo and Dorte Verner 2000. *Revisiting the link between poverty and child labor: The Ghanaian experience*. Policy Research Working Paper WPS2488. Washington, DC: World Bank.

Burra, N. 1989. *Child labour and education*. Paris: UNESCO-UNICEF Co-operative Programme.

———. 1995. Born To Work: Child Labour In India. Delhi: Oxford University Press.

Business Line. 2019. J&K records 2936 cases of ceasefire violations by Pakistan in 2018, highest in 15 years. https://www.thehindubusinessline.com/news/national/jk-records-2936-cases-of-ceasefire-violations-by-pakistan-in-2018-highest-in-15-years/article25932363.ece.

Casimir, M., and A. Rao. 1995. Prestige, possessions, and progeny – Cultural goals and reproductive success among the bakkarwal. *Human Nature 6* (3): 241–272. https://doi.org/10.1007/bf02734141.

Child Labour: Amend the Amendment. (2016). Actionaid.org. Retrieved 19 March 2016, from http://www.actionaid.org/india/2015/08/childlabour-amend-amendmentCommittee. New Delhi: Ministry of Labour.

CRIN. 2011. INDIA: JUVENILES OF JAMMU AND KASHMIR - UNEQUAL BEFORE THE LAW & DENIED JUSTICE IN CUSTODY. [online] Available at: [Accessed 6 May 2020].

Convention on the Rights of the Child. (1989). Ohchr.org. https://www.ohchr.org/EN/ProfessionalInterest/Pages/CRC.aspx. Accessed 7 May 2017.

Cotterrell, R. 2013. Rethinking 'embeddedness': Law, economy, community. *Journal of Law and Society 40* (1): 49–67. https://doi.org/10.1111/j.1467-6478.2013.00612.x.
Dandekar, K. 1989. Child labour: Do parents count it as an economic contribution. In *Demographic and socioeconomic aspects of the child in India*, ed. K. Shrinivasan. Bombay: Himalaya.
Deshta, S., and K. Deshta. 2000. *Law and menace of child labour*. New Delhi: Anmol Publications.
Duschinski, H., M. Bhan, A. Zia, and C. Manmood. 2018. *Resisting occupation in Kashmir*. Philadelphia: University of Pennsylvania Press.
Edmonds, E.V. 2009. *Defining child labour: A review of the definitions of child labour in policy research working paper*. International Labour Organisation. http://www.ilo.org/ipecinfo/product/download.do?type=document&id=11247. Accessed 15 Oct 2015.
Edwards, P.K. 1990. The politics of conflict and consent: How the labor contract really works. *Journal of Economic Behaviour and Organization* 13: 41–61.
Evans, P. 1995. *Embedded autonomy*. Princeton, NJ: Princeton University Press.
Fareed, R. 2018. Kashmir rape case: The girl, her family and the accused. https://www.aljazeera.com/indepth/features/india-asifa-rape-killing-girl-family-accused-180416070659470.html.
Folks, H. 1946. *US child labour commission report*. Washington: United States Government.
Fukuda-Parr, S., et al. 2004. *Human development report*. New York: United Nations Development Programme.
Fyfe, A. 1989. *Child labour*. Cambridge: Polity Press.
Gabarrón, L. 1996. *Infancia trabajadora y desarrollo humano: problemas y alternativas*. University of Veracruzana, UNICEF and ILO.
Galaty, J., and D. Johnson. 1990. *The World of pastoralism: Herding systems in comparative perspective*. London: Guilford Press.
Gani, A., and M.A. Shah. 1998. Child labour in carpet industry of Kashmir. *Indian Journal of Industrial Relations* 33 (3): 349–366.
George, Alex, and Sameet Panda. 2015. Child labour law amendment applying the brakes on social mobility. *Economic & Political Weekly* 38: 16–19.
Gomango, S. 2001. *Child labour: A precarious future*. Delhi: Authors Press.
Gupta, C. 2016. *State and capital in independent India: Institutions and accumulation*. Delhi: Cambridge University Press.
Hahnel, R. 2002. *The ABCs of political economy: A modern approach*. London: Pluto Press.

International Labour Office. 2001. *Traditional occupations of indigenous and tribal peoples: Emerging trends*. Geneva: ILO.

International Labour Organisation. 1973. C-138, Minimum age Convention 1973 (No138). http: //www.ilo.org/dyn/normlex/en/f?p=NORMLEXPUB:12100:0::NO::P12100_ILO_CODE:C138. Accessed 19 Oct 2015.

International People's Tribunal on Human Rights and Justice in Indian-Administered Kashmir and Association of Parents of Disappeared Persons 2015. Structures of Violence: The Indian State in Jammu and Kashmir. September. International Sites of Conscience. http://www.sitesofconscience.org/.

Khajuria, R. 2017. Mob attacks nomadic family over suspicions of cattle smuggling in Jammu's Reasi. https://www.hindustantimes.com/india-news/mob-attacks-nomadic-family-over-suspicions-of-cattle-smuggling-in-jammu-s-reasi/story-C3qbO9sgQTivcprlVKebSO.html.

Khan, R.E.A., and K. Ali. 2005. Economically active and home care groups of children in Pakistan: How much they differ. *Indian Journal of Labour Economics* 48 (3): 605–618.

Knual (1988) in Explaining the demand and supply of child labour: A review of the underlying theories. (2007). Retrieved from https://www.ilo.org/ipec/Informationresources/WCMS_IPEC_PUB_7870/lang--en/index.htm

Larsen, P.B. 2003. Indigenous and tribal children: Assessing child labour and education challenges: Child labour and education working paper. International Labour Organisation. http://www.ilo.org/ipecinfo/product/download.do?type=document&id=1100. Accessed 5 Sept 2015.

Marx, K. 1867. Capital: *A critique of political economy*. [References to 1954 ed., Moscow: Progress Publishers.] [References to 1962 ed. London: Macmillan.]

———. 1976. *Capital*. Vol. 1. Trans. Ben Fowkes. London: Lawrence and Wishart.

Mbembe, Achilles. 2003. Necropolitics. *Public Culture* 15 (1): 11–40.

Mehendale, A. 2016. One step forward, two steps back – Amendments to child labour legislation in India. https://www.right-to-education.org/blog/one-step-forward-two-steps-back-amendments-child-labour-legislation-india.

Mohanty, P.K. 2006. *Encyclopaedia of scheduled tribes in India*. Delhi: Isha Books.

National Policy on Child Labour. 1987. New Delhi: Government of India.

Nieuwenhuys, O. 1994. *Children's lifeworlds: Gender, welfare, and labour in the developing world*. Psychology Press.

Nieuwenhuys, Olga. 1996. The paradox of child labor and anthropology. *Annual Review of Anthropology* 25 (1): 237–251. https://doi.org/10.1146/annurev.anthro.25.1.237.

Nika, Fayaz Ahmad. 2007. *Socio-economic and ethical dimensions of child labour in Kashmir*. Doctor of Philosophy, University of Kashmir.

Noorani, A. 2011. *Article 370: A constitutional history of Jammu and Kashmir*. New Delhi: Oxford University Press.

———. 2014. *The Kashmir dispute, 1947–2012*. New Delhi: Oxford University Press.

Perappadan, B. 2012. No hope of a Life of dignity for these bonded labourers. [online] The Hindu. Accessed 6 May 2017.

Pandit, M. 1991. Handicraft, child labour in Jammu and Kashmir: A status paper. In *Towards eradication of child labour*, ed. H. Indira et al. Ahmedabad: Gandhi Labour Institute.

Parliamentary Standing Committee on Labour on Child Labour Prohibition and Regulation Act Amendment Bill 2012 (PSCL) (2013–14): 40th Report. pp. 38–39. http://164.100.47.134/lsscommittee/Labour/15_Labour_40.pdf. Accessed 20 Oct 2015.

Press Information Bureau. 2015. Approval to move official amendments to the child labour (Prohibition & Regulation) Amendment Bill, 2012. *Press Information Bureau*. http://pib.nic.in/newsite/PrintRelease.aspx?relid=121636. Accessed 8 Sept 2015.

Registrar General & Census Commissioner of India. 2001 *Census*. New Delhi.

———. 2011. *Census*. New Delhi.

REPORT OF THE NATIONAL COMMISSION ON LABOUR. 1969. https://casi.sas.upenn.edu/sites/casi.sas.upenn.edu/files/iit/National%20Commission%20on%20Labour%20Report.pdf. Accessed 23 July 2017

Roychowdhury, A. 2018. *Labour law reforms in India: All in the name of jobs*. London: Routledge.

Samantroy, E., H. Sekar, and S. Pradhan. 2016. *State of child workers in India: Mapping trends*. New Delhi: V.V. Giri National Labour Institute.

Scheme of National Child Labour Project Revised-2003. 2003. https://labour.gov.in/sites/default/files/SchemeofNationalChildLabourProjectRevised.pdf.

Schlemmer, B. 2000. *The exploited Child*. London: Zed Books.

Second National Commission on Labour Report. 2002. *Ministry of labour*. Government of India.

Sharma, A. 2009. *The Bakkarwals of Jammu and Kashmir navigating through nomadism*. New Delhi: Niyogi Books.

Siddiqi, M. 2003. *Child labour: How to investigate?* New Delhi: Deep & Deep.

Spenser, David A. 2009. *The political economy of work*. London: Routledge.

Stein, E., and J. Davis. 1940. *Labor problems in America*. New York: Farrar & Rinehart.

Sudha, B.G., and Smita Tewari. 1985. Child labour in rural areas: Some factors. *Kurukshetra* XXXIII (7): 31–33.

Suri, K. 2014a. Challenges in education of Tribal children in Poonch district of Jammu and Kashmir. *Asian Journal Of Multidisciplinary Studies 2* (1): 142–145.

———. 2014b. Education, conflict and development: A case study of mobile schools for pastoralists in Jammu and Kashmir. *IOSR Journal of Research & Method in Education (IOSRJRME) 4* (1): 12–19. https://doi.org/10.9790/7388-04151219.

———. 2014c. Impact of armed conflict on the seasonal migratory practices of Gujjar and Bakkarwal tribes in Jammu and Kashmir. *IOSR Journal of Humanities and Social Science 19* (2): 54–62. https://doi.org/10.9790/0837-19235462.

———. 2014d. Teaching the nomads in the wild: An analysis of seasonal educational schools for nomadic populations in Jammu and Kashmir. *Asian Journal of Multidisciplinary Studies 2* (3): 29–33.

———. 2014e. Impact of armed conflict on the seasonal migratory practices of Gujjar and Bakkarwal Tribes in Jammu and Kashmir. *IOSR Journal of Humanities and Social Science* 19 (2): 54–62. https://doi.org/10.9790/0837-19235462.

Suri, K., & Raina, P. (2016). A Study of Educational Status of Tribal Bakkarwal Children of Kalakote block of Rajouri District in Jammu and Kashmir. *Asian Journal Of Multidisciplinary Studies, 4*(11), 72–81.

Suri, K., and D. Hooda. 2014. *Gujjars and Bakkarwals of Jammu & Kashmir*. Gurgaon: Shubhi Publications.

The Armed Forces (Special Powers) Act 1958. New Delhi: Government of India.

The Child Labour (Prohibition and Regulation) Act 1986. New Delhi: Government of India.

The Child Labour (Prohibition and Regulation) Amendment Act. 2016. New Delhi: Government of India.

The Child Labour (Prohibition and Regulation) Amendment Bill 2012. New Delhi: Government of India.

The Constitution of India. 1950.

The Employment of Children (Amendment) Act 1978. New Delhi: Government of India.

The Factories Act 19481987. New Delhi: Government of India.
The Gazette of India. The Constitution (Application to Jammu and Kashmir) Order, 2019 2019. New Delhi.
The Government of India. 1979. Report of the Committee on Child Labour (Gurupadaswamy Committee).
The Industrial Disputes Act. 1956. New Delhi: Government of India.
The Jammu and Kashmir Public Safety Act 1978. New Delhi: Government of India.
The Juvenile Justice (Care and Protection) of Children Act. 2015. New Delhi: Government of India.
The Right of Children to Free and Compulsory Education Act. 2009. New Delhi: Government of India.
Tripathy, S.N. 1991. *Exploitation of child labour in Tribal India*. Delhi: Daya Publishing House.
World Bank. 2010. *India's Employment challenge: Creating jobs, helping workers*. New Delhi: Oxford University Press.
World Bank Report. 1998. Washington, DC.

10

Conclusions and Generalised Policy Inferences

Alberto Posso

This volume presents readers with new information regarding the causes of child labour in developing countries. As highlighted throughout the volume, poverty is considered the primordial cause of this phenomenon, and as such reducing poverty is likely to significantly impact child labour.

In Chap. 2, Joydeb Sasmal and Ritwik Sasmal argue that policies that promote economic growth are likely going to decrease poverty, which in turn will lower child labour. In Chap. 5, Eva Rodríguez Cuevas and Lorena Vieira Costa similarly argue that policies that aim to reduce vulnerability to poverty are likely to be effective in reducing child labour. They argue that exposure to negative shocks pushes households in poverty and children into labour, so facilitating access to credit and other resilience mechanisms is going to be important.

The approach to economic policy in these two chapters is somewhat outdated yet remains relevant. Reducing poverty is likely to result in a decrease in child labour. The economics literature, however, widely

A. Posso (✉)
RMIT University, Melbourne, VIC, Australia
e-mail: alberto.posso@rmit.edu.au

A. Posso (ed.), *Child Labor in the Developing World*,
https://doi.org/10.1007/978-981-15-3106-4_10

acknowledges that targeted expenditures are likely to accelerate the pace by which countries can reduce poverty and child labour. The discussion in Chap. 3 aims to highlight in a theoretical setting that child labour and poverty require a combination of policies. The author discusses how educational policies, combined with credit and income transfers, provide the right policy mix. However, Indrajit Thakurata also warns that while certain policies may work for some aspects of the population, they may prove ineffective for others. The author provides an example and notes that because of parental educational background, financial inclusion policies and free education may not be strong enough for certain households to induce higher educational investments and lower child labour. The author argues that in this case, only income support can push the household beyond a minimum threshold, which effectively incentivises greater investments in human capital.

Building on this theme, the point of Chap. 8 is mainly to highlight that even those policies that are generally thought to be ineffective may prove useful in certain settings. Fabien Sundjo argues that a legal ban on child labour is unlikely to push children into the streets or put families at starvation risk according to Cameroonian data. Rather, the legal ban may prove effective in this country.

Overall, be it legal bans or credit transfers, policies need to be harmonised to be effective. Indeed, even addressing cultural issues may be relevant. In Chaps. 4 and 9, Dakhina Mitra and Afreen Gani Faridi, respectively, highlight that child labour is often an intrinsic cultural factor. Dakhina Mitra therefore calls for a broader multidimensional approach to deal with child labour—one that aims to catalyse behavioural change. She also calls for mass media behavioural-change campaigns to break caste barriers. The author finds that households in poor regions adopt discourses that promote and justify the notion that poor children should work and produce a culture of child labour. In turn, these societal discourses of caste hierarchies, cultural practices, traditional norms, gender biases and efficacy of schooling further impede children's right to exercise their choice or influence decisions. These complimentary policies should be aimed at changing the culture of child labour in poor societies. In turn, these activities are likely to compliment broader economic policies.

Similarly, targeted policies, particularly education subsidies, may be an effective complimentary tool to incentivise households to increase their children's educational attainment. Indeed, Roselaine Bonfim de Almeida's work in Chap. 7 suggests that keeping children out of poverty is likely to enhance future educational outcomes and help future households build resilience against shocks.

However, these policy tools may not be effective for all groups, and considering group heterogeneity when designing policies is going to be important. In Chap. 6, Peter J. Morgan and Trinh Q. Long make this evident when they find that changing household composition can have different effects on schooling and child labour even within similar communities. The authors show that different types of migration have different effects on child schooling and labour. For example, children living in households with migrants who migrated for work are not found to be different in terms of school time from those living in households without any migrants, and children living in households with migrants who migrated for education or other purposes tend to have a higher probability of attending school. In this case, understanding changes in the family structure, not only cultural factors, is likely to lead to better policy recommendations. Thus targeting policies to specific circumstances and communities, as well as targeting the general causes of child labour, is possibly the most effective way to tackling this phenomenon.

Index[1]

[1] Note: Page numbers followed by 'n' refer to notes.

A. Posso (ed.), *Child Labor in the Developing World*,
https://doi.org/10.1007/978-981-15-3106-4

The manufacturer's authorised representative in the EU is Springer Nature Customer Service Centre GmbH, Europaplatz 3, 69115 Heidelberg, Germany. If you have any concerns regarding our products, please contact ProductSafety@springernature.com

Printed and bound by CPI Group (UK) Ltd, Croydon, CR0 4YY
30/09/2026
02225460-0007